James Heron

The Church of the Sub-Apostolic Age

Its Life, Worship and Organization

James Heron

The Church of the Sub-Apostolic Age
Its Life, Worship and Organization

ISBN/EAN: 9783337058210

Printed in Europe, USA, Canada, Australia, Japan

Cover: Foto ©Lupo / pixelio.de

More available books at **www.hansebooks.com**

THE CHURCH

OF

THE SUB-APOSTOLIC AGE:

*ITS LIFE, WORSHIP, AND ORGANIZATION, IN THE
LIGHT OF "THE TEACHING OF THE TWELVE APOSTLES.*

BY THE
REV. JAMES HERON, B.A.

London:
HODDER AND STOUGHTON,
27, PATERNOSTER ROW.
MDCCCLXXXVIII.

[*All rights reserved.*]

PREFACE.

NOTWITHSTANDING the proverb *qui s'excuse s'accuse*, a word must be said by way of justifying the publication of this book. Though several works of various dimensions have appeared on the *Didaché* in this country, there seemed not only abundant room but occasion and need for such treatment of it as is here attempted. Some short treatises had been published dealing with special aspects of that ancient writing, such as Professor J. Rendel Harris's work, *The Teaching of the Apostles and the Sibylline Books*, and that of Dr. Taylor supplying illustrations from the Talmud; both most valuable for their purpose, but confined to limited departments of the subject. Canon Spence's book is more general, but less thorough than those just named, and much progress has been made in the exposition of the *Didaché* since it was written. The most comprehensive discussion available to English readers is that by Dr. Schaff, entitled *The Oldest Church Manual.* Containing as it does, along with translations, the Greek text of the *Teaching* and of the related documents, embodying also an exhaustive analysis of the style and vocabulary, and being especially copious on the bibliography of the manual, Dr. Schaff's book is both useful and interesting.

I would fain hope, however, that the present work, which has grown out of an independent study of the early literature, which has kept in view the most recent discussions on the *Teaching*, and which differs from any I am acquainted with in entering more fully into the questions touched and illustrated by that old writing, which are indeed all the important and interesting questions of the early Church, will be found to have a sufficiently distinct purpose and *raison d'être* of its own. The closing chapter on *Church Organization* has been prepared with much care, with a regard solely to the facts and what seemed the truest solution of them, and with the latest discussions on that topic constantly in view. In order to deal thoroughly and satisfactorily with the *data* which the early literature presents on this question, I have found it necessary to examine and test the theories by which it has been sought to explain and harmonize them,—the theories associated with the names of Bishop Lightfoot, Dr. Hatch, Dr. Harnack, and Canon Liddon.

The most recent hypothesis with respect to the origin of the Christian ministry is that put forward by Professor Milligan in *The Expositor* for November, to the effect that the term "presbyter" did not signify office, but was, like "*Reverend*," a general term of honour applied to religious officers. This view, however, seems distinctly at variance with the history of the genesis of the Christian office-bearers, and of their nomenclature as given in the Acts of the Apostles. Paul and Barnabas find a body of Christian administrators, called "elders," at Jerusalem (Acts xi. 30), and who, there can be no doubt, were mainly a transcript of the Jewish eldership. Shortly after having been in intercourse with "the elders" of the mother Church, these brethren have office-bearers called "elders" *elected* and *solemnly appointed* in all the Churches of Asia Minor hitherto founded by them (Acts xiv. 23). They are thus, according to the writer of the Acts, not only officials, but their official title, and as yet the only title by which they are known, is "elders." This is the title by which these office-bearers, whether at Jerusalem or in Asia Minor, are habitually called in the Acts. It is employed to designate them ten times, while the term "bishop" occurs only *once* (Acts xx. 28), and then as another name for the "elders," and as descriptive of their functions. Nothing could be more manifest than that, in the terminology of the writer, the primary official title is "elder," and that of bishop only secondary, and descriptive of work. When it is recognised, further, that the primary official title of the members of the Jewish Synedrion was "elders"; that (as is pointed out in the following pages) these same Jewish elders were also, in a secondary way, called both "shepherds" and "bishops" or "overseers"; and that precisely the same qualifications were required in the Jewish elder as those which, in his epistles to Timothy and Titus, the apostle demands in the Christian "elder" or "bishop"—as, that he should be the husband of one wife, blameless, having his children in subjection under him, while his election depended on the suffrages of the members of the synagogue—it is impossible to resist the conclusion that the Jewish was the original and archetype of the Christian functionary, and that the true history of the nomenclature is that indicated above. The use of the titles in the subsequent literature is in perfect harmony with the foregoing history. It is true that in 1 Tim. iii., and in Phil. i. 1, the designation employed is "bishop," showing that by this time it, too, has become a familiar official title for these functionaries; but in Tit. i. 5-9 it still occurs as secondary to that of "elder"; and in 1 Pet. v. 1, 2, it appears, just as in Acts xx. 28, as descriptive of the work of those immediately before called "elders." In the Epistle of Clement of Rome the persons who have been thrust out of the episcopate are uniformly called "elders"—"duly-appointed elders"—while the title "bishop" occurs only once in the whole letter. In Polycarp's Epistle these officers are known only as "elders," and are by this very title officially distinguished from the "deacons," who are here associated with the presbyters, as elsewhere they are associated with the bishops. And, finally, when one of the presbyters rises above the others, and monopolises the title "bishop," those from among whom he emerges continue to be known by the official title of "presbyters."

The advice of Mephistopheles to the Student of Theology, in Goethe's *Faust*, is to be indifferent to *thoughts* and *things*, and to make *words* his chief concern. "Words, words alone are your best hope!" There is some danger of the discussion on the ministry in the early Church degenerating into a mere strife about words. It is therefore necessary to recall attention to the fact that, by whatever name or names they may have been designated—whether they were called bishops or presbyters, or both—there was a *plurality* of these office-bearers in each congregation, and they were elected by the free choice of the Christian people.

DUNDELA MANSE, BELFAST,
December, 1887.

CONTENTS.

	PAGE
INTRODUCTORY	1

PART I.

THE DIDACHÉ.

CHAPTER I.
Translation of the "Didaché" — 15

CHAPTER II.
The Discovery of the "Didaché" — 34

CHAPTER III.
The Design and Character of the "Didaché" — 41

CHAPTER IV.
The "Didaché" in the Early Church — 47

CHAPTER V.
The Age of the "Didaché" — 73

PART II.

CHURCH QUESTIONS ILLUSTRATED BY THE DIDACHÉ.

PAGE

CHAPTER I.
THE NEW TESTAMENT CANON . . . 87

CHAPTER II.
FAMILY AND SOCIAL LIFE . . . 105

CHAPTER III.
CHRISTIAN UNITY AND CHARITY . . 117

CHAPTER IV.
BAPTISM 129

CHAPTER V.
THE EUCHARIST 146

CHAPTER VI.
THE LORD'S DAY . . . 163

CHAPTER VII.
CHURCH ORGANIZATION . . . 190

    A. THE ITINERANT MINISTRY. 193
        i. Teachers . . 193
        ii. Apostles . . 195
        iii. Prophets . . 198

		PAGE
B.	THE LOCAL MINISTRY	200
	I. The Natural History of the Local Officers	201
	(*a*) The " Elder " . . .	204
	(*b*) The " Bishop "	206
	(Dr. Hatch's view examined)	
	II. Were " Presbyter " and " Bishop " names of the same office-bearers?	218
	(Dr. Harnack's view examined)	
	III. Was Monarchical Episcopacy set up by the Apostles?	238
	(Bishop Lightfoot's view examined)	
	IV. Apostolical Succession . . .	266
	(Canon Liddon's view examined)	
	V. Sacerdotalism . . .	285
	VI. Ministerial Support . .	291
	VII. The Diaconate . .	294

INTRODUCTORY.

IT is told of the late Isaac Taylor that, when he was a young man, his mother, observing him one day leaning pensively against the mantelpiece, inquired what he was troubled about. He replied that he was thinking of the many evils which had come upon Christianity. As his mind matured, and his researches in Primitive Church history became more extended and profound, he saw no reason to alter his opinion, or to regard the changes which were made on Apostolic Christianity as other than corruptions. In fact, no thoughtful person, with open mind, can look at the simple, spiritual religion of the New Testament, so little burthened with ceremonial trappings, so full of buoyant life and aggressive energy, so free and so expansive, and then contemplate the elaborate system of rigid sacerdotalism into which it was afterwards transformed, and perceive that, in being so modified, it was losing much of its early virtue as a regenerating and reforming power in society, without being impressed and saddened with the contrast. On such a question, at any rate, Renan may be accepted as an unprejudiced witness; and Renan describes the change as "the most profound transformation in history."

[margin notes: Corruption of Primitive Christianity; borne witness to by Isaac Taylor; by Renan;]

At once the calmest and the most comprehensive survey of the moral influence of Christianity that we possess, is probably that given by Mr. Lecky in his " History of European Morals from Augustus to Charlemagne." Standing, as he does, outside the different Church parties, and looking at the facts, not with the eye of an ecclesiastic, but through the dry light of philosophy, no writer could be more free from ecclesiastical leanings. What is his verdict in the case?

by Mr. Lecky.

" There can be little doubt," he says, "that for nearly two hundred years after its establishment in Europe, the Christian community exhibited a moral purity, which, if it has been equalled, has never for any long period been surpassed." " In the first two centuries of the Christian Church the moral elevation was extremely high. In the century before Constantine a marked depression was already manifest. The two centuries after Constantine are universally represented by the Fathers as a period of general and scandalous vice." He shows that the very period during which Catholicism was so supreme, was one " of the most contemptible in history." The new Byzantine Empire, founded by Constantine, the first Christian emperor,—an empire which derived all its ethics from Catholic sources, and continued for 1,100 years,—he characterizes as "the most thoroughly base and despicable form that civilization has yet assumed." It was the age of treachery. Its vices were the vices of men who had ceased to be brave without learning to be virtuous. Its history is a monotonous story of the intrigues of priests, eunuchs, and women, of

Its deterioration under the Byzantine Empire;

poisonings, of conspiracies, of uniform ingratitude, of perpetual fratricide.

The condition of the Western Empire was different externally, but morally not dissimilar. Not a century after Constantine, Rome was captured by Alaric, Roman society was dissolved, and the barbarians who adopted the Christian faith became a virgin soil for Catholicity to work on. She exercised for many centuries an almost absolute supremacy over the thoughts and actions of mankind, and created a civilization which was permeated in every part by ecclesiastical influence. But the age of Catholic ascendency " ranks immeasurably below the best Pagan civilizations in civic and patriotic virtues, in the love of liberty, in the number and splendour of the great characters they produced, in the dignity and beauty of the type of character they formed." Boundless intolerance of all divergence of opinion was united with a boundless toleration of falsehood and fraud, which debauched the conscience of society. A deadly torpor sank upon the human mind, which, for many centuries, almost suspended its action ; and moral corruption, deep and wide-spread, prevailed. Why was it, Lecky asks, that a religion which was not more remarkable for the beauty of its moral teaching than for the power with which it acted upon mankind, and which had been so effective in the opening centuries, had proved itself unable to reform and elevate society? He points out, that while Catholicism contained elements which proved efficient in abating infanticide, suppressing gladiatorial shows, and promoting charity and manumission of slaves, it had other elements which worked with a sinister and

[marginal note: and in the West.]

evil influence. The tolerant Roman legislation was displaced by laws of the most minute and stringent intolerance, administered by an aggressive and despotic priesthood, crushing and enfeebling both the intellectual and moral nature. In its conflicts with the paganism of the Empire, and with the barbarian hordes, Christianity underwent a profound modification, and was deeply adulterated and materialized. Pagan *religions* as well as Pagan worshippers had been baptized. Though apparently defeated, the old gods still retained, under a new faith, no small part of their influence over the world. The ascetic and monastic spirit, which became so dominant, threw discredit on the domestic virtues and affections, weakened the social ties, extinguished all public spirit and patriotic feeling,[1] withdrew from active life the moral enthusiasm which is the leaven of society, and made a sordid and emaciated maniac, without knowledge, without patriotism, without natural affection, passing his life in a long routine of useless and atrocious self-torture, and quailing before the phantoms of his own delirious brain, the ideal of the nations. And this system, instead of cutting off its votaries from the temptations of life and the pursuit of riches, drew towards them vast accumulations of wealth, generated rapacity and avarice as characteristic vices of the monks, and bred immorality of the grossest character. Substantially the same sentence is pronounced by Hallam in his "View of the State of Europe during the Middle Ages."[2] On the matter just adverted to

This view corroborated by Milman; and Hallam.

---

[1] See for further illustration Milman's "History of Latin Christianity," vol. ii.   [2] See vol. ii. chap. vii.

he says, "It would be easy to bring evidence from the writings of every successive century to the general viciousness of the regular clergy, whose memory it is sometimes the fashion to treat with respect."

What a contrast when we turn from such a history to the little work before us! It is like passing from an atmosphere fetid and stifling with unwholesome vapours into a bracing mountain air. How entirely different the simple, spiritual faith which here expresses itself from the elaborate sacerdotal and ascetic system which afterwards prevailed! What is here set forth is to all intents and purposes the religion of the New Testament, laying much stress on the spirit and the life, little on the form. And what strikes one most is the high moral tone which pervades it. It is pre-eminently ethical, and its ethics are free from subtlety and casuistry, and strike directly and powerfully at the evils of the time. The thing which it primarily and peremptorily demands is self-forgetting love, and purity of heart and life. As we contemplate the religion which it depicts—a religion at once simple, pure, and lofty, and appealing to the better and nobler feelings of our nature—and compare it with the development of a later age, adulterated by additions from Judaism on the one side and paganism on the other, ruthlessly mutilating and destroying nature by its asceticism, crushing and enslaving it by its priestly despotism, and appealing chiefly to the baser parts of man's being, we have no difficulty in understanding how, after the first two centuries,—that is, after the transformation referred to set in,—it

Compared with the simple spiritual religion of the Didaché,

which is pre-eminently ethical,

and severely pure.

began to lose its virtue as a purifying and elevating force in the world.

<small>To reconcile the antagonisms of modern society, we need the brotherhood this old book exhibits.</small> The seemingly growing antagonism between different classes and interests in our time, is a common subject of remark. Wealth, and all those advantages which wealth secures, tend, it is said, under our present social system, to accumulate in the hands of a comparatively few, who are often charged by those less fortunate with selfishness and rapacity, and who retort by accusing their opponents of unwarrantable assaults upon the rights of property. The truth really is, that the upper and lower strata of our social fabric are kept asunder now by a much narrower gulf than that which separated classes in the early age of Christianity. But since political power has been getting more and more into the hands of the democracy, who are now more alive to their grievances, and more bent on redressing them, those on the other side, doubtless, have more reason to dread serious inroads on what they regard as their rights and interests. How are these antagonisms in the social body to be mitigated and allayed? How are the conflicting interests of the classes and masses to be reconciled and harmonized? Various nostrums have been advertised as infallible. We know of none so likely to succeed as that which, at the beginning of our era, drew men together over much wider gulfs of separation, and fused them into one. We refer to that spirit of brotherhood and love which lies not far from the heart and core of Christianity, which constituted such a real, living, unifying force in the Church of the early age ; which did not for a moment

subvert the right or principle of personal property, but recognised and sanctioned it ; but which taught the individual to forget and deny himself, and to live in and for the community; which for the first time gave men the idea of a *community;* which led them not only to toil and fast to procure the means of helping their poorer brethren, but inspired them often to put themselves in the place of prisoners or slaves, or those doomed to die, that the latter might go free. The spirit which our modern life needs is that enforced so earnestly and powerfully in this ancient Christian writing, and illustrated at length in the third chapter of the second part of this volume.

Again, what serious person can avoid feeling that the power of modern Christianity is greatly paralyzed by its division into innumerable sects, which waste some of their best re- sources in waging war and making reprisals upon one another? Is there no hope of finding a healing and remedial measure? Is there no possibility of discovering a common meeting-ground in what is now generally acknowledged to have been the polity of the primitive Christians? In its essence we under- stand it to have been government by a council or committee chosen by the people. This was the Jewish mode of government. As Dr. Hatch has shown, it was the form of self-government adopted by the countless clubs and associations which flourished in the opening centuries of our era over the Roman Empire. It is the method which obtains everywhere in all such associations to-day. It is the organ of self-management had recourse to in every free society of men. The spirit of this method, or, in other words,

The Church polity it prescribes.

the democratic spirit, is invading and being felt in Churches which have been hitherto most averse to it. Whether they will or no, they are being compelled to return more or less to the freer spirit of the Apostolic times. May we not discern in this the germ and basis, the promise and the potency of greater unity among the Churches of the future? Some progress had been made of late years to a better understanding of the polity of the Apostolic and Sub-apostolic age. But there was still considerable divergence of opinion. Over this region, darkened with the dust of many a controversy, our little book pours a flood of light, affording us clearer insight into the Church Organization of that time. I propose to make liberal use of the guidance which it offers, and to discuss somewhat in detail the Church arrangements of that period; and my sincere desire is to look at the facts fairly, and without prejudice or bias. The tendency of the historian to read the peculiarities and features of his own denomination into the ancient records, has been the bane of Church history. The claims of truth should be supreme and paramount for every man; but the Church historian especially needs to be on his guard against the "idols" both of "the den" and of "the theatre."

One of the most determined assaults to which Christianity has ever been exposed, is that which has been aimed against it in recent times by what is known as the Tübingen school of critics. Their contention has been, that there is a breach of continuity in the history in the first half of the second century; that it was really during that period, which they call "the

The Didaché refutes the Tübingen hypothesis.

dark age" of Church history, that many of the New Testament writings were produced, and produced by way of an *irenicum* between Ebionism and Paulinism; that the original form of Christianity, as taught by Christ and His apostles, was Ebionistic, and not Pauline. To clear up such matters more fully, and to enable us to trace up the New Testament writings nearer to their sources, more light was certainly desirable. The literature of the age referred to is far from being copious. The First Epistle of Clement of Rome, the Epistles of Barnabas and Polycarp, the letter to Diognetus, the Pastor of Hermas, the doubtful Epistles of Ignatius, a few fragments such as those of Papias, the Jewish-Christian "Testaments of the Twelve Patriarchs," and the Sibylline books, with some inscriptions and other memorial records, have been our only sources of information—stars few and far between to guide our footsteps through the history of those momentous formative years. It is true they were enough to enable scholars to make a satisfactory answer to the above-mentioned school of critics. At the same time, fuller information respecting the period in question was greatly to be welcomed. Nor has the wish for more light been altogether in vain. Within some years past several important works relating to those times, and making large accessions to our knowledge of them, have been brought to light; such as the "Philosophumena" of Hippolytus, which affords much insight into the heresies of the second century; a complete MS. of the First Epistle of Clement of Rome—the only complete one existing; fragments of Tatian's "Diatessaron"; and the texts of Barnabas and Hermas, in Greek; not to speak of various fragments and inscriptions. At the present time, historical researches and topographical explorations of an organized and thorough character are being carried forward in Asia Minor and in Egypt—labours which may yet yield valuable fruit. Two works of the second century, quoted by Irenæus and Eusebius, works which would be of great interest and value, have hitherto escaped discovery—the "Exposition of the Oracles of our Lord," by Papias, a pupil of the Apostle John, and a friend of Polycarp; and the "Chronicles" of Hegesippus, the earliest history of the Christian Church known to have been written, and belonging to the middle of the second century. The former still existed in MS. at Nismes in 1218, in the MSS. collection of the Church there, and is also mentioned in the Library Catalogue of the Benedictine monastery of Christ Church, Canterbury, in the Cotton MS. of the thirteenth or fourteenth century. The latter was extant in the sixteenth century. It is not at all unlikely that these books, as well as some works of a third and still more productive second century writer, Melito of Sardis, may yet be discovered in the still imperfectly explored archives of ancient libraries. In the meantime, the work discovered by Bryennios makes a material contribution to our knowledge of that period, and tends still further to discredit the Tübingen hypothesis. It gives no indication of a protracted conflict between Paul and the rest of the apostles, but combines the Pauline and the Petrine types of thought; and it seems, as we shall see, to point distinctly to the existence of written Gospels such as we possess, and of other New Testament writings.

A good deal of fresh light is thrown by our little treatise on Baptism and the Eucharist, and on other institutions and practices of the Primitive Church. We shall find its statements on all these matters most instructive and suggestive, and on the whole, thoroughly in keeping with the earliest post-apostolic literature we possess; and, brief as the work is, we shall probably be surprised how much it enlarges, or at least clarifies and illumines our knowledge of all the main matters of interest connected with the life, worship, and organization of the Sub-apostolic Church.

Throws light on Baptism, the Eucharist, etc.

PART I.

THE DIDACHÉ.

CHAPTER I.

TRANSLATION OF THE "DIDACHÉ."

THE TEACHING OF THE TWELVE APOSTLES.[1]

The Teaching of the Lord through the Twelve Apostles to the Gentiles.

CHAPTER I.

1. THERE are two ways, one of life, and one of death, and there is much difference between the two ways.[2]

2. The way of life, then, is this: First, thou shalt love God thy Maker; Secondly, thy neighbour as thyself; and all things whatsoever thou mayest wish not to be done to thee, do not thou to another.[3]

3. And the teaching of these words is this: Bless them that curse you, and pray for your enemies, and fast for them that persecute you; for what thanks can ye expect if ye love them that love you? Do not even the Gentiles the same? But do ye love them that hate you, and ye shall not have an enemy.

---

[1] Διδαχὴ τῶν δώδεκα ἀποστόλων. For explanation of the title see Part I. chap. iii. of this book. The double title is found as above in the MS. discovered by Bryennios.

[2] For an exposition of "the two ways" see Part II. chap. ii. p. 105, of this work.

[3] See this negative form of the golden rule illustrated in Part II. chap. iii. p. 117.

4. Abstain from fleshly and bodily lusts. If any one give thee a blow on the right cheek, turn to him the other also, and thou shalt be perfect.[1] And if any one compel thee to go one mile, go with him twain. If any one take thy cloak, give him thy coat also. If any one take from thee what is thine, ask it not again; for neither canst thou.

5. To every one who asketh thee give, and ask not again; for the Father wisheth men to give to all from their own private portion.[2] Blessed is he who gives according to the commandment, for he is free from penalty. Woe to him that receiveth; for if any one receiveth when he is in need, he shall be unpunished, but he who doth so when he is not in need shall give satisfaction concerning his purpose and end in receiving; and, coming under discipline,[3] he shall be questioned about what he did; and he shall not come out thence until he pay the last farthing.

6. But about this too it has been said, *Let thine alms sweat into thine hands, until thou know to whom thou mayest give.*[4]

---

[1] τέλειος. Cf. Matt. v. 48; xix. 21; Jas. i. 4.

[2] ἐκ τῶν ἰδίων χαρισμάτων, conveying the double idea that, though their goods are in a sense their own, they have been *freely bestowed* on them by God.

[3] ἐν συνοχῇ δὲ γενόμενος. Some render ἐν συνοχῇ, *in distress*, and some, *in prison*. Prof. Rendal Harris, for example, supposes it to mean a real prison—not a Roman prison, but one which the Church itself kept for offenders. But there is no trace of such a thing in the early literature. Surely *discipline* is not only a legitimate rendering, but one that meets all the requirements of the passage.

[4] Dr. Taylor well shows this to mean that the alms in their hands should be alms acquired by sweat or toil. See Part II. chap. iii. p. 117 of this volume.

Chapter II.

1 Second Commandment of the Teaching:

2 Thou shalt not kill; thou shalt not commit adultery; thou shalt not corrupt boys;[1] thou shalt not commit fornication; thou shalt not steal; thou shalt not use enchantments; thou shalt not practice sorcery; thou shalt not kill a child by abortion, nor shalt thou put to death what has been born;[2] thou shalt not covet what is thy neighbour's.

3 Thou shalt not swear falsely; thou shalt not bear false witness; thou shalt not slander; thou shalt bear no malice.

4 Thou shalt not be double-minded, nor double-tongued, for a double tongue is a snare of death.

5 Thy word shall not be false nor empty, but fulfilled by deed.[3]

6 Thou shalt not be covetous, nor grasping, nor a hypocrite, nor malicious, nor arrogant. Thou shalt not devise evil against thy neighbour.

7 Thou shalt not hate any man, but some thou shalt reprove, on behalf of some thou shalt pray, and some thou shalt love more than thy life.

Chapter III.

1 My son, flee from every evil thing, and from every semblance of it.[4]

---

[1] παιδοφθορήσεις. The reference is to a loathsome vice very prevalent in the heathen world, hinted at in Rom. i. 27, and one which is not altogether unknown in modern society.

[2] For the prevalence of infanticide in the ancient world, see Part II. chap. ii. p. 105.

[3] Or, *filled with fact*: μεμεστωμένος πράξει.

[4] Dr. Taylor illustrates this paragraph by the Jewish saying, "*make a fence to the law*," that is, not only keep away from evil, but from anything that would lead to it, from anything that

2 Be not passionate, for passion leads to murder; nor a zealot, nor quarrelsome, nor soon angry, for from all these things murders are generated.

3 My son, be not lascivious, for lust leads to fornication; nor a filthy talker; nor of lofty eye; for from all these things adulteries are generated.

4 My son, be not an augur, since it leads to idolatry; nor an enchanter, nor an astrologer, nor one who uses purifications; nor disposed to look on these things; for from all these things idolatry is generated.

5 My son, be not a liar, since lying leads to theft,[1] nor covetous, nor vainglorious, for from all these things thefts are generated.

6 My son, be not a murmurer, since it leads to blasphemy, nor self-willed, nor evil-minded; for from all these things blasphemies are generated.

7 But be meek, since the meek shall inherit the earth.

8 Be patient, and merciful, and guileless, and gentle and good, and always trembling at the words thou hast heard.

9 Thou shalt not exalt thyself, nor give presumption to thy soul. Thy soul shall not cleave to the lofty, but thou shalt have thy conversation with the just and lowly.

---

is like it. In the second chapter of the *Aboth* of Rabbi Nathan "it is shown that the Law or Pentateuch makes a fence to its words when it says 'thou shalt not *approach unto*' this or that forbidden thing." See Taylor, *Two Lectures*, p. 24.

[1] A saying which is quoted as *Scripture* by Clement of Alexandria thus: "He who appropriates what belongs to barbarians, and boasts of it as his own, errs, magnifying his own glory, and falsifying the truth. Such an one is called a thief by Scripture. It says at least: *Son, be not a liar, for lying leads to theft.*"—*Strom.*, i. 20.

10 The operations (of Providence) which befall thee thou shalt accept as good, knowing that nothing comes to pass without God.¹

CHAPTER IV.

1 My son, thou shalt remember night and day him that speaketh unto thee the word of God, and thou shalt honour him as the Lord, for whence the Lordship is proclaimed there is the Lord.²

2 And thou shalt seek out daily the faces of the saints, that thou mayest rest on their words.

---

¹ This saying is quoted by Origen as *Scripture* thus: "Propterea docet nos scriptura divina omnia quæ accidunt nobis tanquam a Deo illata suscipere, scientes quod sine Deo nihil fit" (*De Princ.*, iii. 2). But as the saying occurs in Barnabas, and as Origen elsewhere quotes from Barnabas as Scripture, this saying also he may have taken from Barnabas. It occurs likewise in the "Church Ordinances," and there seem to be references to it by Clement of Alexandria (*Strom.*, vii. 12, 13). Something akin to it is found in the Talmud, which informs us that Rabbi Akiba (who in early life was a shepherd in the service of the wealthiest man in Jerusalem, but ultimately was married to his daughter) was wont when any trouble befell him to repeat the motto of his master, "All is for good." He once arrived at nightfall at a certain village, whose inhabitants refused to entertain him. He remarked, "All is for good," and spent the night in the open air. He had a lamp to read with, a cock to wake him in the morning, and an ass to carry him. The lamp was blown out by the wind, the cock was carried off by a fox, and his ass by a lion. "All is for good," he said. The refusal of hospitality by the villagers did, in the result, turn out to be for his good; for he found that the village had been attacked during the night by a band of robbers, who carried off the inhabitants and made them slaves. Subsequently Rabbi Akiba joined the insurrection of Bar Cochba early in the second century, was taken prisoner, and put to death for his part in the rebellion.

² Taylor refers for illustration to a favourite principle of the Jewish rabbis, that those who sit and occupy themselves with the "Thorah," or Law of the Lord, have the Shekinah amongst them, according to Exod. xx. 24.

3 Thou shalt not desire division, but shalt reconcile those at strife. Thou shalt judge justly; thou shalt not respect the person in rebuking for transgressions.

4 Thou shalt not waver whether it shall be or not.

5 Be not one that stretcheth out his hands to receive, but, when he is called upon to give, closeth them.

6 If thou hast, thou shalt give with thy hands a ransom for thy sins.[1]

7 Thou shalt not hesitate to give, nor when thou dost give shalt thou murmur, for thou shalt know who is the fair recompenser of the reward.

8 Thou shalt not turn away from the needy, but thou shalt share all things with thy brother, and shalt not say that they are thine own, for if ye have fellowship in that which is imperishable, how much more in the perishable.

9 Thou shalt not take away thy hand from thy son or from thy daughter, but from their youth up thou shalt teach them the fear of God.

10 In thy bitterness thou shalt not lay commands

---

[1] The statement is no doubt based on such passages as Prov. xvi. 6, " By mercy and truth iniquity is purged " (margin of Revised Version, *atoned for*), and Dan. iv. 27, " Break off " (Revised margin, *redeem*) " thy sins by righteousness, and thine iniquities by shewing mercy to the poor." In the " Testaments of the Twelve Patriarchs " we read: " In proportion as a man is pitiful towards his neighbour, will the Lord be pitiful towards him " ("Zebulon," 8). The idea is doubtless similar to that in Matt. vi. 14, " If ye forgive men their trespasses, your heavenly Father will also forgive you," and in James ii. 13, " He shall have judgment without mercy that shewed no mercy." But the pity towards others, without which we cannot expect the Divine pity, soon came to be erroneously regarded as *a meritorious and procuring cause* of the Divine pity.

on thy bondman or bondwoman, who hope in the same God, lest at any time they may not fear him who is God over both. For he doth not come to call according to outward appearance, but to those whom the Spirit hath prepared.

11 And ye bondmen shall submit yourselves unto your masters as the image of God in modesty and fear.

12 Thou shalt hate all hypocrisy, and everything displeasing to the Lord.

13 Thou shalt not forsake the Lord's commandments, but thou shalt keep the things thou receivedst and shalt neither add to nor take away from them.

14 In the congregation[1] thou shalt confess thy transgressions, and thou shalt not go to thy prayer with an evil conscience.

This is the way of life.

CHAPTER V.

1 But the way of death is this. First of all, it is evil, and full of curse: murders, adulteries, lusts, fornications, thefts, idolatries, enchantments, sorceries, plunderings, perjuries, hypocrisies, doubleheartedness, guile, arrogance, wickedness, self-will, covetousness, filthy-talking, envy, presumption, pride, vaunting.

2 Persecutors of the good, hating truth, loving a lie, not knowing the reward of righteousness, not

---

[1] ἐν ἐκκλησίᾳ, without the article. Some have inferred from the absence of the article that not the congregation, but church, in the sense of *building* is meant, and have seen in this a sign of late workmanship. But ἐν ἐκκλησίᾳ without the article occurs in the sense of congregation in 1 Cor. xi. 18; xiv. 19, 28, 35, that is, in four places within a brief space in one of Paul's epistles.

cleaving to what is good, nor to righteous judgment, intent not upon what is good, but what is evil; far from whom are meekness and patience; loving vain things, seeking reward, not pitying the poor, not grieving with him who is in sore distress, not knowing their maker, murderers of children, destroyers of the image of God, turning away from the needy, vexing the afflicted, advocates of the rich, lawless judges of the poor, sinners in all things. May ye be delivered, children, from all these.

Chapter VI.

1 See to it that no one lead thee astray from this way of the teaching, since he teacheth thee without God.

2 For if thou canst bear the whole yoke of the Lord thou shalt be perfect,[1] but if thou art not able do what thou canst.

3 And concerning food, bear (the yoke) as far as thou art able; and turn your mind away entirely from meat sacrificed to idols; for it is serving dead gods.

---

[1] By "the yoke of the Lord" here some understand very absurdly the ceremonial law, and others, as Harnack, asceticism, and especially celibacy. But there is not the least support for either view in the context. The "whole yoke of the Lord" means obviously the precepts of the Lord, which have just been summarized in the first part of the *Didaché*, and which our Lord Himself expressly designates *His* yoke (Matt. xi. 29). In those precepts there is no reference either to Jewish ceremonial or to celibacy. But to observe just such precepts as are enjoined here is by Christ Himself represented as leading to perfection. Cf. Matt. v. 39-48 with *Did.* i. 4, and Matt. xix. 21 with *Did.* iv. 7, 8; v. 2; vi. 2.

Chapter VII.

1 And concerning baptism, baptize thus: Having first gone over all these instructions, baptize into the name of the Father, and of the Son, and of the Holy Ghost, in living water.[1]

2 But if thou hast not living water, baptize into other water, and if thou canst not in cold, then in warm.

3 But if thou hast neither, pour out water on the head thrice, into the name of the Father, and of the Son, and of the Holy Ghost.

4 And before the baptism let the baptizer and him who is being baptized fast, and whoever else are able; but thou shalt command him who is being baptized to fast one or two days before.

Chapter VIII.

1 Let not your fasts be with the hypocrites, for they fast on the second day of the week and on the fifth, but fast ye on the fourth day and on the preparation.[2]

2 Neither pray ye as the hypocrites, but as the Lord commanded in His Gospel, after this manner pray ye:

---

[1] "Living water," that is, the running water of a stream or fountain, prescribed on account both of its freshness and abundance. For commentary on this chapter, see the chapter on Baptism in this work, p. 129.

[2] The Jews fasted on Monday and Thursday, because these were the days on which Moses was supposed to have ascended and descended from Mount Sinai. Christians fasted on Wednesday and Friday, as the days of our Lord's betrayal and crucifixion. "The preparation" ($\pi\alpha\rho\alpha\sigma\kappa\epsilon\upsilon\dot{\eta}$) was the Jewish name for Friday, which was so called because it was the day of preparation for the Sabbath.

Our Father, which art in heaven, hallowed be thy name; thy kingdom come; thy will be done on earth as it is in heaven; give us this day our daily bread; and forgive us our debt as we forgive our debtors; and lead us not into temptation, but deliver us from evil; for thine is the power and the glory for ever.[1]

Thrice [2] a day pray after this manner.

CHAPTER IX.

1 And concerning the Eucharist,[3] after this manner give thanks:

2 First, concerning the cup:[4] We thank thee, our

---

[1] With slight variations the prayer is the same as in Matthew's Gospel: ἐν τῷ οὐρανῷ for ἐν τοῖς οὐρανοῖς in the invocation; ἐλθέτω for ἐλθάτω in the second petition; τὴν ὀφειλήν for τὰ ὀφειλήματα, and ἀφίεμεν for ἀφήκαμεν in the fifth; and the omission of ἡ βασιλεία (the kingdom) in the doxology. In the most ancient MSS. of the New Testament the doxology is wanting. It no doubt originated as a response, at the close of the prayer, on the part of the congregation, like *Amen*. See 1 Cor. xiv. 6. "There can be little doubt" (say Westcott and Hort: *New Test. App.*) "that the doxology originated in liturgical use in Syria, and was thence adopted into the Greek and Syriac-Syrian texts of the New Testament." Hence the variations in the terms of it.

[2] A continuation of the Jewish practice of praying three times a day. See Dan. vi. 10; Acts iii. 1; x. 9. Tertullian (*de Orat.*, 25, and *de Jejun.*, 10) and Clement of Alexandria refer to and justify this usage; but Clement adds, "Yet the Gnostic prays throughout his whole life, endeavouring by prayer to have fellowship with God" (*Strom.*, vii. 7).

[3] Referring to the bread and wine of the Lord's Supper, "over which the thanksgiving is pronounced," Justin Martyr says: "This food is called among us the Eucharist (εὐχαριστία), of which no one is allowed to partake but the man who believes that the things which we teach are true" (*Apol.*, i. 66). For further elucidation of the passage, see chap. v., Part II. of this treatise.

[4] The mention of the cup before the bread as in Luke xxii. 17–20; 1 Cor. x. 16, is probably due to the fact that as the Pass-

Father, for the holy vine[1] of David thy Son, which thou madest known to us through Jesus thy Son:[2] to thee be glory for ever.

3 And concerning the broken bread: We thank thee, our Father, for the life and knowledge which thou madest known to us through Jesus thy Son: to thee be the glory for ever.

4 As this broken bread was scattered abroad upon the mountains,[3] and, when gathered together became

---

over was combined with a feast, so was the Lord's Supper with a love-feast, in which there may have been some imitation of what took place at the first observance of the Supper as recorded in Luke xxii. 17–20. The "cup of blessing," answering to the third of the four Passover cups, came after the distribution of the bread.

[1] Christ calls Himself "the True Vine," and is called also "the Root and Offspring of David" (Rev. xxii. 16). It was natural enough for the *Didaché* in giving thanks over "the fruit of the vine," which symbolized Christ's blood, to combine the two designations. Clement of Alexandria employs the phrase. He says: Jesus was "He who poured out for us the wine of the vine of David; that is to say, His blood" (*Quis div. salv.*, 29). He says again: "The vine produces wine, as the Word produces blood, and each drink for health to men; for the body, wine, and blood for the spirit" (*Pæd.*, i. 5). Clement in all likelihood learned the phrase from the *Didaché*, with which, we know by another quotation of his from it, he was familiar.

[2] τοῦ παιδός σου, which may be rendered "son" or "servant." The term is applied to both David and our Lord in the Acts (iii. 13, 26; iv. 25, 27, 30).

[3] This prayer appears again in the pseudo-Athanasian *De Virginitate*, in which the virgin says in partaking of the bread: "We thank thee, O our Father, for Thy holy resurrection, that through Thy Child Jesus Thou didst make it known to us. And as this bread was once scattered that is *upon this table*, and being gathered together became one, so may Thy Church be gathered together from the ends of the earth unto Thy kingdom. For Thine is the power and the glory for ever. Amen." The substitution of *table* for *mountains* was no doubt made to suit the prayer for use in Egypt, and makes it almost certain that it originated elsewhere.

one, so let thy Church be gathered together from the ends of the earth into thy kingdom; for thine is the glory and the power through Jesus Christ for ever.

5 But let no one eat or drink of your Eucharist but those baptized into the name of the Lord; for concerning this the Lord hath said, *Give not that which is holy to the dogs.*[1]

Chapter X.

1 And after being filled[2] give thanks after this manner:

2 We thank thee, Holy Father, for thy holy name[3] which thou hast made to dwell in our hearts, and for the knowledge and faith and immortality which thou hast made known to us through Jesus thy Son: to thee be the glory for ever.

3 Thou, O Almighty Sovereign, didst create all things for thy name's sake, and thou gavest both food and drink to men for their enjoyment, that they might thank thee; but to us thou freely gavest spiritual food and drink and life everlasting through thy Son.

4 Before all things we thank thee that thou art mighty: thine is the glory for ever.

---

[1] Here no doubt we have the origin of the formula, the repetition of which preceded the administration of the ordinance in the early Church: "Holy things to the holy."

[2] An expression which shows that among those for whom the *Didaché* was intended, the Eucharist was accompanied with the love-feast. When it is asked why the *chagigah* was eaten before the Passover, the answer which the Talmud gives is, "It was eaten first, that the Passover might be eaten *after being filled.*" See Taylor's *Two Lectures*, p. 130.

[3] A Hebraism: "There shall be a place where the Lord your God shall choose, to cause His name to dwell there" (Deut. xii. 11). The name stands for God Himself.

5 Remember, O Lord,[1] thy church to deliver her from all evil, and to perfect her in thy love; and gather her together from the four winds, sanctified unto thy kingdom to which thou didst prepare for her; for thine is the power and the glory for ever.

6 Let grace come and this world pass away. Hosanna to the God of David. If any one is holy let him come, if any one is not holy let him repent. Maranatha. Amen.

7 But allow the prophets to give thanks in such terms as they wish.[2]

Chapter XI.

1 Whosoever therefore cometh and teacheth you all these things aforesaid, him receive.

2 But if he that teacheth, himself perverted, teach other teaching to the undoing thereof, do not hear him;[3] but if to the advancement of righteousness and knowledge of the Lord, receive him as the Lord.[4]

---

[1] Harnack has pointed out how the titles in which God is addressed in this prayer harmonize respectively with the several divisions of the prayer. When thanks are given for the blessings of redemption, He is addressed as "Holy Father"; when the blessings of Creation are acknowledged, He is called "Almighty Sovereign"; and when prayer is offered for the Church, He is addressed as "Lord."

[2] εὐχαριστεῖν ὅσα θέλουσιν, perhaps *as much as they wish*. According to Justin Martyr, the presiding minister, when the bread and wine are brought, "offers prayers and thanksgivings to the best of his ability" (ὅση δύναμις αὐτῷ).

[3] 2 John 10: "If there come any unto you, and bring not this doctrine, receive him not into your house, neither bid him God speed."

[4] John xiii. 20: "Verily, verily I say unto you, He that receiveth whomsoever I send, receiveth me; and he that receiveth me, receiveth Him that sent me."

3 And concerning the apostles and prophets, according to the ordinance of the Gospel, so do ye.

4 And let every apostle that cometh to you be received as the Lord.

5 And he shall not remain (beyond) one day; but, if there be need, the next also; but if he remain three days he is a false prophet.

6 And let the apostle, when going away, take nothing but bread to last him till he reach his next lodging-place; and if he ask for money he is a false prophet.

7 And every prophet that speaketh in the Spirit,[1] ye shall not try nor judge; for every sin shall be forgiven, but this sin shall not be forgiven.[2]

8 Yet not every one that speaketh in the Spirit is a prophet, but only if he have the ways of the Lord. From their ways therefore shall the false prophet and the prophet be known.

9 And no prophet that appointeth a table,[3] in the Spirit shall eat of it; but if he do so he is a false prophet.

10 And every prophet that teacheth the truth, if he doeth not what he teacheth, is a false prophet.

11 And no prophet, approved and true, that doth any thing with a view to a worldly mystery of the Church,[4] but teacheth not others to do as he doeth,

---

[1] Cf. 1 Cor. xii. 3; xiv. 2; Rev. i. 10.

[2] Matt. xii. 31: "Every sin and blasphemy shall be forgiven unto men; but the blasphemy against the Spirit shall not be forgiven." See also 1 Thess. v. 19, 20.

[3] A "table" is here no doubt a love-feast. The prophet might be tempted to appoint such a "table" or feast for his own indulgence.

[4] This has been regarded by critics as the most obscure passage—the *crux*—of the *Didaché*. Among the many interpreta-

shall be judged by you, for his judgment is with God; for in like manner also did the ancient prophets.

12 And should any one say in the Spirit, Give me money or some other thing, ye shall not hear him; but if he tells you to give in behalf of others that are in want, let no one judge him.

Chapter XII.

1 And let every one that cometh in the name of the Lord be received; and then after ye have tested him, ye shall know him; for ye shall have understanding of right and left.[1]

---

tions that have been offered by far the most satisfactory is that given by Dr. Taylor. It seems to clear away all difficulty. "Worldly" or "cosmic" has much the same meaning as in Heb. ix. 1. "As the cosmic sanctuary made with hands, was a pattern of the heavenly, so a cosmic mystery is an idea depicted in the world of sense by emblematic actions or material objects." It is teaching by symbolical objects or actions, as the prophets often did, that is referred to. But why is the prophet not to teach others to do as he himself doeth? Dr. Taylor answers by quoting Barnabas, who says that "that very Moses who gave commandment, *Ye shall have neither molten nor graven thing for a god unto you*, himself maketh such that he may shew a type of Jesus. Moses then maketh a brazen serpent" (c. xii.). Moses made a graven image with reference to (εἰς) Jesus, though he says *Cursed be the man that maketh a molten or graven image*. So Justin Martyr says that under the old dispensation there was an element of *precept* and *action*, which was commanded with reference to the mystery of Christ (εἰς μυστήριον Χριστοῦ)—(*Dial. c. Tryph.*, 44). He too refers (c. 94) to Moses making the serpent of brass as a sign, though God had commanded that no image or likeness of any thing in heaven or earth should be made. But in doing this he was free from sin, because "he proclaimed the mystery by which He would break the power of the serpent"—Christ crucified. There is every indication that both Barnabas and Justin had this very passage of the *Didaché* in view in their remarks on this subject.

[1] The *Apostolical Constitutions* have in the corresponding

2 If he that comes is a wayfarer, give him as much help as you can ; but he shall only remain with you two or three days, if there be necessity.

3 But if he be a craftsman, and wish to take up his abode with you, let him work and eat.

4 But if he have not a trade, provide according to your own discretion that he shall not live idle among you as a christian.

5 And if he is not disposed to do so he is a Christ-trafficker.[1] Beware of such.

Chapter XIII.

1 But every true prophet who wishes to take up his abode among you is worthy of his food.[2]

2 In like manner a true teacher is also worthy, like the workman, of his food.

3 All the first-fruit then of the produce of wine-vat and threshing floor, oxen and sheep, shalt thou take and give to the prophets ; for they are your chief priests.[3]

4 And if ye have not a prophet, give to the poor.

5 If thou makest a batch of bread, take the first-fruits, and give according to the commandment.[4]

6 Likewise when thou hast opened a jar of wine or oil, take the first-fruits and give them to the prophets.

7 And of money, and raiment, and every possession, take the first-fruit as seemeth good to thee, and give according to the commandment.

---

passage : " Ye are able to know the right hand from the left and to distinguish false teachers from true teachers " (vii. 28).

[1] Χριστέμπορος, one who makes gain of Christ.
[2] τῆς τροφῆς αὐτοῦ.
[3] Cf. Num. xviii. 12, 13 ; Deut. xviii. 3, 4.
[4] That is, according to the commandment indicated in the preceding note.

Chapter XIV.

1 And on the Lord's day of the Lord, being assembled together, break bread and give thanks, after confession of your trespasses, that our sacrifice may be pure.[1]

2 Let no one who has a dispute with his companion come with you till they are reconciled, that our sacrifice may not be defiled.

3 For this is that which was spoken by the Lord: *In every place and time offer unto me a pure sacrifice; for I am a great King, saith the Lord, and my name is wonderful among the Gentiles.*[2]

Chapter XV.

1 Elect[3] therefore for yourselves bishops and deacons worthy of the Lord, men meek, not avaricious, and true and approved; for they too minister to you the ministry[4] of the prophets and teachers.

2 Disregard them not therefore; for they are those of you that are honoured with the prophets and teachers.

3 And reprove one another, not in anger but in

---

[1] The gifts brought by the Christian people by way of providing for the Lord's Supper and the love-feast, and for the poor, etc., the thanksgiving prayers, and the dedication of themselves to God in the ordinance, were all conceived in the early Church as a spiritual sacrifice offered up to God. Hence the use of the word "sacrifice" here. It contains no reference whatever to the Lord's Supper being a real repetition of the sacrifice of Calvary.

[2] Mal. i. 11. There is no reference to *time* in Malachi. The passage is habitually quoted in the early literature with reference to the Eucharist.

[3] *Elect*—χειροτονήσατε. *Lit.*, to elect by *show of hands*, but then simply *to elect*.

[4] Literally, *liturgy the liturgy*—λειτουροῦσι τὴν λειτουργίαν.

peace, as ye have it in the Gospel; and to any one that wrongs another, let no one speak, nor let him hear from you till he repent.

4 But so pray, and do all your alms and actions as ye have it in the Gospel of our Lord.

Chapter XVI.

1 Watch for your life. Let not your lamps be quenched, and let not your loins be ungirt, but be ye ready; for ye know not the hour in which our Lord cometh.

2 And be ye often gathered together, seeking the things that concern your souls; for the whole time of your faith shall not profit you, unless in the last season ye be made perfect.

3 For in the last days the false prophets and perverters shall be multiplied, and the sheep shall be turned into wolves, and love into hatred.

4 For as lawlessness increaseth, they shall hate, persecute and betray one another, and then shall appear the world-deceiver as the Son of God, and shall work signs and wonders, and the earth shall be given over into his hands, and he shall work lawless deeds which have never been done from everlasting.

5 Then shall the work[1] of men come into the fire of trial, and many shall be offended, and shall perish, but those who have endured in their faith shall be saved by the curse itself.[2]

---

[1] ἡ κτίσις, perhaps *the creation* or *race* of men.

[2] *Saved by the curse.* Taylor illustrates this from Barnabas who describes the goat, spit upon, and pierced, and cast out into the wilderness, as "a type of Jesus set forth to the Church, signifying that whosoever would take up the scarlet wool must needs suffer many things, because the thorn is terrible, and

6 And then shall appear the signs of the truth; first the sign of an outspreading in heaven;[1] then the sign of the voice of a trumpet; and the third a resurrection of the dead;

7 Not indeed of all, but as was said, *the Lord shall come and all the saints with Him.*

8 Then shall the world see the Lord coming upon the clouds of heaven.

must by being afflicted master it. Thus (he saith) they that would see me, and lay hold of my kingdom, *must through affliction and suffering obtain me.*" Again with reference to the sacrifice of the red heifer: "Wherefore the wool withal and the hyssop? Because in his kingdom there shall be *days evil and corrupt in which we shall be saved; because he that aileth in the flesh is healed by the corruption of the hyssop.*"

[1] What is meant by "the sign of the *outspreading* in heaven"? Archdeacon Edwin Palmer has shown that it means the outspreading of the hands so as to form a *cross* with the body. In Moses stretching out his hands, and enabling Israel to prevail over Amalek (Exod. xvii.), and in the words of Isaiah lxv. 2, "All the day long have I spread out my hands;" Barnabas and Justin Martyr see a foreshadowing of the cross, as do later patristic writers. Further illustrations are given by Prof. Rendel Harris in *The Teaching of the Apostles and the Sibylline Books.*

CHAPTER II.

THE DISCOVERY OF THE DIDACHÉ.

A BRIEF account of the discovery of the manuscript of this early writing, which, after having disappeared for many centuries, has now at length been disinterred from the dust of ages, should be here put on record, and may interest the reader.

The discoverer, Philotheos Bryennios, was born of poor parents at Constantinople, in 1833, and received his elementary training in the schools of Tataüla, a Greek suburb of Constantinople. Lutherlike, he provided the means of his early education by singing, and by conducting the music in a Greek church. By native talent and perseverance he pushed his way until, through the goodwill and patronage of a leading ecclesiastic, he gained admission into an important patriarchal college near Byzantium, called "The Theological School of Chalce." Having completed his studies he was ordained a deacon, and appointed "Teacher of the Orthodox Theology." At this period, through the kindness and liberality of a Greek banker of Constantinople, he was enabled to visit Germany, and to attend lectures in the Universities of Leipzig, Berlin, and Munich. In 1861 he was summoned home to be appointed to the office of Professor of Ecclesiastical History in the Theological School of Chalce. Soon after this he became principal of the college, and a little later he was promoted to be master and professor of what is known as "The Great School of the Nation," over which he presided for seven years. *Promotion.*

He paid a second visit to Germany in 1875, when he attended the conference of Old Catholics in Bonn. It was here that the news reached him of his having been chosen Metropolitan of Serræ, in Macedonia. In 1877 he became Metropolitan of Nicomedia, and next in rank to the Patriarch of Constantinople. He has proved himself to be a varied and accomplished scholar, especially well versed in early patristic literature. He is well known among European scholars, and the University of Edinburgh, at its tercentenary celebration in 1884, conferred on him the degree of doctor of divinity. *Becomes Metropolitan of Nicomedia.*

Professor Edmund A. Grosvenor of Robert College, Constantinople, has had several interviews with Bryennios, of which he gives a graphic account in the *Century* magazine of May, 1885, with minute personal and domestic details. The colour of his hair, the condition of his beard, the peculiarities of his dress, and even the furniture and arrangements of his private apartments, are picturesquely described! Suffice it to say, that Archbishop Bryennios seems to be a man of great force of character, remarkably intelligent and courteous, with exceptional conversational gifts. When Professor Grosvenor visited him, his place of residence was in Phanar, the Greek quarter of Constantinople, where the Greek patriarch and *Personal characteristics.*

several Greek bishops also reside, and where the great patriarchal church is situated. In the same quarter is the Jerusalem monastery of the Holy Sepulchre, adjoining which is the library in which Bryennios discovered the MS. of the long lost *Didaché*. In this library there are, it would appear, "from four to six hundred manuscripts." Professor Grosvenor relates the incident of the actual discovery, as he learned it from Bryennios himself. In 1873 the bishop was engaged examining the MSS., when his eye fell on a volume he had not seen before—a small thick book covered with black leather, containing 120 leaves of vellum, or 240 pages. Taking it up indifferently to glance at its contents, he found embodied in it a number of MSS. in Greek, written by the same hand, and among which with great elation he observed the first and second Epistles of Clement of Rome, and the Epistle of Barnabas. He was so much interested in these, that he seems scarcely to have noticed another MS. which was embraced in the volume, and immediately succeeding the two Epistles of Clement. His attention was meanwhile almost exclusively devoted to the MSS. of the Epistles of Clement, and in 1875 he published the text of these epistles with Prolegomena and notes. They were happily made public in time to be used by Dr. Lightfoot in his edition of that Father. In that first publication Bryennios simply announced the contents of the MS. volume discovered by him to be as follows :—

The discovery of the MS. in the monastery of the Holy Sepulchre, Constantinople.

1. *A Synopsis of the Old and New Testaments in the order of Books by St. Chrysostom.* The New Testa-

ment, however, is not given in it. In his edition of the *Didaché* now before us, Bryennios gives at great length the variations upon the text previously published by Migne, as well as the portions which were wanting.

<small>Contents of the MS. discovered.</small>

2. *The Epistle of Barnabas.* The first complete edition of Barnabas in Greek was that given by Tischendorf from the *Codex Sinaiticus* published in 1862. The Bryennios MS., which is also complete, has new readings which have been used by Hilgenfeld, by Gebhardt and Harnack, and by Funk in their most recent editions of the Epistle of Barnabas.

3. *The First Epistle of Clement of Rome to the Corinthians.* The only other MS. which exists of this epistle is that contained in the *Codex Alexandrinus* in the British Museum, in which, however, portions are wanting at the end. The Bryennios MS. of Clement is the only complete one which we possess, and is therefore of great value. It has been used by Lightfoot in his edition of Clement.

4. *The so-called Second Epistle of Clement to the Corinthians.* The Bryennios MS. is also the only complete one extant of this work, which is now regarded as being not an epistle of Clement, but the earliest specimen of a post-apostolic sermon or Christian homily which we possess, and which Lightfoot and others from internal evidence assign to the early part of the second century, anterior to 140 A.D. It is interesting also as being the first example of a *read* discourse which is on record.

5. *The Teaching of the Twelve Apostles* (Διδαχὴ τῶν δώδεκα ἀποστόλων). This is, with one exception, the briefest of all the works in the Bryennios collec-

tion, covering as it does less than ten pages of the original MS., but it is much the most important, and is none other than the long-lost book referred to by the early writers.

6. *The Spurious Epistle of Mary of Cassoboli to Ignatius of Antioch.* It is of little or no value.

7. *Twelve Pseudo-Ignatian Epistles* in the longer Greek recension. The MS. containing these seven works has appended on the last page by the hand of the copyist the following subscription :—

<small>When the MS. was copied.</small> "Finished in the month of June on the 11th, day 3d, Indiction 9, of the year 6564. By the hand of Leon, notary and sinner." The year 6564 in the Byzantine mode of reckoning is equivalent to 1056 of our era, that having been the year in which the MS. was completed by the scribe Leon.

<small>Publication of the work.</small> It was not till 1880, seven years after the discovery, that Bryennios resumed his perusal of that part of the MS. volume which contained the *Didaché*, and began to realize its extraordinary value and importance. From that time forward he devoted every spare moment to the study of it; and at length in 1883 he gave it to the world, with scholarly Prolegomena and Notes, written in modern Greek. The title of his work as translated into English is :

"Teaching of the Twelve Apostles from the Jerusalem Manuscript, now first published with Prolegomena and Notes, embracing both a Collation of the Synopsis of the Old Testament by John Chrysostom, and an unpublished portion from the same Manuscript. By Philotheos Bryennios, Metropolitan of Nicomedia."

Never before probably did the discovery of an early writing awaken an interest at once so immediate, so wide-spread, and so profound. It was instantly seized upon with eager avidity by German scholars, early copies having been sent to those experts in patristic learning, Harnack, Hilgenfeld and Zahn. In the United States and in this country the interest excited by it was if possible still deeper and more general. There was hardly a review, scarcely even a newspaper in the three kingdoms and throughout the United States but contained some notice of it, and some recognition of its importance.

Interest excited by it.

The cause of its awakening such a deep and lively interest is not far to seek. The most cursory examination is sufficient to convince the reader of the value which attaches to it. It is exceedingly brief—not longer than the Epistle to the Galatians—and yet there is scarcely a debated question of importance connected with the sub-apostolic age on which it does not throw some rays of light. It is like the uprising of a new star to shine on regions which heretofore had been somewhat dark and shadowy. The discovery has been called an epoch-making event; and, without doubt, it marks the beginning of a new chapter in the history of the early Church. "Its interest and importance," says Bishop Lightfoot,[1] "have far exceeded our highest expectations. Its chief value consists in the light which it throws on the condition of the infant Church. . . . Of the genuineness of this document there can be no shadow

The interest awakened by it accounted for.

[1] *Expositor* for January, 1885.

of doubt. No one could or would have forged it: it pleases nobody." "Remembering," he adds, "that the whole work occupies only a little more than six octavo pages, we are surprised at the amount of testimony—certainly much more than we had any right to expect—which it bears to the Canon of the New Testament." Canon Venables,[1] describes it as "the most remarkable addition to our knowledge of the sub-apostolic age since the publication of the *editio princeps* of St. Clement in 1633, the value of which cannot be too highly estimated. If its revelations are startling and unexpected, such as are calculated to disturb pre-conceived views on some points of considerable importance, it all the more deserves, and we are sure will receive, patient investigation, and unprejudiced consideration from all who deserve the name of theologians and scholars."

[1] *British Quarterly Review*, April, 1885.

CHAPTER III.

THE DESIGN AND CHARACTER OF THE DIDACHÉ.

THE title, "The Teaching of the Twelve Apostles" (Διδαχὴ τῶν δώδεκα ἀποστόλων), or as it is in the longer form, "The Teaching of the Lord, through the Twelve Apostles, to the Gentiles," does not mean, of course, that the work came directly from the hands of the apostles, but only that it contains a summary of the teaching which they were wont to give. Their Divine Master had laid on them an obligation to make disciples of all nations, baptizing them, and "*teaching them to observe all things whatsoever He had commanded them*" (Matt. xxviii. 20). The New Testament makes frequent reference to a certain body of teaching which the apostles were wont to give to their converts; which in course of time assumed a more or less definite form, easily distinguishable from the false teaching then rife; which, before the Gospels and Epistles were written, was necessarily *oral*, and which must have continued current after they were written. Thus, we are informed (Acts ii. 42) that the early Christians continued stedfastly "*in the apostles' teaching*" (τῇ διδαχῇ τῶν ἀποστόλων). At Athens, Paul is taken to the Areopagus by the multitude, and pressed to tell them what "this new teaching" whereof he

The title explained.

had spoken is (Acts xvii. 19). He thanks God that the Romans had obeyed "that form of teaching which was delivered" to them (Rom. vi. 17). He refers to it repeatedly in his epistles to Timothy and Titus. John again exhorts his readers, if any one comes to them and brings not "this teaching," not to receive him into their house (2 John 10). It is a collection of such apostolic teaching, made, as the book itself informs us, for a specific purpose, that our *Didaché* professes to offer to its readers.

It naturally divides itself into two parts. The first part, comprising the first six chapters, treats of "the two ways, one of life and one of death." This mode of representing the life which a man may live under the figure of two ways, one or other of which he must pursue, is a very common one in ancient literature, sacred and secular. Moses says, "I have set before thee this day life and good, and death and evil," etc. (Deut. xxx. 15). Jeremiah says, "Thus saith the Lord, Behold I set before you the way of life, and the way of death" (Jer. xxi. 8). The Talmud has a similar representation. Prodicus in Xenophon's *Memorabilia* represents the hero in his youth as standing between the way of pleasure and the way of virtue. And the parable of the narrow way and the broad, in the Sermon on the Mount is too familiar to need repetition. It appears from the Acts of the Apostles that "the way" was a recognised and familiar designation of Christianity itself (see Acts ix. 2; xix. 9, 23; xxii.

margin notes: The "Two Ways" treated of in the first part. A similar representation of life in Jeremiah; in the Talmud; in Xenophon; in the Sermon on the Mount; in the Acts of the Apostles;

4; xxiv. 14, 22). When thus used in the singular, it is no doubt meant to convey that it is the way of life, the way of light, the way of truth, the way of righteousness. In 2 Pet. ii. 2, 15, it is described as "the way of truth" and "the way of righteousness" in opposition to "the way of Balaam." As we shall see farther on, Barnabas and Hermas, and other early writers, repeat this parabolic teaching about the two ways. *The Testaments of the Twelve Patriarchs*, a Jewish-Christian work, belonging to the first half of the second century, has not a little in common with our *Didaché*, and among other things, this image of the two ways: "God gave to the sons of men two ways, two counsels, and two lines of action, and two places and two ends . . . two ways, of good and evil." And, referring to the frequent use of the parable, Clement of Alexandria says: "The gospel proposes two ways, as do likewise the apostles, and all the prophets. They call the one narrow and circumscribed, which is hemmed in according to the commandments and prohibitions, and the opposite one which leads to destruction, broad and wrong, open to pleasures and to wrath."[1]

in 2 Peter;

in the early Fathers;

"Testaments of the Twelve Patriarchs;"

in Clement of Alexandria.

In the *Didaché* "the way of life" is described first. It is the way of love to God and man— the way of good works. This is first put positively in a brief summary of duties taken chiefly from the Sermon on the Mount; and then negatively, in an expansion of the second table of the law—

The "Way of Life."

[1] *Stromata*, Book v.

"thou shalt not" do so and so—with a warning against the inward feelings and desires, which might lead to an outward breach of the precepts. The negative prohibitions, however, under this head frequently pass into positive exhortations to duty.

The fifth chapter, which describes "the way of death," consists chiefly of a list of sins such as we have enumerated in various parts of the New Testament, but with the gross and shameful immoralities of the heathen world around especially in view.

<small>The "Way of Death."</small>

We learn from the *Didaché* itself that this first part of it was employed as a sort of textbook for the instruction of candidates for baptism; for the second part opens thus: "Having first taught all these things, baptize," etc. The thing that strikes one most in it is the almost exclusively *ethical* character of the teaching which this earliest Christian handbook embodies. This indeed should hardly surprise us: it was in keeping with the directions which had been given by our Lord Himself. "Go ye, therefore, and make disciples of all nations, baptizing them . . . *teaching them to observe all things whatsoever I have commanded you* (Matt. xxviii. 19). This is literally and exactly what our little manual does for those about to be baptized. It sets before them a summary of the commands of Christ adapted to their circumstances, and earnestly urges their observance. It implies, no doubt, a knowledge of the main facts of the gospel, or that these will be communicated by the teachers, but its own teaching is predominantly moral and practical. It warns against

<small>First part used as a textbook for Catechumens.</small>

<small>Why so ethical?</small>

prevailing evils, and exhorts to purity, quietness, meekness, self-denial, kindliness and charity. It was felt to be vital and essential that the members of the Church just emerging from heathenism, and still surrounded by it, should keep themselves free from its defilements. As Hatch points out strikingly in his Bampton Lecture,[1] "moral purity was the very condition of their existence." If the salt had lost its savour wherewith was it to be salted? It was the holy lives of the early Christians which beyond aught else were like salt to the heathen world, and served pre-eminently to commend and propagate Christianity. They were more powerful and convincing apologies than any ever written by Justin Martyr or by Tertullian. Stanley, the American traveller, who went to Africa in search of Livingstone, says that he went to him as prejudiced against religion as any atheist in London. But the sight of the solitary old man living there not for himself but for others, translating into life and action the teaching of Christ, he informs us, completely overcame his prejudice, and converted him to Christ, though Livingstone had not tried directly to do it. The occurrence related by Stanley enables us to understand the power of early Christianity.

The second part of the *Didaché* contains instructions as to the manner of observing Baptism, Fasting, Prayer, the Eucharist, and Love-feast, and also with regard to the Teachers and Rulers of the Church, closing appropriately with an exhortation to watch-

Second part: a Directory of Worship and Government.

---

[1] *The Organisation of the Early Christian Churches*, Lecture III.

fulness, and preparation for the coming of the Lord. As the first part constituted a little manual for the religious and moral training of catechumens, so in this second part we have a Directory for the worship, government and discipline of the Church.

I ought to mention that in the MS. discovered by Bryennios, the work is not divided into chapters and verses. It was Bryennios himself who divided the book into sixteen chapters. Professor Harnack has divided it into verses; and, though his arrangement is in many respects unsatisfactory, I have adopted it for convenience of reference.

<small>Division into chapters by Bryennios, into verses by Harnack.</small>

CHAPTER IV.

THE DIDACHÉ IN THE EARLY CHURCH.

IN the introductory chapter, reference was made to two works which were well-known to early Christian writers, but which are not now extant—the *Exposition of the Oracles of our Lord* by Papias, and the *Chronicles* of Hegesippus. Another book entitled *The Teaching of the Apostles*, or, in the plural form, *The Teachings of the Apostles*, is also mentioned by the early Fathers, and sometimes quoted by them. Thus, in his chapter, "Concerning the Sacred Scriptures acknowledged to be genuine and Those that are not,"[1] Eusebius mentions "the Teachings of the Apostles" among the latter. After referring to those "acknowledged to be genuine," he proceeds to give the "disputed" Scriptures, and the "spurious" (νόθαι), and puts among the latter "the epistle bearing the name of Barnabas," and "what are called the Teachings of the Apostles" (τῶν ἀποστόλων αἱ λεγόμεναι Διδαχαί). Dr. Salmon thinks that the book whose title Eusebius quotes in the plural, is likely to have been that form of the "Teaching" which distributes the matter among the several apostles, that is, the "Ecclesiastical Canons" or "Church Ordi-

Mentioned by Eusebius among the spurious Scriptures;

---
[1] *H.E.*, Book iii. c. 25.

nances" (as he calls the work).[1] But we have no evidence that in that form it was ever called "The Teaching" or "The Teachings." The work which appears to be substituted for "The Teaching" of Athanasius in the list of Rufinus, and which Rufinus calls "the Two Ways, or the Judgment of Peter," is associated with only *one* of the apostles. The treatise which we now possess under the name of the *Didaché* belongs manifestly to a very early date, not later even in its present form than the earlier part of the second century, and may have existed still earlier in a somewhat briefer text corresponding to the Latin version. This book contains evidence in itself of having been called "The Teaching of the Apostles," and we see no satisfactory reason to doubt its having been the work referred to by the early writers, whether under the title "Teaching" or "Teachings of the Apostles." The plural title applies appropriately enough to our *Didaché*.

The second Pfaff Fragment, generally attributed to Irenæus, but, as Zahn points out, probably the work of some other writer, mentions what it calls "The Second Ordinances of the Apostles" (δεύτεραι τῶν ἀποστόλων διατάξεις). The writer says "those who have become acquainted with the Second Ordinances of the Apostles, are aware that the Lord instituted a new oblation in the new covenant, according to Malachi the prophet. 'For from the rising of the sun even to the setting,

referred to probably by the Pfaff Fragment.

---

[1] See *Non-Canonical Books*, supplementary to his *Introduction to the Study of the Books of the New Testament*, by George Salmon, D.D., F.R.S., Regius Professor of Divinity, Dublin.

My name has been glorified among the Gentiles, and in every place incense is offered to My name, and a pure sacrifice.'" He then goes on to explain how the oblation referred to is the oblation of thanksgiving in the Eucharist, which he describes. Now the *Didaché* speaks largely of the Eucharist under the aspect in which it is presented in this passage, and quotes with reference to it those words of Malachi. It is, therefore, supposed by many, and not without reason, that under this title, "The Second Ordinances of the Apostles," the writer is referring to the *Didaché*. Rothe, it is true, conceived that, after the fall of Jerusalem, a council of the surviving apostles, John, Philip, and Andrew, with other Christian teachers, was held; that at this council, and in order to meet the great emergency created by dissensions and factions in the Church, and by the growing Gnostic heresies, episcopacy was established, and that it is the decrees of this council that are designated in the Pfaff fragment, "the Second Ordinances of the Apostles." But Rothe's speculation, though advocated by him with much plausibility, has no firm basis to rest upon, and is inconsistent with the plain facts of history, which shows that the spread of monarchical episcopacy was slow and gradual, and did not come into general operation till long after this. The theory has, therefore, been thrown over as untenable by writers like Bishop Lightfoot. It is now generally conceded that "The Teaching of the Apostles" is in all probability the work referred to in the fragment.

Again, Clement of Alexandria, writing about the beginning of the third century, does not indeed mention the "Teaching" by name, but cites a statement contained in it, and speaks of it as "Scripture" thus: "He who appropriates what belongs to the barbarians, and vaunts it as his own, does wrong, increasing his own glory and falsifying the truth. It is such an one that is by Scripture called 'a thief.' It is therefore said, 'Son, be not a liar; for falsehood leads to theft.' "[1] Dr. Salmon thinks that Clement may have quoted from the Egyptian form of the work, and not from the Palestinian form, which our *Didaché* represents. But there is no evidence that the "Ecclesiastical Canons" existed in any form so early that it would be quoted by Clement as Scripture. It was, no doubt, as Harnack has endeavoured to show, compiled from several earlier documents, but the earliest of these was in Dr. Salmon's view, a Jewish manual, which certainly would not be quoted by Clement as "Scripture." If it was the Egyptian form that was quoted by him, it must have been the Jewish manual as reproduced by some Christian editor, and adapted to the use of Christians. As we have no evidence that such an Egyptian edition had appeared in Egypt sufficiently early to enable Clement to cite it as Scripture, and as our *Didaché* bears the clearest evidence on the face of it of having been very much earlier than his time, we see no valid reason to doubt its having been the work from which he quotes. With the exception of that part which it has in common with the *Didache*, it is manifest that the "Ecclesiastical Canons" or "Church Ordinances," is very much later than the *Didaché*. And it seems exceedingly unlikely that Barnabas, the writer of the *Didaché*, the editor of the "Ecclesiastical

Quoted as "Scripture" by Clement of Alexandria.

---

[1] Cf. Clement's *Stromata*, i. 20, with the *Didaché*, chap. iii. 5.

Canons," and also the Latin version of the " Teaching," should all, or most of them, independently of one another (as Dr. Salmon appears to hold), have drawn from a Jewish manual the materials for Christian instruction. As to Clement, there are other indications of acquaintance on his part with the *Didaché* as we have it, as, for example, in his use of that very peculiar expression, "the Vine of David."[1] I shall afterwards give reasons for supposing that both Barnabas and Hermas were acquainted with a Christian (not a Jewish) manual, substantially the same as our *Didaché*, though possibly a little briefer; and that there is really no good ground for supposing, with Drs. Taylor and Salmon, that the original manual which supplied the material from which so many later editors or compilers have drawn, was a Jewish one.

Athanasius, the Bishop of Alexandria, in the fourth century, mentions "what is called the Teaching of the Apostles" (Διδαχὴ καλουμένη τῶν ἀποστόλων) among the books which are not canonical, but which had been framed (τετυπωμένα) by the Fathers to be read to those coming and desiring to be instructed in the doctrine of piety.[2] *Named by Athanasius among non-canonical books to be read for instruction.* Dr. Salmon would "willingly believe the *Didaché*, as we know it, to be the book intended [by Athanasius] if he did not feel some hesitation arising from doubts as to whether this book is one which Athanasius would have put into the hands of catechumens." He refers to the information given in the prayers as to the sacred mysteries, which he hardly thinks Athanasius would have

---

[1] Cf. *Quis Dives Salvus*, 29, with *Did.* ix.
[2] Athanasius, *ep. Fest.*, 39.

employed in catechetical instruction. But the very thing that has struck most readers of the *Didaché*, is the little that is said about the Lord's Supper itself, either in the prayers or elsewhere. As Dr. Salmon confesses, there is no mention of the institution of the rite, and no express mention of our Lord's body and blood. So little specific reference is there to the Supper, that Dr. Salmon in another place adopts the theory that these prayers do not apply to that ordinance at all, but to solemn meals like the love-feast. We cannot accept of the view that the Lord's Supper is not contemplated, but the absence of specific information as to the "sacred mysteries" of the Eucharist, is enough to satisfy us that it might have been very well used even so late as the time of Athanasius in the instruction of catechumens; and therefore we have no difficulty in believing that the work referred to by Athanasius is none other than the *Didaché*.

Rufinus, in the fifth century, repeats the statement of Athanasius, except that in place of the title, "The Teaching of the Apostles," he substitutes "The Two Ways, or the Judgment of Peter."[1] Jerome also names "The Judgment of Peter" among the apocryphal Scriptures attributed to that apostle.[2] This book entitled "The Two Ways," or "The Judgment of Peter," is by the majority of critics identified with the first part of the "Teaching," which treats of the two ways, and which appears to have existed in a separate form.

First part of it probably mentioned by Rufinus, under title of "The Two Ways," etc.

And, lastly, a book called "The Teaching of the

---

[1] Qui appellatur Duæ Viæ vel judicium Petri, *Com. in Symb. Apost.*, chap. 38.   [2] *De vir. illustr.* cap. 1.

Apostles," is mentioned by Nicephorus in the ninth century. He refers to it along with the Epistles of Clement, Ignatius, and Polycarp and the *Pastor* of Hermas as being among the New Testament Apocrypha, and as containing two hundred lines or verses, which, however, varied with the size of the page or column. *(Nicephorus in ninth century names it.)*

It should be added that a fragment of a Latin version, identical in substance with the first two chapters of the *Didaché*, but with one notable omission to be noticed afterwards, and with some striking variations, has been discovered recently by Dr. Oscar von Gebhardt, and given to the world by Dr. Harnack in his work on the *Didaché*. In some respects it seems in closer affinity with the Barnabas appendix than with our "Teaching," though in others again it is nearer to the "Teaching." The shortness of the fragment makes it unsafe to build much upon it. *(Fragment of a Latin version of it has been found.)*

It thus appears that a treatise called "The Teaching of the Apostles," but sometimes apparently bearing other designations, was pretty widely known, and held in much esteem in the early Church. From the circumstance that Tertullian has no reference to the *Didaché*, Dr. Salmon infers that it was not known to that Father, that its circulation was limited, and that it spread slowly outside the Jewish section of the Church. But neither does Tertullian quote, nor once mention, nor betray any acquaintance with, the Epistle of Barnabas, from which it would be very unsafe to draw sweeping inferences as to the very limited circulation of that epistle, or even to conclude that Tertullian did not know of it.

Another series of facts not less interesting now demands attention. It has been found, on close examination, that our *Didaché* has much in common with other important and well-known writings of the early Church.

Has much in common with certain early writings;

At the close of the Epistle of Barnabas, which was written some time after A.D. 70, and before A.D. 120, there are three chapters added apparently in the form of an appendix, and consisting of an exposition of what it calls "the two ways." Between these chapters and the first part of the *Didaché* which treats of "the two ways," there is a great deal of common matter—they are, in fact, in substance identical—only that in Barnabas the arrangement is more at random, and the statements more expanded and enlarged. Nor is the kinship between the two confined to the exposition of "the two ways." All through the epistle we find here and there sayings similar to those in the *Didaché*, just as in all parts of the *Didaché* we find sentences which have a manifest affinity to statements in the epistle.

with the Epistle of Barnabas;

In the *Shepherd* of Hermas, who was in all probability a contemporary of Clement of Rome, and whose book in that case was written about the close of the first century, we find not indeed so much as in Barnabas, but still a considerable amount of matter in common with the "Teaching," showing that they either borrowed from one another, or from a common source, or from related sources.

with the Shepherd of Hermas;

Justin Martyr, as we shall see, betrays in many places a knowledge of our *Didaché*, or of some kindred document, with somewhat similar contents.

But there is another work, different from these, known as "The Apostolical Church Order," or "The Ecclesiastical Canons of the Holy Apostles," or "Church Ordinances," or "The Epitome" (for each of these titles has been applied to it). *with the Ecclesiastical Canons;* A considerable proportion of this work consists of later additions, which have been made not earlier, certainly, than the third century; but it has a basis of earlier date, particularly that part which it has substantially in common with the *Didaché* and Barnabas about the two ways; differing from them, however, in this respect, that in it the statements are represented as having been spoken by the several apostles of our Lord successively. In some matters the recension in the "Ecclesiastical Canons" has a closer affinity with that in Barnabas and in the Latin version than with the *Didaché*; though on the other hand it has some striking sayings in common with the *Didaché*, which are not found in Barnabas. With Barnabas it omits *Didaché* i. 3–6, but it has the whole of *Didaché* iii., the golden rule, and other things not contained in Barnabas, and as regards both its order of arrangement and its terse phraseology, it is much nearer to the *Didaché* than to Barnabas. It could not have been taken from Barnabas, as its order is so similar to "the Teaching," and so unlike Barnabas; but especially as it contains so much not found in the latter.

A work of still later date is "The Apostolical Constitutions," which was a sort of Directory, or Book of Order and Discipline for the Eastern Church. It, too, was evidently a gradual formation, having as its earliest *substratum* *with the "Apostolical Constitutions."*

the same matter as the *Didaché,* but embodying also the ecclesiastical rules and usages of a later age, having been enlarged and modified from time to time as new laws and usages arose, and assuming its present or final form about the beginning of the fourth century.

Now it had been noticed long since what a close kinship there seemed to be, and how much in common there was, between these three works—"The Epistle of Barnabas," "The Ecclesiastical Canons," and "The Apostolical Constitutions"; and, so early as 1843, Professor Bickell, of Marburg, had suggested their possible connection with "The Teaching of the Apostles," not then discovered. Acting upon this hint, Dr. Krawutzcky, a Roman Catholic scholar, two years before the discovery of Bryennios, had endeavoured to reconstruct from these three sources the older document from which he supposed them to be derived. His reconstruction is found to agree substantially with the first part of the *Didaché,* and has been appropriately enough described as "a brilliant example of legitimate and successful higher criticism," though it should be added that Krawutzcky himself, owing apparently to his Roman Catholic prepossessions, refuses to accept of the *Didaché* as the original in question, which he supposes to have come from the Apostle Peter.

<small>Krawutzcky reconstructs a common original, agreeing generally with the *Didaché.*</small>

Now the question is, What is the relation of these different works to one another? Especially, what is the original document from which they have been ultimately derived? Is it the Epistle of Barnabas, or

<small>Relation of these works to one another.</small>

the *Didaché*, or some earlier form of the Two Ways, which in course of time underwent various modifications? The weight of opinion at present leans to the conclusion that neither Barnabas nor the *Didaché* in the form in which we now have it, is the original, but that both depend upon some earlier document.

The ablest and most thorough discussion of the question we have seen is that by Dr. Taylor, Master of St. John's, Cambridge.[1] Dr. Taylor's chief object is to show the Hebraic spirit and character of the *Didaché*, and to illustrate its more obscure sayings from Jewish sources. In this object Dr. Taylor has succeeded admirably, and has greatly contributed to the elucidation of many of its more difficult and dark passages. He has made it as certain as anything of the kind can be that the author of the original document was a writer with Jewish training—that he was, in all likelihood, originally a Jew. Dr. Taylor goes even further. He points out that, if you eliminate a certain passage in the first chapter of the *Didaché*, which reproduces some sentences from the Sermon on the Mount—a passage which is not contained in the Latin version, in Barnabas, nor in the "Ecclesiastical Canons"—there is in that case nothing distinctively Christian in the first half of the work which treats of the two ways; and he suggests that it may have been originally not a Christian, but a Jewish manual, which at

The question well discussed by Taylor, who suggests that the basis of the Didaché may have been a Jewish manual.

---

[1] *The Teaching of the Twelve Apostles; with Illustrations from the Talmud.* Two Lectures given at the Royal Institution. By C. Taylor, D.D., Master of St. John's College, Cambridge. Cambridge, 1886.

a later period had some additions made to it by Christian writers, and was adapted to Christian uses. Dr. Taylor puts forward this hypothesis by no means positively, but tentatively, and with some reserve.

Dr. Salmon goes still farther. But Dr. Salmon, in his recently-published *Supplement* to his "Introduction to the Study of the Books of the New Testament," already mentioned, carries Dr. Taylor's argument a step farther, and regards the hypothesis as demonstrated. While admitting that (leaving out of consideration the sentences from the Sermon on the Mount) the *Didaché* form of the Two Ways is a more exact representation of the original than that in Barnabas, which, as Taylor shows, deranges the natural order of the thoughts, clumsily expands them, and attempts to smooth the Hebraic ruggedness of the original, Dr. Salmon thinks that, taking the *Didaché* as a whole, Barnabas is prior to the Christianized form of it; that, in fact, the writer of the *Didaché* had seen Barnabas and used him. He thinks the circumstance that the Christian element does not appear in Barnabas, that in this part of his epistle there is not a word which might not have been written before Christ was born, evidence sufficient that the *Didaché* was unknown to Barnabas; while he supposes the Christian adapter of the "Teaching" to have had Barnabas before him. "I find it impossible to believe" (Dr. Salmon says) "that if he [Barnabas] knew that work [the *Didaché*] he would have gone over it, adapting it to his use by carefully erasing every line which contained anything of specially Christian teaching." Dr. Salmon's judgment very properly carries great weight, and deserves to be treated with the greatest consideration and respect. It is with the utmost diffidence that I venture to differ from his opinion in this matter. But when all the facts are taken into account they do not seem to me to justify the conclusion hinted at by Dr. Taylor, but accepted as proved by Dr. Salmon—that the original source both of the *Didaché* and of the Barnabas appendix, was a Jewish manual, prepared and used as a manual for instructing proselytes to Judaism. Let me, with as much brevity as possible, recite the facts which should enter into a consideration of the case.

(1) Whatever the original was from which Barnabas drew, whether Jewish or Christian, the excerpts made by him are fragmentary and deranged. As we shall see, a great deal was, in any case, omitted by him, so that we need hardly be surprised at any particular omission. [Reasons for believing that the original was a Christian writing.]

(2) To say that, supposing Barnabas had the *Didaché* before him, he went over the work "carefully erasing every line of specially Christian teaching," is very far from being an adequate representation of the case. It was not the Christian element *merely* that he left out, and it is misleading to say that it was. The Christian teaching left out by him constituted in the *Didaché* only the first part of a long paragraph, *all* of which was omitted by him; so that there was no picking out of the Christian part exclusively for rejection. And let it be observed that a large portion of the *Didaché* paragraph omitted by Barnabas is given in the *Shepherd* of Hermas,[1] which I hope to show depends upon the *Didaché*, and not *vice*

[1] See Commandment II.

versa, so that there is good reason for feeling certain that at least a portion of this passage omitted in Barnabas was in the original document. Besides, an equally long paragraph which appears in chapter iii. of the *Didaché*, not distinctively Christian, but one which Dr. Taylor holds to be peculiarly Hebraic in its spirit and structure, is also wanting in Barnabas, though it appears in the "Ecclesiastical Canons," which Dr. Salmon believes to have been independent of the *Didaché*. There is indeed in Barnabas (chap. 4) what Dr. Taylor regards as a reminiscence of this part of the "Teaching," and which also points to the fact that the paragraph in question, though omitted by Barnabas, was in the original. It should be added here that several of the most characteristic sayings which the *Didaché* has in common with the other recensions, and which there is, therefore, good reason to believe were in the original document, are left out by Barnabas, as the golden rule, which is in the Latin version and in the "Ecclesiastical Canons," and the sayings : "Lying leads to theft," "Let thine alms sweat into thine hand," both of which are in the "Ecclesiastical Canons." There are also distinct echoes of them in the *Shepherd*, and of the latter at least in Barnabas himself (chap. 10). We are, therefore, justified in concluding that they, too, were in the original. In presence of these facts it is hardly putting the case fairly to say that, supposing Barnabas had the *Didaché* before him, he must have gone over it "carefully erasing every line which contained anything of specially Christian teaching."

(3) There is after all distinctively Christian teaching in common between Barnabas and the *Didaché*,

and also between the *Didaché* and the "Ecclesiastical Canons," the most simple and natural explanation of which is a *Christian* original which they all knew and drew from. The passage in *Did.* iv. 8 is admittedly based on Acts iv. 32; Rom. xv. 27; and 1 Cor. ix. 11; yet this passage occurs also both in Barnabas (c. 19) and in the "Ecclesiastical Canons." Dr. Salmon supposes Barnabas to be the original; but we find it easier to believe that the original *Didaché* contained the passage, as we shall have occasion to prove it far more likely that Barnabas had seen some text of the *Didaché*, than that the writer of the latter had seen the former. It is also significant that the words, "spiritual food and drink and eternal life" in one of the Eucharistic prayers, and which are unmistakably Christian, are reproduced exactly in the "Ecclesiastical Canons." It is to me far more probable that these were in the original source than that a work which bears so many marks of a very early date as the *Didaché*, took them from the "Canons."

(4) Even in the strongest instances cited by Dr. Taylor of sayings derived, as he thinks, from Jewish sources, they bear marks of New Testament colouring, and of having been, in part at least, suggested by kindred sayings in the New Testament. One of his strongest is the negative form of the golden saying, "All things whatsoever thou wouldest not have done to thee do not thou to another." It appears in Tobit iv. 15 thus: "What thou hatest do to no one"; and in the Babylonian Talmud thus: "What to thyself is hateful thou shalt not do: this is the whole law, and the rest is comment." We say nothing of the fact that this saying is by no means exclusively

Jewish; that as Taylor himself shows, it appears in the Confucian Analects, and that, as might be added, it is found not only in Plato, but in Isocrates 400 years before Christ. Gibbon cites it from the latter in his "Decline and Fall" (chap. liv. note 38): "Ἃ πάσχοντες ὑφ' ἑτέρων ὀργίζεσθε ταῦτα τοῖς ἄλλοις μὴ ποιεῖτε." No doubt the original writer of our manual, who was, we imagine, a Jewish Christian, was familiar with the negative form of the saying; but the πάντα ὅσα ἐὰν θελήσῃς μὴ ("all things whatsoever thou wouldest not,") of the *Didaché* and the "Canons," and the *omne quod tibi non vis fieri* of the Latin version, all of which omit the word *hatest*, and reproduce the first part of the saying as it appears in Matthew, seem to combine a reminiscence of the Christian form of the saying with the Jewish form of it; while the fact that it appears in Matthew in immediate connection with the picture of the "two ways" by our Lord, leaves the impression that the original author knew the saying and its connection as it occurs in the Sermon on the Mount, but that being familiar with the negative form of it, which was likely current and more or less familiar as a proverb, this form combined with the other in his reproduction of it. In the "Ecclesiastical Canons" it is given as from Matthew. Elsewhere Dr. Taylor himself notices the remarkable reading of Acts xv. 28, 29, in *Codex Bezæ* and other MSS. of the Western type: "It seemed good to the Holy Ghost and to us to lay upon you no greater burden as necessary than these things, that ye abstain from things sacrificed to idols, and from blood, and from fornication; and whatsoever things ye would not have happen to yourselves, that ye do not to another."

Another of the sayings which Dr. Taylor illustrates from the Talmud is, " Let thine alms sweat into thy hands" (*Did.* i. 6), which, as he well brings out, simply means, " Let the alms in your hands be the result of sweat or labour on your part." He gives instances from the Talmud—not much to the point, indeed—where "sweat" connotes "toil." But his aptest illustrations are found not in Jewish, but quite other literature; as in the Greek comic poet Aristophanes, one of whose characters says: "I will not cast away my sweat and savings till I know how the matter stands"; and in the pseudo-Athanasian *Quæstiones ad Antiochum Ducem* (Q. 88, Migne, xxviii. 651), where it is said "there is almsgiving and almsgiving. And of one kind is the reward of the labourer who *out of his own sweat* shows compassion; but quite another is that of the ruler who gives from endowments and revenues." Dr. Taylor shows that, as this part of the "Teaching" appears in Hermas (Com. II.) in the " Ecclesiastical Canons " (where it is put into the mouth of Thomas), and in the " Apostolical Constitutions " (vii. 1), "sweat " is paraphrased by " labour," the two words occurring in the " Ecclesiastical Canons." But the usage which makes " sweat " synonymous with "labour" is a perfectly natural and common one everywhere, and not in the least peculiar to Jewish literature. The idea of the precept in the *Didaché* and in the other versions of it is precisely that of Ephesians iv. 28 : " Let him that stole steal no more: but rather let him labour, working with his hands the thing that is good, that he may have whereof to give to him that hath need "; and appears far more likely to have been derived from this passage in Ephesians with a possible recollection of Genesis iii. 9, than from any purely Jewish source to which Dr. Taylor has been able to refer.

In like manner Dr. Taylor cites elaborately from Hebrew literature, in order to find some parallel to the saying, "Lying leads to theft"; but what he adduces from that source illustrates not this saying, but its converse, that "theft leads to lying"! And as to the whole passage in *Did.* iii., "Be not prone to anger, for anger leads to murder. Be not lustful, for lust leads to fornication," etc., in which Dr. Taylor finds a specimen of the Talmudic rule to "make a fence to the law," it is to our mind far more likely to have been suggested by Christ's teaching in His Sermon on the Mount, where He points out that the inward feeling, whether of anger, or lust, or the like, from which the outward act proceeds, is to be avoided, as a breach of the commandment as well as the overt act. I must say, indeed, that while reading Dr. Taylor's two lectures, and admiring their erudition, one could not help feeling that in such cases erudition is in great danger of running into pedantry, and of wasting its strength raking among the dust-bins of ancient literature for what is all the time lying patent and at hand in familiar writings. Hitherto, then, we have found nothing to make it probable that the original source of the *Didaché* was a Jewish document, but a good deal that points to a Christian original. No doubt it is largely Hebraic in its style and mode of thought, but its having been written by a Jewish Christian would account for that. Nor is there anything in its predominantly ethical character to prove that it was not originally Christian. Look at the

Epistle of James. The name of Christ occurs only twice in it: in the opening clause, and at the beginning of the second chapter. For the rest it is not only purely ethical, but Jewish in its spirit and cast. Witness the many parallels traced by the commentators between it and the Books of Ecclesiasticus and Wisdom. With far more plausibility might it be maintained that the Epistle of James was originally a Jewish document, addressed to Jews and not to Christians, but adapted to Christian uses by the insertion of one or two phrases. If Dr. Taylor sets himself to find parallels to James in Jewish literature with as much industry as he has devoted to the *Didaché*, I have no doubt that in that case his erudition will be equally fruitful; but he will still be far from proving that James's epistle was originally a Jewish one, addressed to Jews and not to Christians in the first instance. Is it not, moreover, antecedently improbable that a man like Barnabas would draw his materials directly from a Jewish manual? We know his strong anti-Jewish spirit. In his conception the Jewish system is utterly abolished for "the new law of Christ." Dr. Salmon himself speaks, though not in this connection, of Barnabas's "total want of respect" for Jewish institutions. "His whole tone of feeling towards the Jewish nation is such" (he says) as he thinks "impossible in one born a Jew," and therefore he supposes him a Gentile, though afterwards in a note, to account for his acquaintance with the imaginary Jewish manual for proselytes about "the two ways," he suspects Barnabas to have been a Gentile proselyte to Judaism before he became a Christian. Is it at all likely that a man so hostile to

Judaism would make such use of a Jewish manual? It is still more improbable that three or four Christian compilers, most of them independently of one another, drew their materials for Christian instruction from the same Jewish source.

(5) We have seen that the *Didaché* has not a little in common with Hermas and the "Ecclesiastical Canons," while in common with the Latin version it has something which is not in Barnabas, and which, therefore, could not have been derived from Barnabas; so that if our treatise drew it from any earlier source, that source was not Barnabas. This view will be still further confirmed when we compare the *Didaché* and Barnabas more closely with one another, and find numerous indications that Barnabas came after the *Didaché*, and knew it in some such form as that in which we now possess it.

In chapter iv. of Barnabas we have, as Taylor well points out, an evident recollection of various parts of the *Didaché*, and so expressed as to make it clear that it is Barnabas who is reproducing the *Didaché* and not *vice versa*. "Let us utterly *flee from* all works of iniquity, lest we *become like them*" (the wicked men who do them) seems an echo of *Did.* iii., " *Flee from all evil,* and *from all that is like unto it ;* " and the passage, " Let us take earnest heed in the last days, for the whole time of our faith shall profit us nothing unless, etc. . . . Do not by retiring apart live a solitary life . . . but, coming together to the same place, seek ye together the things pertaining to salvation," is a manifest reproduction of *Did.* xvi. ; " But be ye frequently gathered together, seeking the things that are profitable to your

The Didaché prior to Barnabas.

souls; for the whole time of your faith shall not profit you except in the last season ye be found perfect. For in the last days," etc. Observe, too, that the sentiment here expressed by both the *Didaché* and Barnabas about holding out in the last days, is a notably Christian one. See Matt. x. 22; xxiv. 13; 2 Tim. iii. 1; Heb. iii. 14.

It is also shown by Taylor that the description by Barnabas (chapter vii.) of the goat taken for an offering for sin, and spit upon, and accursed, and crowned, is a commentary, thoroughly characteristic of Barnabas, on the expression in *Did.* xvi., "saved by the curse."

I have already adverted to the saying, "Let thine alms sweat into thine hands." It is characteristically allegorized by Barnabas thus: "Now wherefore did Moses say, 'Thou shalt not eat the . . . swine, nor the eagle, nor the hawk, nor the raven,' etc. 'Thou shalt not join thyself,' he means, 'to such men as know not how to procure food for themselves by *labour and sweat*, but seize on that of others in their iniquity, and, although wearing an aspect of simplicity, are on the watch to plunder others.' So these birds, while they sit idle, inquire how they may devour the flesh of others, proving themselves pests by their wickedness."[1]

Compare also *Did.* iv.: "Thou shalt remember night and day him that speaks to thee the word of God, and thou shalt honour him as the Lord," with Barnabas (chap. xix.): "Thou shalt love as the apple of thine eye every one that speaketh to thee the

---

[1] *Barn., Ep.*, chap. x.

word of the Lord"; and see the remarks of Taylor on this and on the previous parallel.

Again, in *Did.* iv. we read, "Thou shalt hate all hypocrisy, and every thing that is not pleasing to the Lord. Thou shalt not forsake the commandments of the Lord, but thou shalt keep what thou hast received, neither adding to nor taking from it. In the congregation thou shalt confess thy sins, and shalt not come to thy prayer with an evil conscience." As Dr. Taylor points out, Barnabas divides this into two fragments, putting one at the beginning and the other at the close of chapter xix., attaching to what he gives in each case a moiety of the sentence which next follows in the *Didaché*. Thus, at the beginning of chapter xix. we have the words, "Thou shalt hate doing what is unpleasing to God, thou shalt hate all hypocrisy, thou shalt not forsake the commandments of the Lord"; and at the end of the same chapter the other fragment of the saying, "Thou shalt keep what thou hast received, neither adding to it, nor taking from it. To the last thou shalt hate evil (or the wicked one). Thou shalt confess thy sins. Thou shalt not go to prayer with an evil conscience."

We think that no one who compares carefully these different versions of the same sayings, can have any doubt of the priority of the *Didaché* version to that in Barnabas.

Dr. Salmon cites one instance which he thinks indicates that the *Didaché* came after Barnabas. The *Didaché* in the last chapter mentions as one of the signs of Christ's coming, "the sign of the stretching out in heaven" ($\sigma\eta\mu\epsilon\hat{\iota}ον\ \dot{\epsilon}\kappa\pi\epsilon\tau\dot{\alpha}\sigma\epsilon\omega\varsigma\ \dot{\epsilon}\nu\ ο\dot{\upsilon}\rho\alpha\nu\hat{\omega}$). The explanation of this, given by Archdeacon Edwin

Palmer, is now generally accepted as the most satisfactory. He refers to the words of Isaiah lxv. 2, "I have stretched forth (ἐξεπέτασα) My hands," etc. Barnabas explains Isaiah's words as a prophecy of Christ's stretching forth His hands on the cross, and so do Justin Martyr, and others. Dr. Salmon thinks that if the *Didaché* had been prior to Barnabas, a phrase so obscure would never have suggested to the latter his interpretation of Isaiah. On the contrary, Barnabas with his allegorizing tastes and tendencies, is the very man to have invented such an interpretation, had that been necessary; but Barnabas speaks of having himself received the instruction which he communicates (see chap. i.); so that there is every likelihood that his interpretations were traditional among the Christian teachers. Hence the *Didache* uses the expression without feeling it necessary to explain it.

In comparing the *Pastor* of Hermas with the *Didaché*, we are led to a similar conclusion.

The *Didaché* prior to the *Pastor* of Hermas.

Commandment II. of the *Pastor* is evidently a close paraphrase of the second half of chapter i. of the *Didaché*, a passage which, it will be remembered, is not given in Barnabas. When Hermas says, "From the rewards of your toils which God has given you, give to all the needy in simplicity," he is simply rendering in plain language the saying of the *Didaché*, "Let thine alms sweat into thy hands."

The saying in our treatise, "Lying leads to theft," is thus reproduced and explained in Commandment III. of the *Pastor*: "They therefore who *lie* deny the Lord, and *rob* Him, not giving back to Him the deposit which they have received. For they received from Him a spirit free from falsehood. If they give Him back this spirit untruthful, they pollute the commandment of the Lord, and become *robbers*."

In Commandment VIII. Hermas gives a list of evils resembling that in *Didaché* ii., and then adds the exhortation which follows in the *Didaché*, that they must avoid "all other vices *like* these." In Commandment III. Hermas refers to the "prophets," and instructs his readers how to test them in a manner which closely resembles, and appears to echo, chapter xi. of the *Didaché*; and in Vision iii. c. 5, he mentions other office-bearers similar to those named in our document—"apostles, bishops, teachers and deacons." It should have been noted also that he, too, reproduces the allegory of "the two ways" (see Commandment VI.); and that, like the Latin version of the "Teaching," he refers in the same connection to two angels —one of equity and the other of iniquity. Barnabas speaks of angels also, but with him it is not one, but a number of angels who preside over each of the ways. This representation of the angels appears either to have found a place in the original *Didaché*, or to have been connected with the Two Ways in the traditionary oral teaching, and so to have found its way, at an early stage, into the literature on the subject.

For evidence that Justin Martyr was acquainted with the "Teaching," I must refer to Dr. Taylor's *Lectures*. One instance adduced by him is specially interesting and striking, as it illustrates the most difficult saying in the *Didaché*, that "no prophet, approved and true, that does

The Didaché known to Justin Martyr.

anything with a view to a worldly mystery of the Church, but does not teach others to do as he does, shall be judged by you; for with God he has his judgment, for so did the ancient prophets also." "Doing something with a view to a worldly (or cosmic) mystery" means, no doubt, conveying instruction by symbolical representation, as the prophets often did. Justin Martyr in his *Dialogue with Trypho*, chapter xliv., says that under the old dispensation some precepts were laid upon the Jews with reference to the worship of God and the practice of righteousness, but some precepts and acts were mentioned with a view to the mystery of Christ (εἰς μυστήριον Χριστοῦ). In chapter xciv. he points out how God commanded Moses that no image or likeness of any thing in heaven or earth should be made, yet he caused the brazen serpent to be set up as a sign by which those bitten by serpents were saved. But in doing this he was free from sin, because "he proclaimed the mystery by which He would break the power of the serpent"—Christ crucified. And it was because this purpose was lost sight of, he says, that "the teachings of the prophets are falsely slandered." The key which unlocks the difficult sentence in the *Didaché* is here put into our hand by Justin. In chapters xciv., xcv. of his *Dialogue*, we seem also to have a commentary on another difficult phrase of the *Didaché*, "saved by (or from under) the curse itself."

From a review of all the evidence we are led to the conclusion that, prior to Barnabas, Hermas, Justin, and the rest, there was an original Christian *Didaché*, not very different from our *Didaché*, Conclusion.

but whose text may have had some additions made to it somewhat later from the traditionary oral teaching which no doubt accompanied and supplemented it. And evidently, whatever text was known to them, Barnabas, Hermas, and others did not feel under any obligation to reproduce it literally, but turned it to their own account with much ease and freedom.

CHAPTER V.

THE AGE OF THE DIDACHÉ.

WE have just reached the conclusion that there was an original Christian *Didaché* prior to Hermas and Barnabas, and which must have existed, therefore, before the close of the first century; it may have been considerably before the end of it. But in the shape in which it is now before us, as recovered by Bryennios, later accretions may have been made to it. It is necessary, therefore, as approximately as may be, to fix the date of the *Didaché* in the form in which we now possess it. To what age, in view of its present contents and characteristics, must it be assigned?

1. The first thing that strikes one is its silence with respect to certain Church usages which were prevalent from, at all events, the middle of the second century onwards, and which would have lain directly in its way to mention had it been written after that date. In its instructions with regard to baptism, for example, we have no allusion to any of those observances which began soon after that date to accompany the celebration of the rite. We know that Easter was celebrated in the time of Polycarp before the middle of the century, _{Silence as to Early Church observances; as in the case of Baptismal observances; of Easter;}

and that warm and protracted controversies arose as to the day of celebration. Our manual, though it gives directions about kindred matters, and though it constituted a sort of Church Directory in the locality where it circulated, is silent about Easter.

and of Ascetic Practices. Some, indeed, have imagined that they see in it traces of the ascetic practices of a later time. When our book says, "If thou art able to bear the whole yoke of the Lord thou shalt be perfect; but, if thou art not able, do what thou canst" (*Did.* vi. 2), Harnack attempts to show that celibacy is referred to; but the context is entirely against the supposition. The context makes it clear that "the whole yoke of the Lord" means the commands of the Lord just given in the previous part of the *Didaché*. Having just completed the summary of obligations contained in the first five chapters, the writer goes on: "See to it that no one lead thee astray from this way of the teaching, since he teacheth thee without (the authority of) God. For if thou canst bear the whole yoke of the Lord, thou shalt be perfect; but if thou canst not, what thou canst that do." "The whole yoke of the Lord" thus points back to the precepts which have just been given, which contain no hint about celibacy, but which contain several references which make this statement about "the yoke of the Lord" natural. The yoke which Christ invites men to take upon them (Matt. xi. 29) is, of course, all the obligations laid by Him on His followers. Now just as Jesus had said, "If thou wilt be perfect" (the same word as that used above), "go and sell that thou hast and give to the poor"—the *Didaché* says, "Thou shalt not hesitate to give; nor when thou dost give shalt thou murmur . . . Thou shalt not turn away from the needy, but thou shalt share all things with thy brother, and shalt not say that they are thine own" (iv. 7, 8)—a sentiment which recurs again to the writer's mind at the very moment when he says that he who is "able to bear the whole yoke of the Lord shall be perfect" (cf. v. 2 *ad finem*, with vi. 2). Again, as Jesus had said, "Whosoever shall smite thee on the right cheek, turn to him the other also" (Matt. v. 39); so our *Didaché* has said (i. 4), "If any one give thee a blow on the right cheek, turn to him the other also, *and thou shalt be perfect*;" adding other similar precepts from the Sermon on the Mount. Is there any need to go farther to learn what the writer means by "the yoke of the Lord," in bearing which his readers will be "perfect"? To shut one's eyes to these plain references, and discover in the phrase either monastic asceticism or Jewish ceremonialism, is a typical specimen of the pedantic style of criticism.

I may remark in passing that there is nothing of a Judaizing tendency in the book, and that though the writer was, in all probability, a *Jewish* Christian, he was certainly not a *Judaizing* Christian. Not only is there no hankering after any part of the Mosaic ritual: the Lord's day and not the Jewish sabbath is recognised, and the writer says: "Let not your fasts be with the hypocrites, for they fast on the second and fifth day of the week" (*Did.* viii. 1). The days mentioned were the Jewish fast days, and they who observe them are called "hypocrites." No Judaizer, and no Ebionite could have written thus. The Ebionite held to the

[marginal note: No Judaizing tendency in the book.]

Mosaic law, rejected Paul, and denied the divinity of Christ. But our writer has no predilection for Jewish ceremonial, quotes Paul's writings, strongly asserts Christ's "Lordship," and speaks of Him as "the God of David" (*Did.* x. 6). But this only by the way. What I desire to emphasise is that we look in vain in the *Didaché* for reference to any of those Church observances which began to prevail in the course of the second century.

2. We discover in it just as little trace of the *heresies* of the second century. It is well known how widespread and virulent and alarming to the Church were the Gnostic heresies of that period. In the *Didaché* there is no consciousness of them whatever; leading us to infer that it must have been written long before they became rife.

<small>No trace in it of Gnostic or Montanist heresies.</small>

As to Montanism: it is now being recognised more and more that, while it ran into many exaggerations and extravagances, it was on its better side a continuation, or at least a revival, of the spiritual Christianity of the New Testament, and a vigorous protest against the rigid ecclesiastical and hierarchical system into which apostolic Christianity was being rapidly transformed. While Dr. Sanday, in a recent number of *The Expositor*, has justly pointed out that "there was a conservative element in Montanism, Professor Harris, in a still more recent issue, takes it as beyond doubt that "Montanism was primitive Christianity," only with the primitive traits more pronounced and exaggerated through the opposition of "Catholicism" so called. If the Church of the *Didaché* seems at first sight to have some of the features of Montanism, it soon becomes apparent that it differs from Montanism

THE AGE OF THE DIDACHÉ. 77

in precisely those matters wherein Montanism differs from apostolic Christianity; and that in the teachers, apostles and prophets, as well as in the place held by the bishops of the *Didaché*, we have simply a continuation of apostolic Christianity, and characteristics which bring us close to the apostolic age.

3. At the time when our book was written and in regions where it was current, the Eucharist and love-feast were still united. "After being *filled* (μετὰ τὸ ἐμπλησθῆναι) give thanks after this manner," it says (*Did.* x. 1). A meal is clearly indicated by the expression "being filled." Dr. Taylor cites from the Talmud a striking parallel in the observance of the passover. Referring to the words of Deut. xvi. 2: "Thou shalt sacrifice the passover of the flock and the herd," it is asked, "Why not the flock only?" and the answer is that the herd was the *chagigah* (or feast offering), which, it is said, was "eaten first that the passover might be eaten *after being filled.*" There is no doubt the love-feast took the same place in the Lord's Supper as the paschal meal did in the celebration of the passover. Dr. Salmon, indeed, suggests that in this chapter the Lord's Supper is not contemplated at all, but merely some solemn meal. But it is expressly called "the Eucharist," and there is no evidence that even the love-feast, apart from the Lord's Supper, was ever so designated. We know that from very early times it was the distinctive title of the supper. Again, thanks are given not for "the bread" simply, but "for the *broken* bread"; "no one is to eat or drink of their Eucharist except those baptized"; and the words are applied to it which we

[sidenote: Eucharist and Love-feast still united when and where it was written.]

know were, in a somewhat varied form, applied to the Lord's Supper: "Give not that which is holy to the dogs." And the *oneness* of the bread once scattered on the mountains, used as a symbol of the unity of the Church, is evidently based on 1 Cor. x. 17, which refers to the Lord's Supper. We, therefore, cannot resist the conclusion that the Lord's Supper, as well as the love-feast, is here spoken of. Now it is well known that early in the second century the love-feast was separated from the Eucharist in at least Pontus and Bithynia, and probably over a much wider area. The Roman emperor and his consuls were exceedingly jealous of all clubs and associations (Hetæriæ) as perilous to the safety of the empire, and Trajan issued an edict against them. A great fire broke out in the city of Nicomedia, and as no means of extinguishing it were at hand, much damage was caused by the conflagration. It occurred to Pliny that it would be a prudent precaution to form an association of firemen, but, though he proposed to limit the number to one hundred and fifty members, Trajan refused to sanction it. He reminds Pliny how such societies have disturbed the peace of the empire, and adds that "whatever name we give them, and for whatever purpose they may be established, they are sure to become factious combinations." Trajan's edict was applied by Pliny to Christian assemblies, and one result was that, in that province at least, the love-feast was dissevered from the Eucharist. But there is no reason to believe that the edict took effect only in that region. The separation (partly as an effect of the edict, and partly also, no doubt, to avoid giving occasion to the popular rumours respecting the *epulæ thyesteæ*, the unnatural repasts attributed to the Christians by the heathen) was evidently widespread. In Justin Martyr's time, and in the countries known to him, they are separate. It is true that we find them united amongst the Copts till a late period, but such union appears to have been exceptional after the time referred to. The reference to the mountains in the *Didaché* makes it probable that it did not originate in Egypt. Its native soil was likely either Palestine or Asia Minor; and the circumstance that the Eucharist and the love-feast are represented by it as still observed together, raises at least a strong presumption that its age was not later than the early part of the second century.

4. The rules laid down regarding *Church organization*, point with still greater certainty to an early date. We know that some time in the first half of the second century the "bishop" begins to be distinguished from the "presbyters," and we begin to hear of the three orders, "bishop, presbyters and deacons," as congregational officials. *The notices of the ministry point to an early date;* Our document, however, just like Paul in his epistles, knows only of two orders of local office-bearers, "bishops and deacons." "Presbyters" are not named, because, as is admitted generally, "bishops" here are equivalent to "presbyters." It is suggestive that the fourth-century edition of the *Didaché*, the "Apostolical Constitutions," has "bishops, presbyters and deacons," where our treatise has only "bishops and deacons." When in addition to these we find "teachers," "apostles," and "prophets," with similar characteristics and similar means of testing them to those described in the New Testament (see

Did. x. 13 and Acts xiii. 1–4; xiv. 4, 14; 1 Thess. ii. 6; Rom. xvi. 7; 1 Cor. xv. 5–7), we are forced to the conclusion that the state of things which our little volume sets before us is one not far removed from the apostolic age.

5. The style and vocabulary are also more akin to those of the New Testament than those of any other post-apostolic writing; and technical and ecclesiastical terms which come into use from the second century onward are here conspicuous by their absence. Again, words which changed their meaning early in the history are here employed in the New Testament sense, as χειροτονεῖν, which means in the *Didaché* and in the New Testament *to elect*, but in later literature *to ordain*. At the close of the fourth chapter of our document we read, "In the congregation (ἐν ἐκκλησίᾳ) thou shalt confess thy transgressions." Some critics have taken ἐν ἐκκλησίᾳ, without the article, to mean "in church," and have seen in this a clear sign of "late workmanship." It is quite true that in early times the word "Church" was not applied to the place of meeting, but only to the Christian assembly. "I do not call the place, but the congregation of the elect, a church," says Clement of Alexandria.[1] But the absence of the article is no evidence that the place and not the congregation is intended in the passage before us. If the critics who suggest this had only opened their Greek Testament, they would have found that in at least four places in the First Epistle to the Corinthians ἐν ἐκκλησίᾳ occurs without the article, and in precisely the same sense as in the case before us, *i.e.*, in the

[1] *Strom.*, vii. 5. 29.

sense of congregation (see 1 Cor. xi. 18; xiv. 19, 28, 35.

The *substance* of our little book is in keeping with its style. "There is an archaic simplicity —I had almost said a childishness—in its practical directions, which is only consistent with the early infancy of a Church. Such is the test which it suggests of truth and falsehood. 'A true apostle,' says the writer, 'will only remain in a place a single day, or two at most; if a man who sets up for an apostle stays a third, he is a false prophet.'"[1]

[margin: as well as the substance of the Didaché;]

6. Another evidence of early date appears in the manner in which the Gospels and other New Testament books are cited. The Apostolic Fathers quote the Old Testament as Scripture, but, with one exception,[2] they never cite the Gospels or Epistles as such, or as written documents at all, the reason being twofold; first, because the New Testament writings, though familiar to them, as we know by their references, and their reproduction of many statements from them, that they were; and carrying, as they manifestly did in their view, quite exceptional authority, nevertheless have not yet been consciously and formally put by them in the canon along with the Old Testament Scripture, though we can already see in reading them the beginning of the process; and, secondly, because

[margin: and the manner of citing the New Testament.]

---

[1] Bishop Lightfoot, in *Expositor* for January, 1885.

[2] The exception is Barnabas (*Ep.* c. iv. 14) who quotes the words of Christ, "many are called, but few are chosen," with the formula, "it is written"; another sign that the epistle was written later than the *Didaché*, which never quotes the New Testament in this way.

those early Fathers, who either immediately succeeded the apostles, or had been in close intercourse with those who knew the apostles personally, naturally enough attached primary importance to the *oral* Gospel which they were able to trace back certainly and directly to apostolic teaching, and which enabled them thus to test the written Gospels and Epistles, and confirm their genuineness. So long as they were able to assure themselves by intercourse with those who had been in intimate fellowship with Peter, or Paul, or John, or James, that the Gospel which they possessed was the same as that which had been taught by those apostles of our Lord, the *writings* which also contained this Gospel had only a secondary value for them. "On any occasion," says Papias,[1] "when a person came in my way who had been a follower of the elders, I would inquire about the discourses of the elders—what was said by Andrew, or by Peter, or by Philip, or by Thomas or James, or by John or Matthew, or any other of the Lord's disciples, and what Aristion, and the elder John, the disciples of the Lord would say. For I did not think that I could get so much profit from the contents of books, as from the utterances of a living and abiding voice." It is manifest that books were already in existence and accessible. But I give the passage from Papias in order to point out that the *Didaché* accords exactly with the state of feeling prevalent in the sub-apostolic age. The Gospel is referred to as a whole, and in a way which I shall notice afterwards, and statements are evidently taken from several epistles, but no New Testament books are specified or cited as Scripture.

[1] Eusebius, *H.E.*, iii. 39.

In view of all the considerations I have presented, I feel coerced to the conclusion that the *Didaché* assumed the form with which Bryennios has made us familiar, not later than the opening of the second century, and it may have been a good deal earlier.

PART II.

CHURCH QUESTIONS ILLUSTRATED BY THE DIDACHÉ.

CHAPTER I.

THE NEW TESTAMENT CANON.

WHEN trying to ascertain the date of our document I had occasion to advert to the manner in which it quotes the Gospels and Epistles. It is a prior question, however, and one of still greater moment: Does it contain any evidence of the existence of New Testament books at the time when it was written? Let us now direct our attention to the facts which it offers in answer to this question.

It makes repeated reference to what it calls "the Gospel," "His (*i.e.* our Lord's) Gospel," and "the Gospel of our Lord," employing the word "Gospel" in the singular; and in one place quoting certain words as something which our Lord "has said." In *Did.* viii. 2 we read: "Neither pray ye as the hypocrites; but as the Lord commanded in His Gospel, so pray ye: 'Our Father, which art in heaven,'" etc. Then we have the Lord's prayer as it appears in Matthew. Again, *Did.* ix. 5: "Let no one eat or drink of your Eucharist except those who have been baptized into the name of the Lord, for concerning this the Lord hath said, *Give not that which is holy to the dogs.*" The Gospel is not named here, but a saying of our Lord is given which is peculiar to Matthew. These two

^{What evidence does it afford of New Testament writings?}

references, it is true, might point to an *oral* Gospel current and familiar in the Church, but the fact that in the one case a saying, and in the other a form of the Lord's prayer is cited, which is found only in Matthew, combined with the further circumstance that this is only one among many instances in which the words of Matthew's Gospel are reproduced, makes it probable that the source from which our author drew was none other than the Gospel of Matthew as we have it. This probability is greatly heightened by the further references in our treatise. Thus: " Concerning the Apostles and Prophets, according to the ordinance of the Gospel, so do ye " (*Did.* xi. 3). The writer has in view evidently, as we may gather from the context, such ordinances as those in Matt. x. 5-12 and Luke ix. 1-6. Here our author refers to a particular ordinance of the Gospel (which he supposes his readers to be possessed of and familiar with), instructing them to act in accordance with it. He could hardly take it for granted that they knew of such a particular precept unless he knew that they had within reach the written Gospel which contained it. But this is not all. " Reprove one another, not in wrath, but in peace, *as ye have it in the Gospel*" (ὡς ἔχετε ἐν τῷ εὐαγγελίῳ), says our author (*Did.* xv. 3). And again : "Your prayers and alms and all your actions so perform *as ye have it* in the Gospel of our Lord." This appeal of the writer to a definite fixed Gospel which he knows them to have in their possession, and which, he is also certain, embodies the details which he specifies, seems to carry us beyond a mere oral, traditionary Gospel, which would be more or less vague and fluctuating, and which could not be counted on to embrace such particular details. It supposes and points to a written Gospel; and has its parallel in such a statement as this in Clement of Alexandria: "We have not this saying in the four Gospels which have been handed down to us; it is found in the Gospel according to the Egyptians" (*Strom.* iii. 13). That our author himself had access to such a Gospel there can be little doubt. In this short work of his we have reproduced large portions of the Sermon on the Mount, and numerous other sayings of our Lord, some of them verbatim, and others substantially as they appear in Matthew—a fact all the more significant when it is remembered with what want of literal exactness the early Fathers are in the habit of quoting both Old Testament and New. It is, therefore, highly probable that the writer was familiar with, and knew that his readers were familiar with, a written Gospel the same as our Gospel of Matthew.

But now another circumstance has to be noted. It is remarkable that in some places the writer follows Luke's version of the sayings rather than Matthew's, showing that he either knew Luke's version also, or the oral version which it represents; while in the Eucharistic prayers we have distinct echoes of certain words of Christ in the sixth, fifteenth, and seventeenth chapters of John. It is no valid argument against his using more Gospels than one that he so often employs the word "Gospel" in the singular number. Justin Martyr does the very same thing, though we know that he was acquainted with the four Gospels or "memoirs" (cf. *Apol.* i. 66 with *Dial.* c. 10). And so does Irenæus (*Against Heresies*, iii. 11, 7, 8, 9).

There are also manifest citations and allusions in the *Didaché* which indicate acquaintance with the Acts of the Apostles, First and Second Thessalonians, the Epistle to the Romans, the First Epistle to the Corinthians, and that to the Ephesians; and there are reminiscences of John's First and Second Epistles, and of the Apocalypse.

If I am correct in the view just presented, and in the conclusion already reached as to the date of our treatise, it contains the earliest testimony we possess to a written Gospel or Gospels, and is on that account peculiarly interesting. But in order to a proper appreciation of the testimony which it offers it will be necessary and, I think, not without interest and advantage, to give a brief and rapid *résumé* of the first and second century evidence on this subject.

Apart from the *Didaché*, our earliest witnesses are of course the Apostolic Fathers, those early writers who are supposed to have been in personal communication with the Apostles; and of these Clement of Rome is generally placed first. The date of his epistle is probably about 96 A.D. Clement cites copiously from the Old Testament as Scripture, without specifying the particular books from which his citations are taken. He embodies in his letter not a little from the New Testament writings also, though he never refers to these as "Scripture," as he does in the case of the Old Testament, because the idea of a New Testament canon had not yet taken formal shape. And his quotations are what have been called "silent," without any mention of the source; only that the sayings of Christ are given

Other early evidence of New Testament writings.

The testimony of Clement of Rome;

as His thus: "Remember the words of the Lord Jesus, for He said, Woe to that man: it were better for him that he had not been born, than," etc. Peter and Paul are spoken of as "apostles" and "pillars." Paul's First Epistle to the Corinthians is, as we might have expected in a letter to the Church of Corinth, expressly mentioned, and the writer manifests acquaintance not only with the Epistles of Paul, but with James and First Peter, and in particular with the Epistle to the Hebrews.

Barnabas in like manner has sayings from the Gospels, the Epistles of Paul, First Peter, and the Apocalypse; and one of these, *of Barnabas;* the saying, "many are called, but few are chosen" (Matt. xxii. 14), is introduced with the formula "as it is written." Here, then, we have the first express quotation from a *written* Gospel. For obvious reasons I pass over Ignatius, and come to Polycarp, who wrote from Smyrna to the Philippian Christians.

Probably not much less than a quarter of a century has elapsed since the Epistles of Clement *of Polycarp.* and Barnabas were written. And Polycarp's letter has evident marks of progress; for whereas Clement's citations from the Old Testament are far more numerous than those made by him from the New Testament writings, those of Polycarp from the latter are far more abundant than from the former. Indeed he hardly ever, if at all, refers to the Old Testament, except as it appears in the New. The authoritativeness of the New Testament books is more expressly recognised than by Clement, and the process is well-nigh complete which puts them formally in the category with Old Testament Scripture

Polycarp reproduces not a little from Matthew, Mark, and Luke's Gospels, the Acts, ten or eleven of Paul's Epistles, James and First John, and he is especially profuse in his use of First Peter. He quotes anonymously like the others, but he makes express mention of Paul's Epistle to the Philippians, adding "neither I nor any other such one can come up to the wisdom of the blessed and glorified Paul." But perhaps the remark of his which is most noticeable in this connection, is that in his seventh chapter, where he says, "Whosoever perverts *the oracles of the Lord* to his own lusts, and says there is neither a resurrection, nor a judgment, he is the first-born of Satan." We know from Irenæus that Polycarp applied this very designation, the "first-born of Satan" to Marcion. Irenæus informs us, that on the two happening to meet on one occasion, Marcion said to Polycarp, "Acknowledge (or salute) us," and that the latter replied, "I acknowledge the first-born of Satan." In other respects the description here given by Polycarp applies to Marcion. We know from other sources that he formed a collection of sacred books in keeping with his heretical views, his Gospel having been an adaptation of that of Luke, and his Apostolicon including the Epistles of Paul. It is with reference to him that Dionysius says, "Some have attempted to mutilate the dominical Scriptures." I am satisfied by Harnack's argument as against Lightfoot, that it is Marcion to whom Polycarp refers in this place. There is no reason, therefore, to doubt that "the oracles of the Lord" to which Polycarp refers, were written oracles, which, though perverted by Marcion, were already well established and known in the Church.

With regard to the Apostolic Fathers generally, it should be observed that, though they make use of many sayings and passages which are found in our Gospels without informing us that they are taken from written documents, indeed without referring to any source at all, this is really no proof, no presumption even, that they did not use such documents; for they do precisely the same thing in the case of other writings—Paul's Epistles, for example—from which undoubtedly, and as is generally admitted, they reproduce not a little without any indication of the source, written or otherwise. But considering the brevity of the writings of the Apostolic Fathers, and that most of them were written in the form of letters to individuals or to Churches, it is remarkable that we discover in them traces of all the New Testament writings except Jude, 3 John, and 2 Peter.

Our next witness is Papias, who is supposed by Lightfoot to have been born not later than 70 A.D., but whose work belongs to the first quarter of the second century. He wrote a book entitled, "Exposition of Oracles of the Lord." The book itself has been lost, but valuable and interesting extracts from it have been preserved by Irenæus and Eusebius. In the preface to his work Papias says, "I shall not hesitate also to add for your benefit along with my interpretations, such things as I formerly carefully learnt and carefully remembered from the elders, guaranteeing their truth. For I did not, like many, take pleasure in those who have many things to say, but in those who teach the truth; nor in those who relate strange commands, but in those (who relate) such as were given from the

[marginal note: The testimony of Papias.]

Lord to the faith, and which came from the Truth itself. But if at any time any one came who had been a follower of the elders, I inquired what were the discourses of the elders—what was said by Andrew, or by Peter, or by Philip, or by Thomas, or by James, what John or Matthew or any other of the Lord's disciples said; and what Aristion and the presbyter John, the disciples of the Lord, say. For I did not think that I could profit so much from the contents of books as from the utterances of a living and abiding voice." After stating that he understands Papias to refer in this passage to two persons called John, John the apostle and John the presbyter, Eusebius says, "Papias professes to have received the sayings of the apostles from those who had been their followers, but says that he himself was an immediate hearer of Aristion and the presbyter John. Certainly he often mentions them by name, and gives their traditions in his writings." Having referred to several traditions which Papias had recorded, Eusebius goes on: "He has also handed down in his writing other accounts of the before-mentioned Aristion of the sayings of the Lord, and traditions of the presbyter John; to which referring those who desire to learn them, we shall now add to the extracts already given from him, a tradition which he sets forth concerning Mark, who wrote the Gospel, in the following words:—'And this also the Presbyter said: Mark having become the interpreter of Peter, wrote down accurately whatever he remembered, not indeed in order, of what was either said or done by Christ. For neither did he hear the Lord, nor follow Him; but afterwards, as I said, (he followed) Peter, who suited the instructions to the needs (of those who heard him), but not so as to make a connected narrative of the oracles (or discourses) of the Lord. So that Mark committed no mistake in thus writing down some things as he remembered them; for to one thing he gave heed, to omit nothing of what he had heard, nor to falsify anything in them.'" Eusebius then proceeds: "these things, then, are told by Papias with regard to Mark. But concerning Matthew he has said this: 'Matthew, then, compiled the oracles in the Hebrew dialect, but each one interpreted them as he was able.' He also made use of testimonies from the First Epistle of John, and likewise from that of Peter."[1]

Critics are not agreed on the point whether "the presbyter John" mentioned by Papias above is the same person as the John of the previous clause, the same, that is, as the apostle. Eusebius, as we have seen, distinguishes between them; but Irenæus, who had the treatise of Papias before him, and who in addition as a pupil of Polycarp, an intimate friend of Papias, was likely to have been better informed as to the facts than Eusebius, seems to have no doubt on the subject. Irenæus speaks of Papias as "a hearer of John [clearly meaning the apostle] and a companion of Polycarp."[2] But the point is immaterial for our purpose. What is worthy of notice is that the very object of Papias's book was to give "an exposition of the dominical oracles." There is no reasonable ground to doubt that by this term he means the Gospels. He actually connects the word with Matthew, who he says, "compiled the oracles in the Hebrew dialect;" and he expressly mentions in the passage

[1] Eus., *H.E.*, iii. 39.   [2] *Iren.*, v. 33, 4.

cited from him by Eusebius, the Gospel of Mark, supplying us with interesting information as to the way in which Mark derived it from Peter. There is every probability that Papias in his book referred to the other Gospels, but it did not lie in the way of Eusebius, nor serve his object, to employ the references. Even in the brief fragments of his which have been preserved, there are indications of his familiarity with both Luke and John, as well as the Acts of the Apostles. What is of special interest is that it is in Papias that we have the first express reference to any of the Gospels by *name*, and that their existence as written documents is implied at a period long antecedent to the date at which Papias wrote, that at the time when he was in intercourse with Aristion, and with the presbyter John, that is, probably, before the beginning of the second century, these writings were not only in existence, but recognised as genuine and authentic by immediate disciples of the Lord.

A contemporary of Papias was Quadratus, who addressed an Apology to Adrian. In an extract from this given by Eusebius,[1] Quadratus says, that "some of those [who had been healed and raised from the dead by Christ] have survived to our own times." Quadratus must have been born, therefore, long before the close of the first century, probably as early as A.D. 70 or 80, or it may have been earlier still. This same Quadratus and others Eusebius describes[2] as immediate disciples of the apostles, who built up the Churches whose foundations had been previously laid by the apostles, and who "afterwards, leaving their own

The testimony of Quadratus.

[1] *H.E.*, iv. 3.   [2] *H.E.*, iii. c. 37.

country, performed the office of evangelists to those who had not yet heard the faith; whilst, with a noble ambition to serve Christ, they also delivered to them the writing of the Divine Gospels." Eusebius gives as his authority the account preserved in the Memorials of apostolic teaching still extant, he says, when he wrote his history—referring, no doubt, to such books as that of Papias and the Memorials of Hegesippus. There is not the slightest reason, then, to doubt the thorough trustworthiness of the statement, that those immediate disciples of the apostles who became Evangelists to those who had not yet heard the faith, delivered to them also "the writing (τὴν γραφήν) of the Divine Gospels"—a most important testimony to the existence of written Gospels at a very early date, and as having been in the keeping of immediate disciples of the apostles, who, therefore, were in the best position to judge of their genuineness.

It is singular that among the most conclusive and striking testimonies on behalf of the Gospels and other New Testament writings are those borne by the heretics of that time. Hippolytus, in his *Philosophumena*, or *Refutation of all Heresies*, recently discovered and published in 1851, quotes largely from Basilides and Valentinus, Gnostic heretics who wrote, the former about A.D. 125, and the latter a few years later. Basilides, who belonged to the reign of Hadrian (Clem. Alex., *Strom.* vii. 17), had a work in twenty-four books on "the Gospel." The important thing is that both he and Valentinus accept of the four Gospels as genuine, and quote them as well as Paul's Epistles freely, and particularly the Gospel of John.

The testimonies of the heretics Basilides and Valentinus.

Basilides, for example, is represented by Hippolytus as saying, "this is that which is spoken of in the Gospels: 'that was the true light which lighteth every man that cometh into the world.'" Here is John's Gospel, along with the others, accepted by the Gnostic heresiarchs at this early period. What does this fact—that these sacred writings are, in the first quarter of the second century, without question recognised as genuine by orthodox and heterodox alike—imply? It implies that their genuineness must have been accepted and securely established before the heresies and consequent separation originated. Had the writings in question, or any of them, appeared after the development of the Gnostic aberrations, it is not conceivable that they would have been received as apostolic by both, as indeed it is impossible to conceive their acceptance as apostolic writings by any within whose memory they had first become known; supposing, that is to say, that they did not come from the apostles and their fellow-disciples, but were subsequently produced. We are thus able, by another line of evidence, to trace them back as accepted apostolic writings to a date prior to the close of the first century.

Justin Martyr wrote towards the middle of the second century, and was born not far from the beginning of it. He speaks of "the memoirs composed by the apostles, which are called Gospels," and says that when the Christians met on "the day called Sunday," either these or the writings of the prophets were read as long as time permitted. He also makes such abundant and peculiar use of the four Gospels, including John (with

The testimony of Justin Martyr.

whose ideas and phrases his writings are impregnated) and other New Testament writings, as to leave no room for reasonable doubt that the sacred writings used by him were the same as those which we possess. And Justin, who was born in the East, and had travelled and sojourned in the West, has no knowledge of any other state of things than that which he describes. The assured place held by these apostolic writings over the whole Church is the place which they have held so far back as his memory and knowledge reach. Let the reader again ask himself how long time it must have taken before they could have been thus established in the unquestioning faith and confidence of the Church.

Justin had a pupil called Tatian, who after the death of his master became a heretic. Tatian made a harmony of the four Gospels, which he called "*Diatessaron*" (a term in music, which means here, doubtless, a concord of four), which began with the opening sentence of John's Gospel: "In the beginning was the word"; and which got into, and for centuries continued in, large use in the orthodox Churches. Ephraem Syrus, who died in 373, wrote a commentary on it, of which an Armenian translation exists. A Latin translation of the Armenian was published in 1876, and from this, with other aids, the original text of the *Diatessaron* has been approximately reconstructed; and puts it beyond doubt that Tatian's work was based on the four Gospels as we have them. Let it be remembered that Tatian was a pupil of Justin, and that the Gospels used by the pupil must have been the same as those employed by the master.

The testimony of Tatian;

Theophilus of Antioch, about 170, quotes from the prologue of John's Gospel, ascribing it expressly to John, and representing it as inspired. Apollinaris, about the same date, speaks of "the teaching of the New Testament, to which it is impossible that anything should be added or anything diminished from it." He describes some as "showing the Gospels to be at variance with one another" with regard to the time of the paschal observance, expressly names Matthew, and implies the existence of John. The date assigned to the Muratorian fragment on the canon varies from 160 to the beginning of the third century. In it we have the first formal list of the New Testament writings. The fragment begins with a broken sentence, after which the writer proceeds to speak of "the third book of the Gospel, that according to Luke," next of "the fourth Gospel, that of John"; then of the Acts, of Paul's Epistles, and other New Testament books. There can be no doubt that immediately before the broken sentence with which the mutilated fragment begins, the writer had been referring to Matthew and Mark, for he speaks of "the several books of the Gospels," calling Luke the third and John the fourth Gospel.

Irenæus, Bishop of Lyons, was born in Asia Minor about 130, and had been a pupil of Polycarp, of whose manner and teaching, he tells us, he had a very vivid recollection. A person called Florinus had in early life, along with Irenæus, sat at the feet of Polycarp. Florinus, having subsequently imbibed heretical opinions, is thus addressed by Irenæus

in a letter which has been preserved by Eusebius:—
"These doctrines the presbyters before us, who also were disciples of the apostles, did not deliver to thee. For when I was yet a boy I saw thee in Lower Asia, with Polycarp, moving in splendour in the royal court, and endeavouring to secure his good will. For I remember the incidents of that time better than those of recent occurrence; for the things we have learned in youth, growing with the mind, become united to it; so that I can tell the very place where the blessed Polycarp was accustomed to sit and discourse, and his goings out and comings in, and his way of life, and his personal appearance, and the discourses which he addressed to the people, and how he described his intercourse with John, and with the rest who had seen the Lord, and how he rehearsed their words, and what he had heard from them about the Lord, and about His miracles, and about His teaching; all these Polycarp, having received them from eyewitnesses of the Word of Life, would relate in accordance with the Scriptures."[1] That is, what Polycarp told them he had learned from John and others who had seen the Lord with regard to Christ and His miracles and teaching, was in accordance with the accounts recorded in the New Testament Scriptures. Irenæus was the younger contemporary and successor of Pothinus, who at the time of the persecution of the Christians in Gaul was past the age of ninety, and who was, therefore, born eleven or twelve years before the death of John, and must have been intimate with some of our Lord's immediate disciples and with many disciples of the apostles. Thus,

[1] Euseb., *H.E.*, v. 20.

through two different channels, through Polycarp and through Pothinus, Irenæus has had the means of becoming thoroughly conversant with the real facts as regards the New Testament writings. But he has not a shadow of doubt respecting them. "We have learned," he says, "from none others the plan of our salvation, than from those through whom the Gospel has come down to us, which they did at one time proclaim in public, and, at a later period, by the will of God, handed down to us in the Scriptures, to be the ground and pillar of our faith. . . . Matthew issued a written Gospel among the Hebrews in their own dialect, while Peter and Paul were preaching at Rome, and laying the foundations of the Church. After their departure, Mark, the disciple and interpreter of Peter, also transmitted to us in writing what had been preached by Peter. Luke also, the companion of Paul, recorded in a book the Gospel preached by him. Afterwards John, the disciple of the Lord, who also leaned upon His bosom, himself published a Gospel when residing at Ephesus in Asia."[1] Irenæus refers at length to the four Gospels, and it is admitted on all hands that those known to him were the same as ours. He is also familiar with the other New Testament Scriptures. Nor is it doubted that the New Testament writings familiar to Clement of Alexandria are identical with those known to us.

Here then we have an irrefragable chain of evidence connecting these sacred writings with their apostolic authors, and such as no other ancient literature can pretend to offer in

Conclusion.

[1] Iren., *Against Heresies*, B. iii. c. 1.

support of its genuineness. Is it not, to say the least, a singular Providence that has preserved for us such historical testimony? And are not the facts adduced enough to show that, in supposing that the "Gospel" so often appealed to by the *Didaché* as in possession of its readers was a written Gospel, we are making no unhistorical supposition, but one thoroughly sustained by the evidence of history?

But while the *Didaché* bears early and valuable testimony in behalf of the Gospels and other New Testament books, I may remark further, while on this part of our subject, that it unites with the other early literature to overthrow effectually what is known as the Tübingen hypothesis. It was contended by Baur and his disciples that Christianity at first was but a form of Judaism, or Ebionism; that Jesus was Himself an Ebionite, and claimed to be nothing more than a man; that it was in this form Christianity was preached, and continued to be preached by the original apostles; that it was Paul who took the first great step beyond this and began a wide deviation from the Christianity of Christ Himself; that there was thus a deep and radical difference between Paul's gospel and that of the Twelve—a difference that continued while they lived; that in four of Paul's Epistles —the Epistles to the Romans and Galatians, and the two Epistles to the Corinthians (the only letters of Paul admitted to be genuine by Baur)—there are signs of this antagonism; that in the famous Clementine writings (so-called) we see an example of the Ebionite opposition to Paul, who is covertly assailed under the name of Simon Magus, and that in the Marcionites,

[Sidenote: The Didaché also refutes the Tübingen hypothesis.]

on the other hand, who refuse to recognise any of the apostles except Paul, we have the true Pauline party; that the greater number of the New Testament books, including the Gospels, were written late in the second century, and mainly by way of an Eirenicon for the purpose of representing that there was no real or deep variance between Paul and the Twelve, and in order to reconcile the contending factions; and that in the Gospel of John we see the last result of the struggle between Paulinism and Ebionism—"a treaty of peace signed on the heights of Gnosticism" (Baur). The theory, however, is destitute of any historical basis that can be called even plausible. The Ebionism of the Clementine books was held only by an insignificant faction, and has been shown to be a development of the second century of very limited dimensions, both historically and in its tenets quite distinct from the Judaizing Christianity which so much harassed Paul.[1] Above all, neither in the work before us, nor in the Apostolic Fathers, nor in any of the genuine Christian literature of that time do we detect any sign of the alleged antagonism. On the contrary, the different types of Christian thought—the Pauline, the Petrine, and the Johannine—are combined and blended in one harmonious system. And by the stress of hard historical facts the survivors of this school have been gradually driven from the position which they had taken.

[1] See Lightfoot's Dissertation on "St. Paul and the Three," in his "Epistle to the Galatians."

CHAPTER II.

FAMILY AND SOCIAL LIFE.

IT is only a glimpse of the Christian home life which the *Didaché* affords, but it is exceedingly suggestive:—

"Thou shalt not take away thy hand from thy son, or from thy daughter, but from their youth up shalt teach them the fear of God. Thou shalt not in thy bitterness give orders to thy bondman or thy bondwoman, who hope in the same God, lest they should not fear the God who is over both; for He doth not come to call according to outward appearance, but on those whom the Spirit hath prepared. And ye, bondmen, shall submit yourselves unto your masters, as to the image of God, in modesty and fear."

Not much is said here, but enough is said to speak volumes to any one who knows what domestic life was among the surrounding heathen at the period when our little book was written. Indeed we are quite unable to appreciate what Christianity did for the home unless we have some knowledge of the deplorable condition out of which it was lifted by the new religion, some idea of the evils incident to the pagan family life of that age. It is the dark background necessary to complete and set off the picture of the Christian household, and on

Pagan family life.

which, therefore, we must delay the reader for a moment.

The head of the family, whether as husband, as father, or as master, was, by Roman law, almost omnipotent within the domain of the household. He had almost unlimited control even over his wife, who held a position of abject inferiority, and was little better than his slave. She was, in the legal phrase of the time, *in manu mariti*, under the hand of her husband. His power over her was virtually absolute. Her legal relation to him was that of a child to the parent, and what that was we shall see immediately. She could hold no property. He might lend her to another man, or bequeath her to him by will. After marriage she was shut up for the most part with her slaves, in the seclusion of the *gynæceum*. Her education, and her opportunities of mixing with society being very limited, she usually lacked the intelligence and refinement which these conditions are needed to supply; and her husband was not expected to find any profit or delight in her companionship. He rather looked for these in the *Hetæræ*—the courtesans of the period—who mixed freely with men, even with the noble and the educated, and to increase their charms sedulously cultivated both mind and manners. It was in this class that the Augustan poets found their Lesbias, their Delias, and their Cynthias. Nor was it expected that the husband should be faithful. The marriage tie, at the time I speak of, was not regarded as imposing any obligation. It was inevitable that the moral nature of the woman should be degraded by the inferior status thus assigned to her, and by the treat-

[marginal note: Inferior status of the wife.]

ment naturally arising from it. So much was this the case, so abandoned and profligate had women become, that it was thought that they were naturally more inclined to evil than men. "Nil non permittit mulier sibi, turpe putat nil," says Juvenal, in his sixth Satire. He speaks of a chaste woman as a "rara avis in terris." He represents the woman of his day as laughing in mockery as she passes the altar of modesty. As we learn from Clement of Alexandria and from other sources, she went to the public baths, and bathed promiscuously with the men; and she even fought in the gladiatorial combats in the amphitheatre. Divorces were without number. Seneca refers to a woman who reckoned the years not by the names of the consuls, but by the names of her husbands. Such women with their impure souls within, but adorned as regards their outward persons with paints and perfumes and meretricious finery, Clement of Alexandria likens to an Egyptian temple, with its sacred groves surrounding it, its porticoes and vestibules, its walls gleaming with gold and silver, with artistic paintings and many-coloured gems from India, and its shrines veiled with gold-embroidered hangings; but if you enter the penetralia, and seek the divinity within, the god that is adored, you will be shown—a cat or a crocodile or a serpent. So, he says, withdraw the veil of this temple —take away the dye, and the paint, the gold, the finery, and the cosmetics, and you find, not the image of God, but—a fornicator and adulteress.

I have said that the legal relation of the wife to the husband was somewhat similar to that of the child to the parent. What, *Helpless position of the child.*

then, was the relation of the son to the father? It was one of absolute and helpless subjection. Without violating any law, the Roman father might scourge or imprison his son, appropriate any property he may have acquired by his industry, sell him as a slave, or even put him to death. And the father retained this power while he lived, though his son may have passed middle life, and risen to the highest honours of the state. First of all, when the child was born, it was a matter open to debate whether he would be reared or not. He might be killed, or cast away to be devoured by dogs or wild beasts, or to be picked up as an abandoned child and consigned to slavery, or, in the case of a female child, it might be to the *lupanar*. The children of the proudest patrician families of Rome were thus abandoned, and were often to be found in the foulest and most infamous resorts of the city. The references to child murder in our manual are brief, but pointed and significant (*Did.* ii. and v.), and are abundantly confirmed by contemporary literature. Gibbon says, "The Roman empire was stained with the blood of infants."[1] If the child's life was spared, he or she grew up subject to the unlimited authority of the father, to be disposed of according to his will. He arranged the marriage of his children. The daughter had no option but to take the husband

---

[1] "Decline and Fall," chap. xliv. "It seemed so natural a thing, in the old heathen world, to expose infants, if it was not found convenient to rear them, the crime excited so little remark, was so little regarded as a crime at all, that it was not worth while to find a name for it; and thus it is nothing wonderful to learn that the word 'infanticidium' was first born in the bosom of the Christian Church. Tertullian is the first in whose writings it appears."—Trench, "On the Study of Words," Lect. v.

chosen by the father. She was his property, and her consent was not necessary. He could even sell her into slavery. Their situation being thus helpless and abject, it is no wonder that the children did their best to make up for their lack of independence by cunning and deceit, and by employing the slaves as their accomplices in frustrating the desires of their father. Their training and education were in a great degree in the hands of slaves, and generally of the most incapable of the slaves of the household, who from physical defects were unfit for active labour. And what was the environment amid which they grew up to manhood? Apart from the contemporary literature, the ruins of Pompeii tell us. The walls of the dwellings in which they lived, and the rooms in which they slept, were covered with frescoes and pictures of the most sensual and obscene character; and the very air which they breathed was impregnated with impurity. How could it be otherwise than that such a home was as a rule without purity, without filial respect, and without natural affection?

But the family had other inmates whose position was still more abject and degraded. I refer to the *slaves*. Indeed the word *familia* meant originally the body of slaves connected with a household. Under the Empire the slaves were almost numberless—three or four times as numerous as the rest of the people—and constituted the great mass of the population. A rich Roman would possess thousands of slaves, over whom his power was simply boundless. He could scourge and torture them, and put them to death when he chose, and for the most trivial fault. A master was killed by his slave through jealousy or

<small>Slavery.</small>

passion, and in consequence the four hundred slaves connected with the household were all put to death by the express sanction of the Senate. The slave was merely a piece of property, a thing, a chattel, and the master could deal with him as such. He had no rights. He could not bring an action at law. The law did not recognise even the right of marriage as existing among slaves. They might cohabit at the pleasure of the master, to whom their children belonged as part of his stock. The female slaves were of course in like manner at his disposal. What the result was the reader may imagine. Too generally the slaves were housed in the most loathsome manner, sleeping in the *ergastula*, or private prisons which were kept by the masters. And it should be remembered that the slaves were not of a different colour, nor of an alien race from their masters. They were often their own flesh and blood. Their ranks were being continually recruited by the captives taken in war, by the sale of insolvent debtors, or by children who had been either sold or cast away by their parents. It is easy to understand that a class so numerous and so oppressed constituted a constant and most serious danger to the State. "As many enemies as slaves," Seneca speaks of as a proverb. No doubt the masters were often much kindlier and more considerate than the law required; and no doubt the slaves found some protection in public opinion. But it was inevitable that such a condition should degrade and demoralize them; so that a "servile" spirit became a synonym for meanness and vice. It also filled them with a feeling of hopelessness and despair which made suicide a common occurrence among them.

If it be true, as undoubtedly it is, that the morals of society in general depend upon those of the family, what the outcome of the domestic life which I have sketched was, does not need to be detailed. It would be difficult to exaggerate the corruption which everywhere prevailed, and which was intensified by a variety of causes—such as the grinding political despotism on the one side, and the cringing meanness on the other; the disgrace which was attached to labour, which was therefore left in the hands of the slave-class, while the rest of the people lived in idleness and pleasure. Whatever restraining influence religion may have previously exerted, was relaxed by the withering scepticism which was now so widespread. In such worship as there was, Bacchus and Venus, the Egyptian Isis, the Cybele of Asia Minor and Astarte—the patrons of impurity and pleasure—had taken the place of the superior divinities. And to such a pass had society come that common pleasures and ordinary vicious excesses were insufficient to satisfy the craving of its morbid appetite. At once to excite and gratify it the amphitheatre ran with rivers of human blood, shed in the gladiatorial contests; and unnatural vice of the most abominable description was freely indulged in. One form of it, expressly mentioned by the Didaché, *pæderasty*, was exceedingly prevalent. Clement of Alexandria represents the life of many in his time as "nothing but revel, debauchery, baths, excess . . . idleness, drink. You may see some of them half drunk, staggering . . . vomiting drink on one another in the name of good fellowship. . . . It is well, my friends, it is well to make an

Moral putrefaction of society.

acquaintance with this picture at the greatest possible distance from it, and to frame our lives to what is better." He gives a contemptuous picture of the dandies of the time having their hair pulled out by means of pitch-plasters in order that they may look soft and effeminate. It would make them more beautiful, he remarks, to pluck out not hairs but lusts.

Christianity regenerated family life; Christianity met these evils by beginning at the fountain-head, and by casting its healing salt into the spring of waters. Its first care was to revolutionize and regenerate the family life. It lifted woman from the inferior status to which she had been depressed, and made the mar- *elevated woman;* riage union one of equality and of mutual respect and affection. "If the God of both is one," says Clement,[1] "the master of both is also one: one Church, one temperance, one modesty; their food is common, their marriage an equal yoke. . . . And those whose life is common, have common grace, and a common salvation. Common, therefore, to men and women is the name of man."

required careful upbringing of children. As our manual shows, very special care was given to the proper upbringing of the children in the Christian home. "Thou shalt not take away thy hand from thy son or from thy daughter, but from their youth up shalt teach them the fear of God." The kindred exhortations of Clement of Rome, of Polycarp, and of Hermas on this subject, show how earnest the early teachers were about it.[2] Such counsels were all the more necessary

---

[1] *Pæd.*, chap. iv.
[2] See Clem. Rom., i. *ad Cor.*, c. 21; Polycarp, *Ep.*, c. 4; Hermas, *Pastor*, *Vis.* i. 3.

as the education of Christian children appears to have been carried on exclusively in their own home. Christian parents, so far as we can gather, did not send their children to the pagan schools. And we meet with no traces of primary schools among the Christians till the fourth century, when we find them in charge of priests. As the father's time was taken up with his daily work, the education of the children fell chiefly into the hands of the mother, and very beautiful are the representations in the Catacombs of the mother surrounded by her little ones, whom she is tenderly training in Divine nurture. For the early Church did not think it necessary that children should pass out of childhood before they would be capable of being regenerated. Jesus "came to redeem all," says Irenæus,[1] "all who through Him are born again to God; infants, little children, boys, young men and old. Therefore He passed through every age; for the infants He became an infant, sanctifying the infants; among the little children He became a little child, to sanctify those who are of this age, and present to them an example of piety, uprightness and obedience."

The *régime* of the Christian family was one of severe temperance, and extreme simplicity. "On the road to heaven," says Clement of Alexandria, "the best provision is frugality; moderation is the shoe, and beneficence the staff." He would have been a warm advocate of our modern Bands of Hope; for he says, "I admire those . . . who are fond of water, the medicine of temperance, and flee as far as possible

The family régime severe though not austere or gloomy.

[1] Irenæus, *Against Heresies*, ii. c. 22, s. 4.

from wine, shunning it as they would fire. It is proper that boys and girls should keep as much as possible away from this medicine."[1] On the other hand, the spirit of the Christian home was not austere, cold, nor gloomy. "We are no Brahmins nor Indian gymnosophists," says Tertullian, "no wild men of the woods, nor separatists from life. We are mindful of the gratitude which we owe to the Lord our God, and do not despise the enjoyment of His works. We only so moderate it as to avoid excess and abuse."[2] Gymnastic exercises were strongly recommended. Even angling was encouraged as a lawful and apostolic practice, only it was pointed out that "that was the better sport which the Lord assigned to the disciple when He taught him to catch men." While images in their homes were peremptorily forbidden, the use of Christian symbols was allowed. The figure of a shepherd carrying a lamb on his shoulder was common on their goblets. " Pleasantry is permissible, but not frivolity," says Clement.[3] "Whatever things are natural to men we must not eradicate, but impose limits and times. One needs not be gloomy, but only grave." It is very touching to see the toys of little children depicted on their tombs in the Catacombs. One has the picture of a child holding out a bunch of grapes to a bird.

With regard to the institution of slavery, the early Christian Church had a more difficult and delicate task to perform. How was it to be dealt with? Had the Church entered on a revolutionary crusade against a system so deeply

How Christianity dealt with slavery.

---

[1] *Pæd.*, Book II. chap. I.   [2] *Apol.*, 42.
[3] *Pæd.*, Book II. chap. I.

rooted and so widespread, and encouraged revolt on the part of the slave population, the inevitable result would have been to cause useless bloodshed, to rivet the bonds of the slave more closely; while in all likelihood such a movement would have recoiled with fatal effect on Christianity itself. Perhaps in nothing do we see more the profound wisdom of the apostolic teaching, than in the policy adopted regarding slavery. No direct blow is aimed at it. No encouragement is given to the slave to rebel or escape from his master. On the contrary, as in our little treatise, he is exhorted "to submit himself to his master as the image of God, in modesty and fear." But broad and far-reaching principles are introduced which work silently, and are destined ultimately to overthrow the system. Both masters and their slaves are taught the worth of individual man, no matter what his position in society. They are all equal before Him in whom there is neither bond nor free. And meantime Christian masters are taught to mitigate the evils of the system in every way possible. "Thou shalt not in thy bitterness," says our book, "give orders to thy bondman, or thy bondwoman, who hope in the same God, lest they should not fear the God who is over both; for He doth not come to call according to outward appearance," etc. What a contrast to the customs of pagan society, when masters and slaves were taught to sit down together as equals at a common table in the celebration of the Lord's Supper, and of the love-feast. And inside the Church it was the slaves often who held the superior position, for its offices were all open to them. In the third century, one who had been a slave became Bishop of Rome. It is significant that in the earlier inscriptions in the Catacombs there is no reference to the social condition of those whose bodies rest there. It is only from their names that one can guess whether they were bond or free. And it should not be forgotten that one form assumed by the charity of the early Church, was the subscription of large sums of money for the voluntary emancipation of slaves. "Behold Christ Himself," says Cyprian, "in your captive brethren, and redeem from captivity Him who has redeemed us from death. Snatch from the hands of the barbarians Him who has snatched us from the grasp of the demon, and purchase with money the liberation of Him who purchased us with His blood."[1] Nay, in many instances, prompted by a still more chivalrous charity, Christians sacrificed their own freedom to emancipate their captive brethren. "We know many among ourselves," says Clement of Rome,[2] "who have given themselves up to bonds in order that they might ransom others. Many too have surrendered themselves to slavery that with the price which they received for themselves, they might provide food for others."

Thus did early Christianity regenerate and transform the family in all its relations. And thus too by renovating it at the heart did it seek to sweeten the breath of society.

[1] Cyprian, *Ep.* 62, c. 2.   [2] 1 *Ep.*, c. 55.

CHAPTER III.

CHRISTIAN UNITY AND CHARITY.

TO nothing does our treatise bear more emphatic testimony than to the sense of unity and brotherhood which existed in the primitive Church. It is silent as to any supreme authority of individual or council. It is indeed some- *How Christian unity was maintained* what remarkable that we hear nothing of *and exhibited;* any Church synod from the time of the Council of Jerusalem about the year 50 A.D. (Acts xv.) till after the middle of the second century; and this is all the more singular in view of the wide-spread and virulent Gnostic heresies which at this time disturbed and harassed the Church. Such councils could hardly have been held without attracting the notice, and challenging the interference, and arousing the hostility of the adverse civil power. Besides, so long as any of the first apostles survived, their advice served in a great degree no doubt in place of such a synod, and when they passed away the opinion of men like Polycarp and others, who had been in close contact with the apostles, carried much weight. Yet during this period there was such real inner unity, such brotherhood and true solidarity among Christians everywhere as probably have never been known since. We have ample proof of this in the work before us.

The members of the Church have learned as Catechumens, a common faith. They are all baptized into the Tri-une name. Their lives are regulated by a common law—the law of Christ. The local congregations are uniformly managed by presbyter-bishops and deacons, each congregation having a plurality of both. And, besides the local office-bearers, there are certain ministers called "teachers," "apostles," and "prophets," who belong to the whole Church; itinerate from place to place, and help to keep the more remote Christian communities *en rapport* with one another.

promoted by the itinerant ministry;

Above all, they are partakers of one bread in the Eucharist, and of a common life in Christ, to which there is a beautiful allusion in one of the Eucharistic prayers: as the broken bread of the Eucharist was scattered in ears upon the mountains, and gathered together became one, so they are taught to pray that from the ends of the earth the Church may be gathered together in Christ's kingdom (*Did.* c. 9). And in many and touching ways does this deep sense of brotherhood express itself. On every Lord's day they come together to worship God and to celebrate the Eucharist and love-feast; nor on the Lord's day only: "Be ye gathered together often, seeking the things that concern your souls" (*Did.* xvi. 2). And again: "Thou shalt seek out daily the faces of the saints, that thou mayest rest on their words" (*Did.* iv. 2). And from another source we learn that at an early period the Christian people were wont to hasten every morning, immediately on rising, to the place of Christian meeting, in order to engage in worship, and observe the

by frequent meetings and celebrations of Eucharist and love-feast;

Eucharist.[1] But it is in their hospitality and boundless charities that we see the most striking manifestation of their brotherly feeling. {and boundless hospitality and charity.}

It was a time of movement within the empire, when there was much more travelling to and fro than we should expect in circumstances when the means of transfer from place to place were so much fewer and less rapid than in our age. And as at the time I speak of the majority of Christians belonged to the humbler and poorer classes, a correspondingly great demand was made on the generosity of Christian householders. In fact every Christian home was regarded as an asylum for the stranger and a refuge for the destitute members of the Church. The early Christian teachers lay the greatest stress on this. Melito of Sardis wrote a book on the subject,[2] and there is hardly an early writer who does not insist on it.[3] Our book is particularly urgent on the matter. Every wayfarer who comes in the name of God, no matter where he comes from, is to be received, and, on being duly proved, entertained. "Whosoever cometh in the name of the Lord let him be received. . . . If so be he that cometh is a wayfarer, help him as much as ye are able." As, however, Christian hospitality was liable to be abused by spies and impostors, it was necessary not only to exercise caution, but to be able to test such wanderers. Hence our book speaks of "proving" them. Whether, in addition to the simple, {Yet the hospitality not indiscriminate.}

---

[1] *Egypt. Const.*, ii. 58.   [2] Euseb., *H.E.*, iv. 20.
[3] See Clem., *ad Cor.* i. 1, 11, 12; Hermæ, *Past.* Sim. ix. 27; Tertullian, *ad Ux.*, ii. 4; Euseb., *H.E.*, iv. 23.

practical tests prescribed in it, any credentials were required, we are not informed; but we know that a little later no traveller was entertained who did not bring with him a letter of introduction from the chief official of the Church; and as such letters were sometimes forged it became necessary that they should be written in a certain form which made imitation impossible or difficult. Such letters were called *Literæ Formatæ*. But there is no doubt that the constant intercourse thus kept up between remote Churches brought them into closer relations with one another; made them better acquainted with one another's circumstances and troubles; conveyed suggestions from one to the other; and became a source of encouragement and help in times of difficulty and trial. When

Liberality of the Churches of Carthage the Church of Numidia was unable to pay the sum required for the ransom of their imprisoned members, the Christians of Carthage, consisting of 3,000 or 4,000 poor people, made a collection on their behalf amounting to 100,000 HS. or about £900, and supplied them with what was needed. At an early period the Church of Rome

and Rome. was especially famed for such liberality. Eusebius gives a letter ascribed to Dionysius to the Roman Christians, in which Dionysius says, "this practice has prevailed with you from the very beginning, to do good to all the brethren in every way, and to send contributions to many Churches in every city. Thus refreshing the needy in their want, and furnishing to the brethren condemned to the mines, what was necessary, by those contributions which ye have been accustomed to send from the beginning, you preserve as Romans, the practice of your ancestors the Romans, which was not only observed by your bishop Soter, but also increased; as he not only furnished great supplies to the saints, but also encouraged the brethren that came from abroad, as a loving father his children, with consolatory words."[1] Eusebius informs us that 1,500 widows and poor were supported by the Romish Church. Mommsen (v. 52) says that the cost of a slave's maintenance in the first century was computed at £7 10s. 0d. annually. Reckoning by this, the cost of the 1,500 poor Christians would be £11,250 per annum. Even the half of that would be a large sum for the Roman Church, considering all the demands upon her. The spontaneous and the generous charities of the Christians attracted the notice and excited the surprise of the heathen. "The eagerness of these people" (says Lucian in his *De Morte Peregr.*), "when one of them falls into misfortune is incredible; they spare nothing to bring him aid."

No matter to what class they belonged, the fact of their being in need was a sufficient cause, in any of their fellow-beings, to evoke their charity. But very special care and sympathy went out towards the widow and the orphan. Polycarp in a bold and striking figure describes widows as "the altar of God," the altar on which the Church lays her offerings. Christian householders are exhorted to take charge of orphans, to receive them into their houses, and treat them as if they were their own children. "When any Christian becomes an orphan, whether a young man or a maid, it is good that some one of the brethren who

Care of widows and orphans.

[1] Euseb., *H.E.*, B. iv. c. 23.

is without a child should take the young man, and
esteem him in the place of a son ; and he that has a
son about the same age, who is marriageable, should
marry the maid to him : for they which do so, perform
a great work, and become fathers to the orphans,
and shall receive the reward of this charity from the
Lord God." And instructions are given to bring up
the young men to some trade so that they may not
be burdensome to the brethren.[1] Thus Origen on
the martyrdom of Leonidas his father was taken
home by a wealthy Christian lady of Alexandria and
treated as her own child.[2] And in like manner the
new-born child of Felicitas, the slave-martyr at Carthage, was taken charge of by a Christian woman.

A readiness to place their means at the disposal
of the Church on behalf of the poor and needy is
required of Christians, which reminds us of
the community of goods in the Church of
Pentecost. "Be not one that stretches out
his hands that he may receive, and closeth
them that he may not give . . . thou shalt not
turn away from the needy, but thou shalt share all
things (συγκοινωνήσεις δὲ πάντα) with thy brother,
and shalt not say that they are thine own, for if ye
are joint partakers in what is imperishable, how much
more in perishable things?" (*Did.* iv.) "We who
valued above all things the acquisition of wealth and
possessions, now bring what we have into a common
stock, and communicate to every one in need," says
Justin Martyr (*Apol.* i. 14). "We Christians have
all things in common, except wives," says Tertullian
(*Apol.* 39). The same idea is strongly inculcated even

Sidenote: The Spirit of the Pentecostal Church, continued.

---

[1] *Apost. Const.*, B. iv. 1, 2.   [2] Eusebius, *H.E.*, vi. 2.

in much later times by men like Chrysostom, Ambrose, and Augustine. Chrysostom desires to see reproduced again the state of things among the first Christians at Jerusalem. He thinks it would be like heaven on earth, and would have a powerful influence on the pagan mind.[1] Ambrose argues that "Nature created everything for common use. If then there are men who are excluded from the enjoyment of the products of the earth it is contrary to nature. The unequal division of this wealth is the result of egoism and violence."[2] And Augustine maintains that no one has a right to wealth which he will not use rightly.[3] It is not to be inferred from such statements that the right of personal property was not distinctly recognised in the early Church. What was taught was that no one should look upon his earthly goods as being for his own use alone. They are simply a loan given us by God, to be employed according to His will, and the devotion of which to the poor and needy is eminently agreeable to His will. At the same time, care was taken that their gifts should be without compulsion—should be free and spontaneous. Referring to the oblations, Justin Martyr says, "they who are able, and willing to do so, give what each thinks fit; and what is collected is deposited with the president, who with it succours the widows and orphans, and those who, through sickness or any other cause, are in want, and those who are in bonds, and the strangers among us, and provides for all who are in need."[4] While the Jews gave first-fruits and tithes, Irenæus points out

Christian giving free and spontaneous.

---

[1] *Hom. in Act.* 7, 11.   [2] *De off. Minstr.*, i. 29.
[3] *Ep.* 153.   [4] *Apol.*, i. 67.

that not in a legal or servile spirit, but in the spirit of freemen, like the poor widow who cast all her living into the treasury, Christians "who have received liberty set aside all their possessions for the Lord's purposes, bestowing joyfully and freely not the less valuable portions of their property."[1] To use their possessions thus, and sit loosely to them, was in accordance with the fact that they were sojourners on earth. "Have a care, therefore," says Hermas,[2] "as one living in a foreign land; make no further preparations for thyself than such merely as may be sufficient . . . Instead of lands, therefore, buy afflicted souls, according as each one is able, and visit widows and orphans, and do not overlook them; and spend your wealth and all your preparations, which ye received from the Lord, upon such lands and houses. For to this end did the Master make you rich, that ye might perform these services for Him." And such gifts are constantly thought of, not as mere alms dispensed to men, but as oblations or sacrifices well-pleasing to God. This is beautifully brought out by Justin Martyr in opposition to the heathen, who called the Christians atheists because they had no temples nor altars, and did not offer sacrifices. He shows that to help the needy, to do good and to communicate is the most acceptable sacrifice to the living God.[3] And Irenæus and Clement of Alexandria insist on the same idea.[4] It was partly because they thought of them so, and desired to present a pure

Alms thought of as oblations or sacrifices offered to God.

---

[1] Iren., *Against Heresies*, B. iv. c. 18.
[2] *Pastor, Sim.* i.   [3] *Apol.*, i. 14.
[4] Iren., *Adv. Hær.*, iv. 17; Clem., *Strom.* vii. 6.

offering, that gifts were received only from Christians in communion with the Church. No impure offering might be laid upon God's altar. No gifts were received from the excommunicated, from the impenitent, from heretics or heathen, or of money made in unlawful occupations. The *Apostolical Constitutions* lay it down that "it is better to die of want than to accept of gifts from the ungodly and wicked."[1] When the Gnostic heretic Marcion left the Church, the 200 HS. which he had previously given were handed back to him.[2] The right of presenting offerings was as much a sign of being in communion with the Church as the participation of the Eucharist itself.

No gifts received from the ungodly or impenitent.

The right to present offerings a sign of being in communion.

And not only were the offerings and alms required to be thus free from taint of evil, they were expected to be the fruit of self-denial. "Let thine alms sweat into thine hands," says our book (*Did.* i. 6). We have already seen that this means, "Let your alms be the fruit of sweat or toil," and that it seems an echo of Eph. iv. 28. "Work the thing that is good," says Hermas, "and of thy toils which God giveth thee, give to all that lack, in simplicity."[3] There were few rich Christians at this early period. The gifts which the Church required came, for the most part, from those sons of toil who had to earn their bread by the sweat of their brow. Hence such exhortations as those already quoted, or as that in the *Apostolical Constitutions*: "Work with self-restraint at your business, that you

Giving to be the fruit of toil

---

[1] *Apost. Const.*, iv. 8, 10.   [2] Tertull., *de prescr. Haer.*, c. 20.
[3] *Com.*, ii.

may always have enough for yourselves and the poor, and may not be a burden to the Church of God."[1] They were even expected to give towards such benevolent purposes what they had saved by fasting. "Having fulfilled what is written in the day on which you fast, you will taste nothing but bread and water; and having reckoned up the price of the dishes of that day which you intended to have eaten, you will give it to a widow, or an orphan, or some person in want, and thus you will exhibit humility of mind."[2] "If any one has nothing to give, let him fast, and set apart that day's share for the saints."[3] And after the death of any member of a Christian household, the family continued to give charities and oblations in his name, as if he were still alive.[4] In many instances their self-denial went further still. "We know many among ourselves," says Clement of Rome, in words worth quoting a second time, "who have given themselves up to bonds in order that they might ransom others. Many, too, have surrendered themselves to slavery, that, with the price they received for themselves, they might provide food for others."[5] And it should be borne in mind that in the early Church usury was not permitted. On the contrary, it was denounced with an earnestness and energy which would have refreshed the soul of Mr. Ruskin. "The usurer," says Chrysostom, "helps the poor man only to ruin him afterwards, like one who holds out his hands to a wrecked struggler in the waves, only to plunge him

and fasting.

Usury forbidden and denounced.

---

[1] *Apostol. Const.*, ii. 63. [2] *Pastor* of Hermas, *Sim.* v. 3.
[3] *Apostol. Const.*, v. 1.
[4] Tertull., *de Corona*, c. 3; *de Monog*, c. 10. [5] Clement, i. 5.

more certainly into the deep waters."[1] And all interest on money lent was, in the judgment of the early Fathers, usury. Any brother who needed such assistance should have what he wanted lent him without interest.

But while the early writers and preachers exhaust all their resources in pleading for works of benevolence and charity, on the other hand they are equally careful not to pauperize nor demoralize the poor by encouraging a spirit of dependence, or by impairing the feeling of self-respect and self-reliance. *Care taken not to demoralize or pauperize the poor by charity.* "If he who comes is a wayfarer, help him as much as ye are able; but he shall only remain with you two or three days if there be necessity. But if he be a craftsman, and wish to take up his abode with you, let him work and eat; but, if he have not a trade, provide according to your own discretion, that he shall not live idly among you as a Christian. And if he will not conform in this he is a Christ-trafficker. Beware of such" (*Did.* xii.). It is to be feared that there are still traffickers of this sort sponging upon the Christian community, and ready to sell themselves to any denomination for a suit of clothes; and that, for the sake of making proselytes, there are people who countenance such Christ-mongering. It is instructive to observe how every such practice, fitted as it was to degrade and not to elevate men, was frowned upon in the early Church. Thrift and industry and honest independence were cherished and promoted. Work is no longer, as among the heathen, regarded as a disgrace, but as *Thrift and industry encouraged;*

[1] *Hom.* 5 *in Matth.*

manly and honourable, and a salutary self-discipline. It is idleness that is opprobrious. The implements that represent their trade and business in life are constantly figured on the tombs of the dead in the Catacombs. But while industry was thus encouraged it was not with a view to the accumulation of wealth, or for any selfish object. It was for the benefit of the Christian community.

but not the selfish accumulation of wealth.

And here, indeed, we come upon what was most distinctive of the Christian life of that age. The Christian lived not for himself, but in and for his brethren, and in particular for the poor and the afflicted. The more complete their separation from the world, the more severe their common sufferings and trials, the more closely were Christ's followers drawn together.

The Christian lived for the community.

And thus drawn together not only by common suffering and danger, but by a common life and love, it was those early Christians who first showed the world what is meant by *a community* of people in a district or a country. The very idea of such a thing was virtually unknown before. How wonderful that at a time when society in that old Roman world was decaying and breaking up, and being torn and rent by contending factions and bitter jealousies and hatreds, its separating elements were being re-united in a new bond of union; and Jew and Gentile, Greek and barbarian, patrician and plebeian, the master and his slave, were being taught to sit as brothers and equals at the same table, fused into one living unity in the glowing flame of Christian sympathy and love.

Christianity first taught what is meant by a community.

CHAPTER IV.

BAPTISM.

WE come now to notice the directions which our book contains with respect to the administration of baptism, which, as being the earliest post-apostolic rules that we possess on this subject, are invested with a rare and peculiar interest. They are as follows :—

"And as regards baptism, baptize thus: having first communicated these instructions [*i.e.* The *Didaché* those embodied in the first part of the on baptism. *Didaché*, which immediately precedes], baptize into the name of the Father, and of the Son, and of the Holy Ghost, in living water. But if thou hast not living water, baptize into other water; and if thou canst not in cold, then in warm. But if thou hast neither, pour out water on the head thrice, into the name of the Father, and of the Son, and of the Holy Ghost. And before the baptism, let the baptizer and the person who is being baptized, and any others who can, fast; but thou shalt direct the person who is to be baptized to fast one or two days before." (*Did.* vii.)

There is much here that is worthy of being noted.

(1) We see that, even at this early period, baptism took place only after a course of Christian instruction.

In the early apostolic Church converts appear to have been baptized immediately on their professing faith in Christ (Acts ii. 41 ; viii. 36–38 ; ix. 18 ; x. 47). But already, when our Directory was written, they are put under a course of training before being baptized— a preliminary education which, as we have seen, was predominantly ethical and practical, though we cannot doubt that, in addition to what our book prescribes, the catechumens were orally instructed in the leading facts and verities of the gospel. Indeed, all through, their familiarity with these is taken for granted. The whole passage in the *Didaché* forcibly reminds us of the statement of Justin Martyr on the same subject: "As many as are persuaded and believe that what we teach and say is true, and undertake to be able to live accordingly, are instructed to pray and to entreat God with fasting for the remission of their past sins, we praying and fasting with them. Then they are brought by us to a place where there is water, and are regenerated in the same manner in which we were ourselves regenerated. For in the name of the Father and Lord of the universe, and of our Saviour Jesus Christ, and of the Holy Spirit, they then receive the washing with water."[1] Justin goes on to say that "this washing is called illumination, because they who learn these things are illuminated in their understanding." The converts from heathenism were soon so numerous, and their religious education was felt to be so important, that some of the ablest and most distinguished teachers of the Church, like Origen a little later, devoted them-

Marginal note: Baptism to be preceded by a course of instruction.

[1] *Apol.*, i. 61.

selves to this work under the name of Catechists; and in course of time the ordeal of admission to the Church was made still more difficult than it appears in our Directory, and, with some allowance for exceptions, the period of probation was extended over three years. "Those that first come to the mystery of godliness, let them be brought to the bishop or to the presbyters by the deacons, and let them be examined as to the causes wherefore they come to the word of the Lord; and let those that bring them inquire exactly about their character, and give them their testimony. Let their manners and their life be inquired into, and whether they be slaves or freemen. And if any one be a slave, let him be asked who is his master. If he be a slave to one of the faithful, let his master be asked if he can give him a good character. If he cannot, let him be rejected, until he show himself to be worthy to his master. But if he does give him a good character, let him be admitted. But if he be household slave to an heathen, let him be taught to please his master, that the word be not blasphemed. . . . If a maker of idols come, let him either leave off his employment, or let him be rejected. If one belonging to the theatre come, whether it be man or woman, or charioteer, or dueller, or racer, or player of prizes, or Olympic gamester, or one that plays on the pipe, on the lute, or on the harp at those games, or a dancing-master, or an huckster, either let them leave off their employments, or let them be rejected. If a soldier come, let him be taught to 'do no injustice, to accuse no man falsely, and to be content with his allotted wages:' if he submit to those rules, let him be received; but, if he refuse, let him be rejected. He that is guilty of sins not to be named, a Sodomite, an effeminate person, a magician, an enchanter, an astrologer, a diviner, a user of magic verses, a juggler, a mountebank, one that makes amulets, a charmer, a soothsayer, a fortune-teller, an observer of palmistry; he that, when he meets you, observes defects in the eyes or feet of the birds or cats, or noises, or symbolical sounds: let these be proved for some time, for this sort of wickedness is hard to be washed away; and, if they leave off these practices, let them be received; but if they will not agree to that let them be rejected. . . . Let him that follows the Gentile customs, or Jewish fables, either reform, or let him be rejected. If any one follows the sports of the theatre, their huntings, or horse races, or combats, either let him leave off, or let him be rejected. Let him who is to be a catechumen be a catechumen for three years; but if any one be diligent, and has a goodwill to his business, let him be admitted; for it is not the length of time, but the course of life that is judged. Let him that teaches, although he be one of the laity, yet, if he be skilful in the word, and grave in his manners, teach; for 'they shall be all taught of God.'"[1]

(2) The reference to the instruction of catechumens in the *Didaché* reminds us of another fact which it is important to remember, namely, that the great majority of those admitted to the Church during the period in question were adult converts from heathenism, or at least

Most of the baptized at this time adults.

---

[1] *Apostol. Const.*, viii. 32.

persons capable of being taught. The baptism most prominent in such circumstances will be necessarily adult baptism.

(3) But the chief interest of the passage given from the *Didaché* lies in its prescriptions with respect to the *mode* of baptizing. Let us carefully examine what it says on this point.

(*a*) Baptism is to be administered in " living " water, which means the *running* water of a river or a fountain, as opposed to that which is stagnant, and which was recommended both on account of its freshness and abundance. *"Living," i.e. running water, prescribed.* The general rule, then, was that baptism should be administered in running water, which meant practically baptism in rivers. Accordingly the oldest baptismal pictures in the Catacombs represent the person undergoing baptism as standing in a river unclothed, and the baptizer on the bank; though it ought to be observed that even this does not necessarily imply immersion, for in most cases the subject of baptism is standing ankle-deep in the river, while the baptizer is engaged, not in immersing him, but in pouring water on him. In early Christian literature there is a body of writings known as " Sibylline Books," the production of various authors and times from the beginning of the second century onward, who put what they had to say in the form of Sibylline oracles, in imitation of the mysterious and famous Sibylline books which were offered to Tarquin by the Sibyl. These Christian Sibylline oracles are frequently quoted by early Christian writers. But it is noteworthy that there is not a little in common between the *Didaché* and these Christian Sibylline writings.[1] The celebrated acrostic on the name of Christ occurs in Book viii., and is reproduced by Augustine in a Latin form in his *De Civit.*, xviii. 23. The passage consists of thirty-four lines, the initials of which make the words Ἰησοῦς Χριστὸς Θεοῦ Υἱὸς Σωτήρ = " Jesus Christ, Son of God, Saviour"; ending with the word Σταυρός = cross. The initial letters of this title make the word ΙΧΘΥΣ = fish, which became the familiar symbol of Christ in the early Church. In several parts of this acrostic there are striking coincidences with sayings in the *Didaché*; but one line in it is particularly pertinent to the matter under consideration, a verse which speaks of "illuminating the elect with water by twelve springs," an evident allusion to Christian baptism as taking place in "spring" or living water. Indeed the symbol of the fish swimming in water is itself connected with the baptismal rite by early writers.[2]

The common rule, then, according to our manual, was to baptize in "living" or running water. But to this general practice certain exceptions were admitted.

"Other water" permitted. (*b*) If running water is not accessible, they may baptize in "other water," *i.e.* manifestly, in pools or cisterns.

(*c*) If they are not able to baptize in cold water, they may baptize in *warm* water. This can hardly *Warm water allowed.* refer to occasions when cold water is not available, for if they are in a position to have warm water they are likely to have a supply of

---

[1] See "The Teaching of the Apostles and the Sibylline Books," by J. Rendel Harris (Cambridge, 1885).
[2] See Tertullian, *De Baptismo*, c. 1.

cold water also. The phrase employed in this case—
"if thou canst not" (εἰ δ' οὐ δύνασαι)—may point
rather to instances wherein the candidates were sick,
or to infants. Dr. Taylor produces striking parallels
from the Talmud. An attempt was made to obtain
a dispensation from the practice of purificatory immersion in the interests of the women of Galilee, who
were said to be afflicted with barrenness through the
use of cold water; and it was permitted to warm
the water for the use of the high-priest on the Day
of Atonement, if he was aged or delicate (*Mishnah*,
Joma iii. 5.).[1]

That infant baptism, as well as clinical baptism,
may have been contemplated in this permission to use "warm" water is not at all
improbable. Dr. Taylor also shows from the Talmud
how from very early times all proselytes to Judaism
were baptized, and quotes the Talmudical saying, "A
newly made proselyte is like a new-born child"
(*T. B.* Jebamoth, 48 *b*). He points out that "at the
baptism and reception of a proselyte, three persons,
constituting a *beth din*, or court of law, were in all
cases required to be present. In the case of 'a little
proselyte,' it was said 'they baptize him on the
authority of a *beth din*' (*T. B.* Kethuboth, 11 *a*). But
might this be done to a child without his intelligent
consent? Yes (it was replied), on the principle that
one may act for a person to his advantage, though
not to his disadvantage, without his knowledge and
consent. The case supposed is explained to be that

Infant baptism.

---

[1] See "The Teaching of the Twelve Apostles, with Illustrations from the Talmud," p. 54. By C. Taylor, D.D., Master of St. John's College, Cambridge.

of a child who, having no father, comes, or is brought by his mother, to be made a proselyte. But when children were made proselytes with their father, the act of the father in bringing them was held to imply the assent of the children, independently of the authority of the court of three in attendance at the ceremony."[1] The first Christians, who were Jews, and who were therefore quite familiar with infant baptism in the case of proselytes to Judaism, would as a matter of course observe the same practice in the case of the children of Christian converts; and there is evidence that they actually did so. Even in the New Testament itself there are traces of such baptism. The children of believing parents are said to be "holy" (1 Cor. vii. 14), which means here, as it generally does, brought near to God and dedicated to Him, and which, doubtless, contains, as the word often does, a reference to the dedication which took place in baptism. The words "sanctify" and "baptize" are often used interchangeably. Thus, as the Israelites are said (1 Cor x. 3) to have been "baptized in the cloud and in the sea," Moses himself is described in the Talmud as having been "sanctified in the cloud." So such expressions as "But ye were washed, but ye were sanctified" (not "ye *are*," as in the Authorized Version), referring to an act of dedication which has already taken place, are regarded by the commentators as pointing to baptism. Hence also Christians are called "holy" (ἅγιοι), that is, persons who have been brought near and dedicated to God; and sanctifica-

Children of Jewish proselytes baptized.

---

[1] "The Teaching of the Twelve Apostles, with Illustrations from the Talmud," p. 57.

tion is repeatedly described in the New Testament as something which has already been accomplished (see the Greek of Acts xx. 32; xxvi. 18; 1 Cor. i. 2; vi. 12). (Of course in other places the word carries the deeper moral sense in which it is progressive.) And just as we might have anticipated, we find in post-apostolic Christian literature early traces of the baptism of children. Justin Martyr, writing about the middle of the second century, says "he could produce many men and women sixty or seventy years old who have been Christ's disciples since childhood."[1] Irenæus says that Jesus came "to save all who through Him are born again to God, infants and children, and boys and youths, and old men."[2] A reference to other passages in Irenæus demonstrates that in this phrase, "being born again," he includes, as was customary in his day, baptism. In the very next book of this same work he writes: "Giving to the disciples the power of regeneration unto God, He said to them, Go and teach all nations, baptizing them in the name of the Father, and of the Son, and of the Holy Ghost."[3] And Clement of Alexandria says, "Let our seals be either a dove, or a fish, or a ship scudding before the wind, or a musical lyre, or a ship's anchor [these being all well-known Christian emblems]; and if there be one fishing, he will remember the apostle, and *the children drawn out of the water.*"[4] In this last clause there is an undoubted reference to baptism, and probably to the baptism of children. It is true that adults might be so described as the children of God, but it is more

[1] *Apol.*, i. 15.
[2] *Adv. Hær.*, ii. 22, 4.
[3] *Adv. Hær.*, iii. 17, 1.
[4] Clement, *Pæd.*, iii. 11.

natural to take the expression as designating those who are children in point of age. At all events, Origen, who was thoroughly conversant with the early literature, history, and traditions of the Church antecedent to his own time, derives the practice of infant baptism from apostolic tradition.[1] It is true that Tertullian opposed infant baptism; but there could be no better evidence that it was no recent ecclesiastical development than the ground on which he bases his opposition to it; for he urges its discontinuance not on principle, but for prudential reasons, and not as an innovation, but as an established and prevailing custom.

Baptism by pouring sanctioned. (*d*) But if they have neither running water, nor other water, they are to *pour* water thrice upon the head in the name of Father, Son, and Holy Spirit. This third alternative, in which *pouring* is expressly sanctioned, seems to imply that in the other cases immersion was intended. Indeed the preposition in the phrase "baptize *into* other water," points directly to immersion; and there is little room for doubt that this was the common mode of baptism in early times. As Dr. Taylor, in the work already referred to, shows, the baptism of Jewish proselytes was by immersion; and "according to the Jewish rite a ring on the finger, a band confining the hair, or anything that in the least degree broke the continuity of contact with the water, was held to invalidate the act." The general mode of baptism indicated over and over again by

Immersion.

---

[1] *Ep. ad Rom.* v.: "Ecclesia ab apostolis traditionem accepit parvulis baptismum dare." See also *Levit. Hom.* viii.

the Apostolic Fathers, and by their successors, is undoubtedly immersion.[1]

I have referred already to the Sibylline Oracles of the early Christian age. In Book iv. of these oracles, which describes the eruption of Vesuvius which took place in A.D. 79 as a recent calamity, and which, therefore, must have been one of the earliest of these writings, immersion is distinctly indicated. "Ah! wretched mortals," the writer exclaims, "lay down your swords; away with groans, and murder, and violence, and wash your whole bodies in the perennial waters, and, raising your hands on high, ask pardon for your sins" (vv. 161 ff.).

But what is most interesting and most important here is, that in this old Church Directory of the end of the first century, written probably while the Apostle John was still alive, a certain degree of freedom is allowed as regards the method of baptizing. The validity of the rite is not tied absolutely to any one mode, but pouring as well as immersion is recognised as valid. "This much is lifted above all question" (says Harnack), "namely, that the author regarded as the essential element of the sacrament, not the immersion in water, but chiefly and alone the use of water. From this one is entitled to conclude that, from the beginning, in the Christian world immersion was the rule; but that quite early the sacrament was considered to be complete when the water was applied, not in the form of a bath, but in the form of an aspersion." It is certainly significant that two of the oldest baptismal pictures in the Catacombs

---

[1] See Barnabas, *Ep.*, c. 11; Hermas, *Vision*, iii. c. ii. 7; *Com.* iv. c. 3; Book iii. Sim. ix. c. 16.

represent children as standing in the water ankle-deep, and as having water poured upon them in the form of spray. Indeed the first English Baptists laid no stress on the mode, nor did they practise immersion themselves, but were content with sprinkling. The Reformers took the large and liberal view of this matter. "Whether the person baptized is to be wholly immersed, and that once or thrice, or whether he is only to be sprinkled with water is not of the least consequence," says Calvin. "Churches should be at liberty to adopt either, according to the diversity of climates, although it is evident that the term *baptize* means to immerse, and that this was the form used by the primitive Church."[1] The Westminster Divines took the same position as Calvin : "Dipping of the person into water is not necessary," they say ; "but baptism is rightly administered by pouring or sprinkling water upon the person."[2] I may remark that the vote by which the Westminster Assembly thus pronounced pouring or sprinkling legitimate was a very close one—twenty-five to twenty-four.

(4) Another peculiarity in the baptismal directions of the *Didaché* should be noticed. The authorization to baptize is given here to the Christian people generally, without any restriction of the prerogative to a class of office-bearers. The same instruction is reproduced in the *Apostolical Constitutions*, but there the administration of the ordinance is expressly confined to the bishop or the presbyter. Taylor points out that in Jewish baptism the proselyte, if not an infant, performed the act of immersion himself. Ter-

Administration of the rite not restricted to office-bearers in the Didaché.

---

[1] *Inst.*, iv. c. 15, 19. [2] *West. Conf.*, c. 28, 3.

tullian assigns to laymen the right of administering the ordinance; and Hilary says that in early times, "*omnes docebant, et omnes baptizabant*"—"all taught and all baptized."[1] In the earlier apostolic times there is no hint of any restriction of the right. On the contrary, Paul for the most part leaves the performance of the ceremony to others, and Paul himself was baptized by Ananias, who appears to have been nothing more than an ordinary disciple (Acts ix. 10). The growth of the sacerdotal spirit soon tended to restrict it; but no doubt, though there is no principle involved in it, as a matter of order it is not only expedient but necessary that the administration of such an ordinance should be in the hands of the constituted authorities of the Church.

(5) The association of *fasting* with baptism accords with Justin Martyr's testimony on the same subject.[2] The propriety of this practice as in some circumstances a wholesome self-discipline, and a suitable expression of humiliation and sadness of spirit is clearly enough implied by Christ Himself. Matt. vi. 16; Mark ix. 29; Matt. ix. 15. It seems to have been an accompaniment of almost every solemn act or service in the apostolic Church. The designation of Saul and Barnabas to the work whereto they had been called was marked by fasting, prayer, and the laying on of hands (Acts xiii. 2, 3). And when they went forth on their mission it was with prayer and fasting that they ordained elders in every Church planted by them (Acts xiv. 23). Paul describes himself as having been "in fastings often" (2 Cor. vi. 5; xi. 27), and

Baptism accompanied by fasting.

[1] *Com. ad Ephes.* iv. 11, 12.   [2] *Apol.*, i. 61.

speaks approvingly of the Christians at Corinth "giving themselves for a time to fasting and prayer" (1 Cor. vi. 5).

But observe that in this early writing we hear nothing of the signing of the cross on the forehead, or of giving milk and honey and salt to the candidate, as a sign of citizenship in Christ's kingdom, nothing of the anointing with oil, or the clothing in the white robe, nothing of exorcism, or of the formula of solemn renunciation of the devil and his works, most of which were introduced early as accompaniments of baptism. In the absence of such ceremonies, and in the severe simplicity of the rite as here prescribed, we have another mark of the early date of our Directory.

No mention of sign of cross, etc., in the Didaché.

(6) It is also silent with respect to the purport and significance of this sacred ordinance. There is no remotest hint of baptismal regeneration, the leaven of which we know began to work early. The subtle way in which it insinuated itself is apparent in the early literature. It is well-known how, by what is called the figure of metonymy, we often and naturally enough attribute to signs the properties and effects which in strictness belong only to the things signified. It is a peculiarity of language which attaches necessarily to the use of figure and symbol. The New Testament writers naturally adopt this method of speech in referring to the Lord's Supper. The "cup of blessing" is at once "the new covenant in Christ's blood," and "the communion of the blood of Christ" (1 Cor. x. 16; xi. 25). And they adopt it just as naturally and inevitably in describing baptism. "Repent and be baptized every one

Significance of the rite.

of you in the name of Jesus Christ, unto the remission of your sins" (Acts ii. 38). "Arise and be baptized, and wash away thy sins" (Acts xxii. 16). Of course it is not meant here that sin is washed away or remitted by the baptismal water. It can be only meant that the baptismal washing is the visible sign of that cleansing which in a thousand forms, and in the clearest terms is attributed to the blood of Christ. It is so also when the Roman Christians are said to have been "baptized into Christ's death, buried with Him through baptism into death" (Rom. vi. 3, 4); when the Galatians are told that "as many of them as were baptized into Christ did put on Christ" (Gal. iii. 27); when Titus is reminded that "according to His mercy He saved us through the laver of regeneration, and renewing of the Holy Ghost" (Tit. iii. 5); when Peter writes that as in the days of Noah the few who entered the ark "were saved through water: the like figure whereunto even baptism doth now save us" (1 Pet. iii. 21). Moreover, as Calvin points out, "God does not mock us with empty signs, but by His power inwardly makes good what He demonstrates by the outward sign. Wherefore baptism is congruously and truly called the laver of regeneration. We must connect the sign and the thing signified, so as not to make the sign empty and ineffectual; yet not to honour the sign as to detract from the Holy Spirit what is peculiarly His." Now in their simple earnest faith, the early Christians suppose the thing signified to accompany the sign, and apply the same terms—"regeneration," for example—to both, without sufficiently discriminating between them, but at the same time without intending to teach that the mere sign effected the change. The age was quite destitute of the critical and philosophical faculty, needed to analyze the symbol, and to draw metaphysical distinctions between it and that which it represented. This should always be borne in mind in dealing with the statements of the early Fathers with regard both to Baptism and the Lord's Supper. "Blessed are they," says Barnabas, "who placing their trust in the cross have gone down into the water. . . . We descend into the water full of sin and defilement, but come up bearing fruit in our heart, having the fear of God, and trust in Jesus in our spirit."[1] "They descend into the water dead and arise alive," says Hermas.[2] We have seen already how Justin Martyr and Irenæus apply to baptism the term "regeneration." Now, to take the case of Justin, he evidently does not mean that the mere rite of baptism was the cause and agent of renewal; for he describes the person about to be baptized as having believed already, and as having been "made new through Christ;" and there is much to show that he regarded baptism simply as a sign and a seal (this latter being a common and favourite name for the rite in early times). "For Isaiah" (he says), "did not send you to a bath there to wash away murder and other sins, which not even all the water of the sea were sufficient to purge; but, as might have been expected, this was that saving bath of the olden time which was for those who repented, and who no longer were purified by the blood of goats, and of sheep, or by the ashes of an heifer, or by the offerings of fine flour, but by faith through the blood of Christ, and

[1] *Ep.* of Barnabas, c. xi. [2] Book iii. Sim. ix. c. xvi.

through His death, who died for this very reason."[1] Justin manifestly does not mean to teach that the mere baptismal water washes away sin, and regenerates and renews, but his language is not sufficiently discriminating; and it is not to be wondered at, though it is much to be deplored, that, among converts from heathenism whose early religion taught them to ascribe magical effect to external rites, the magical theory of baptism soon became prevalent.

[1] Justin, *Dial. with Trypho*, c. xii.

CHAPTER V.

THE EUCHARIST.

ON the subject of the Eucharist our document is as striking in its omissions as in its positive prescriptions. It says nothing of the words of institution, and, except in the brief reference in the fourteenth chapter, is almost equally silent with regard to the mode of celebration; evidently taking it for granted that the necessary instructions with regard to such matters would be given orally, or learned from the New Testament itself. Indeed little is here recorded besides the prayers of thanksgiving with which the service was to be accompanied. That room should thus be left for much oral instruction, especially with regard to the mysteries of the faith, is just what we might expect. Taylor points out that "so strong was the predilection for oral teaching in general that, amongst the Jews, the Mishnah, as well as the Gemara, was handed down unwritten for centuries;" and in the early Christian literature there are many traces of a like fondness for it. But, notwithstanding the silence of the *Didaché* on such points as those mentioned, its actual prescriptions are, so far as they go, eminently interesting and instructive. They are as follows:—

Takes for granted oral instructions.

"As regards the Eucharist, give thanks (εὐχαριστήσατε) thus: First with regard to the cup: 'We thank thee, our Father, for the holy vine of David thy servant (or child), which thou hast made known to us through Jesus thy servant. To thee be the glory for ever.' And for the broken bread: 'We thank thee, our Father, for the life and knowledge which thou hast made known to us through Jesus thy servant. To thee be the glory for ever. As this broken bread was scattered upon the mountains, and gathered together became one, so let thy Church be gathered together from the ends of the earth into thy kingdom; for thine is the glory and the power through Jesus Christ for ever.' But let no one eat or drink of your Eucharist except those baptized into the name of the Lord; for regarding this also the Lord hath said, 'Give not that which is holy to the dogs.'"

The Didaché on the Eucharist.

"And after being filled give thanks thus: 'We thank thee, Holy Father, for thy Holy Name which thou hast enshrined in our hearts, and for the knowledge and faith and immortality which thou hast made known to us by Jesus thy servant. To thee be the glory for ever. Thou, O Almighty Lord, didst create all things for thy name's sake, and didst give food and drink to men for their enjoyment, that they might give thee thanks, but to us thou didst freely give spiritual food, drink, and life everlasting through thy servant. Before all things we thank thee that thou art mighty. To thee be the glory for ever. Remember, Lord, thy Church, to deliver her from all evil, and to perfect her in thy love, and gather her together from the four winds, sanctified unto thy kingdom, which thou didst prepare for her;

for thine is the power and the glory for ever. Let grace come, and this world pass away. Hosanna to the God of David. If any one is holy let him come, if any is not, let him repent. Maranatha. Amen.'"

"But allow the prophets to give thanks as much as they wish" (*Did.*, chaps. ix., x.).

Farther on, in the fourteenth chapter, there is another reference to the Eucharist:—

"On the Lord's day of the Lord, being assembled together, break bread, and give thanks, after confession of your trespasses, that our sacrifice may be pure. And let no one who has a dispute with his companion come with you, till they are reconciled, that our sacrifice may not be defiled. For this is the command given by the Lord: 'In every place and time offer unto me a pure sacrifice, for I am a great King; and my name is wonderful among the Gentiles.'"

The Lord's Supper contemplated in cc. ix., x.

That in the former of these two passages the Lord's Supper is referred to, and not such a meal as the love-feast only, I have already given reasons for believing, in opposition to Dr. Salmon's surmise to the contrary. The service is expressly decribed as "the Eucharist," which we know was from early times used as the distinctive name for the Lord's Supper. Thus, speaking of the bread and wine of the Communion, Justin Martyr says, "this food is called among us *the Eucharist.*" In the opening prayer the cup is definitely connected with Christ as the true Vine. Those who drink of it are taught in the thanksgiving to regard it as a symbol of Christ, and to say, "we thank thee for the holy vine of David thy servant, which thou hast made known to us through Jesus thy Son." Jesus is here called "the vine of David," just as He is elsewhere called, "the root of David" (Rev. v. 5; xxii. 16), and "the Son of David" (Matt. xxi. 9, 15; Luke xx. 41, 44). Clement of Alexandria interprets the phrase for us when he describes Jesus as having "poured out for us the wine of the vine of David, that is to say, His blood;"[1] and when he says "the vine produces wine as the Word produces blood, and both the one and the other drink for health to men: wine for the body, and for the spirit blood."[2] And not only is there repeated mention of the broken bread in the passage in the *Didachē*, but the thanksgiving for it is thanksgiving for the life and knowledge which God has made known to us by His Servant Jesus; so that the "broken bread" is also conceived as a symbol of the life that comes through Christ. And the bread for which thanks are given, just like the bread of the Communion in 1 Cor. x., is also regarded as typifying the unity of the Church. It is true that thanks are given for food and drink and the blessings of creation; but this is exactly what we find in Justin Martyr and elsewhere in the case of the Lord's Supper; and in this, as we shall soon see, the Eucharistic prayers simply followed the *Eulogiæ* of the Passover; while thanks are given not for the blessings of creation only, but for "spiritual food and drink and eternal life through thy Servant," in manifest allusion to the words of John vi. 53, "Except ye eat the flesh of the Son of man, and drink His blood, ye have no life in you. Whoso eateth My flesh and drinketh My blood hath eternal life." Nor is it to

---

[1] *Quis. div. salv.*, 29. [2] *Pæd.*, i. 5.

be forgotten that the bread and wine of the Eucharist are spoken of in our book as "holy," and as being only for "the holy," and not to be given to the dogs (see chaps. ix., x.). As Justin Martyr says, the Eucharist, which for him means the Lord's Supper, is only for him "who has been washed with the washing that is for the remission of sins,"[1] so the Eucharist of the *Didaché* is only for those who have been baptized (*Did.* ix. 5). Even the order and connection in which we find this passage respecting the Eucharist prepare us for hearing of the Lord's Supper; for the writer has just given instructions with regard to Baptism; and after an incidental reference to the fasting which should accompany Baptism, and to prayer, he proceeds to speak of the Eucharist. Nor is the circumstance that the same ordinance is touched on afterwards in the fourteenth chapter any valid reason against this view; for *there* the chief duty insisted on is the meeting together of Christians on each Lord's day, and the disposition in which they should assemble—confessing sin, and in a spirit of peace and love—but as the Lord's Supper was the very focus and consummation of each Lord's day service, it was inevitable that it should be mentioned in this connection, just as it is mentioned also by Justin Martyr, though he too had been describing it immediately before.

Assuming, then, that the Lord's Supper is contemplated in the passage, let us notice the more salient points of interest in what is said regarding it. Notwithstanding the omissions to which I have referred there is a good deal that is suggestive.

[1] *Apol.*, lxvi. 1.

(1) We see, in the first place, that in those early times to which the book belonged, the Lord's Supper was observed every Lord's day, and constituted the soul, centre, and crown of Christian worship. And there is no doubt that in this respect it was but a continuation of apostolic practice. *(The Lord's Supper the centre of Christian worship.)*

(2) Commentators have remarked upon the paucity of references to the death of Christ in the Eucharistic instructions of the *Didaché*. We have seen, however, that there are distinct and striking allusions to it; and, considering that the manual does not profess to give a complete representation of the service, and indeed little more than the Eucharistic prayers, the references to Christ's death are far from scanty, and, so far as they go, are deep, rich and significant. *(Reference to death of Christ.)*

(3) What is perhaps most worthy of notice is the almost exclusively *Eucharistical* aspect in which the Lord's supper is presented in the *Didaché*. The fact that the designation, "Eucharist," became a distinctive name for it implies that in the minds of those who gave it that name it was thought of as eminently a thanksgiving service. In this characteristic, indeed, it was only a reproduction in the Christian sacrament of the spirit and example of the Passover. A series of thanksgiving prayers or "blessings" (*Eulogiæ*) accompanied the celebration of the Passover; and how much there was in common between the Passover *Eulogiæ* and the Eucharistical prayers of the *Didaché* will appear immediately. Two words are used in the New Testament to describe the purport and effect of *(Eucharistical aspect of the Lord's supper in the Didaché.)*

the prayers which accompanied the celebration of the Lord's Supper. What is expressed in Matt. xxvi. 26 and in Mark xiv. 22 by the term "blessed" ($εὐλογή-σας$) is expressed in Luke xxii. 17, 19 and in 1 Cor. xi. 24 by the phrase "gave thanks" ($εὐχαριστήσας$). And the words are used, doubtless, because as a matter of fact the prayer offered on the occasion effected the two-fold purpose of blessing and of thanksgiving. In the first place it invoked the divine blessing or benediction on the service, and was regarded as blessing or consecrating the bread and wine to a sacred use. Hence the cup is called by the apostle "the cup of blessing" (1 Cor. x. 16). This might mean the cup over which God is blessed or thanked; but the words are added—"the cup of blessing *which we bless;*" showing that the prayer was regarded as "blessing" or consecrating the cup. Even our common food, the Apostle tells us, is to be received with thanksgiving; and is "sanctified by the word of God and prayer;" being brought thus into relation with God, and the participation of it made a sacred or religious act. In like manner the bread and wine are "blessed" or "sanctified"—have a certain sacredness imparted to them by the prayer which is offered over them, and the spiritual good that is sought through them. They are taken from common uses, and brought into relation to Christ and the higher life of our souls, and made occasions for the holiest and highest exercises of our religion. In accordance with this, even the Westminster divines recommend that in Baptism "prayer should be joined with the word of institution for sanctifying the water to a spiritual use," and that in the Lord's Supper "the minister is to begin the action with sanctifying and blessing the elements of bread and wine, having first showed that those elements, otherwise common, are now set apart and sanctified to this holy use by the word of institution and prayer." But while the bread and wine were thus "blessed" or "sanctified" by prayer, the prayers were at the same time eminently *eucharistic*, vehicles of gratitude and praise for the blessings which the ordinance symbolized, and the whole service was conceived as peculiarly and emphatically a thanksgiving service. Nor was prayer the only channel through which the thanksgiving found expression. The gifts of bread and wine, and the other offerings which the communicants presented, partly by way of providing for the Lord's Supper, and partly for the poor and needy, were gifts of thanksgiving, expressive of their gratitude for the blessings they enjoyed; and the dedication of themselves to God in the ordinance was also regarded as a thankoffering. It was because this aspect of the Lord's Supper stood out so prominently before the minds of the early Christians that it received the name of "Eucharist," and in the Latin Church was known as the "*Actio Gratiarum*," which means the "giving of thanks"; from which, by the way, came the once familiar title "action sermon," which was employed to designate the sermon immediately before the "Eucharist," or "*Actio Gratiarum*." In the French phrase for thanksgiving, "action de grâces," we have still a reminiscence of the Latin one.

(4) We learn here also, what has been touched upon already, that, just as in apostolic days, the Eucharist was at the time and in the region to which

our manual belonged, still associated with the love-feast. Not to delay on other indications of this, it is manifest from the phrase "after being filled," which could only apply to a meal, and which is the same phrase as that applied by the Evangelist to the multitude who, at the miracle of the loaves and fishes had taken "as much as they would." "When they were filled," our Lord directed His disciples to gather up the fragments. And it is remarkable that in Jewish literature the same phrase occurs in connection with the meal which formed a part of the Passover celebration. "Thou shalt sacrifice the passover . . . of the flock and the herd" we read in Deut. xvi. 2. Why not of the flock only (Exod. xii.)? The herd, Rashi writes, was for the *Chagigah*, or feast. When this was joined with the Passover "it was eaten first that the passover might be eaten *after being filled*" (*T. B.* Pesach. 70 *a*).[1]

Still combined with love-feast.

Now the *Agapé* took the same place in the observance of the Lord's Supper as the *Chagigah* did in relation to the passover; and was originally united with the Eucharist as a copy and continuation of the meal which accompanied the Passover; and which indeed was associated with the Eucharist on the first occasion of its observance. See Luke xxii. 17, 19.

Tertullian has a striking picture of the *Agapé* after its severance from the Eucharist. He says: "Our feast explains itself by its name. The Greeks call it love (*agapé*). Whatever it costs, our outlay in the name of piety is gain, since with the good things of the feast we benefit the needy;

Tertullian on the love-feast.

---

[1] See Taylor's "The Teaching, etc., with Illustrations from the Talmud," p. 130.

not as it is with you do parasites aspire to the glory of satisfying their licentious propensities . . . but as it is with God Himself a peculiar respect is shown to the lowly. If the object of your feast be good, in the light of that consider its further regulations. As it is an act of religious service, it permits no vileness or immodesty. The participants, before reclining, taste first of prayer to God. As much is eaten as satisfies the cravings of hunger; as much is drunk as befits the chaste. They say it is enough, as those who remember that even during the night they have to worship God; they talk as those who know that the Lord is one of their auditors. After the washing of hands and the bringing in of lights, each is asked to stand forth and sing, as he can, a hymn to God, either one from the holy Scriptures, or one of his own composing—a test of the measure of our drinking. As the feast commenced with prayer, so with prayer it closed. We go from it, not like troops of mischief-doers, nor bands of roamers, nor to break out into licentious acts, but to have as much care of our modesty and chastity as if we had been at a school of virtue rather than a banquet."[1]

The subterranean galleries at Rome bear silent testimony to this ancient custom—a veritable "testimony of the rocks." One of the earliest of the cemeteries in the Catacombs of Rome is that of Domitilla. Mommsen traces it to the earlier part of the second century, De Rossi to the close of the first. Domitilla was wife of Flavius Clemens, and they were both cousins of the Emperor Domitian. They were accused of atheism

Love-feast in the Catacombs.

[1] Tertullian, *Apol.*, c. 39.

and Jewish manners, by which, there is no doubt, Christianity was meant. Atheism was at that time the standing reproach against the Christians by the heathen. Clemens was put to death, and Domitilla, who is described by Eusebius (by mistake, probably, as Lightfoot shows) as the niece of Clemens, was banished to the island of Pontia in the fifteenth year of Domitian (or about A.D. 95) according to Eusebius, who draws his information from heathen historians.[1] Clement of Rome, who wrote the Epistle to the Corinthians, was probably a member of the same family. We catch a glimpse here of the high social ranks into which Christianity penetrated even at this early date, and of the means by which the Christians were able to secure at least places of sepulture. The imperial government was exceedingly jealous of all secret associations, but, owing to their reverential feelings for the dead, very tolerant towards clubs which united together for purposes of burial. The Christians took advantage of this tolerance, and acquired properties, where, after the Eastern customs, they made tombs in the rocks, excavating subterranean galleries for this purpose. Now, just as the burial clubs among the heathen were accustomed to hold feasts in honour of the dead, the Christians availed themselves of that usage, especially at times when they were hard pressed by persecution, to hold their love-feasts, and doubtless other Christian meetings also in the Catacombs. The hall of the *Agapé* has been found in the Catacomb of Domitilla, with stone seats for the guests, and the cistern from which the supply of water was procured.

[1] Euseb., *H.E.*, B. iii. c. 18.

(5) If it be asked, who were admitted to the Eucharist in those primitive times, and in what spirit were they expected to engage in it, the answer is given by our document. "Let no one eat or drink of your Eucharist, except those baptized into the name of the Lord; for regarding this also the Lord hath said, 'Give not that which is holy to the dogs.'" This agrees very strikingly with the rule which Justin reports as obtaining in his time: "This food is called among us the Eucharist, of which no one is allowed to partake but he who believes that the things which are taught by us are true, and who has been washed with the washing that is for the remission of sins, and unto regeneration, and who is so living as Christ has delivered."[1]

Qualifications of admission to Lord's Supper.

There was no sentiment more deep or strong at that time, and none more sedulously cherished and guarded than that of brotherhood and brotherly love among Christians. It is not surprising, then, that in cases where estrangement had arisen between intending participants, reconciliation was urgently insisted on before they could unite becomingly in the feast of love. "Let no one who hath a dispute with his fellow come together with you, until they be reconciled, that our sacrifice be not defiled. For this is that which is spoken by the Lord, In every place and time offer a pure sacrifice." Applying this same passage of Malachi to the Lord's Supper, Irenæus connects it with the words of Christ, "Therefore when thou offerest thy gift upon the altar, and shalt remember that thy brother hath aught against thee, leave thy

[1] *Apol.*, i. 66.

gift before the altar, and go thy way ; first be reconciled to thy brother, and then return and offer thy gift (Matt. v. 23, 24)." [1] And the further counsel to break bread and to give thanks after confession of sin, Taylor connects with the idea of the passage that the Eucharist is a sacrifice—a spiritual sacrifice of thanksgiving—after the analogy of the Levitical offerings : " He shall confess that wherein he hath sinned : and he shall bring his trespass offering unto the Lord " (Lev. v. 5, 6). Just as the Jew was required to confess his sin before presenting his offering to God, so before the Christian brings his spiritual sacrifice, he is called upon to confess his transgressions.

(6) But the *prayers* prescribed in connection with the Eucharist are particularly worthy of attention. They are notable as being the earliest instance on record of such prescribed prayers in the Christian Church. And they are simple, brief, and spiritual. Nor is the Church tied down to them. On the contrary it is distinctly intimated that room is left for free and extemporaneous prayer, a privilege which is still exercised in the time of Justin Martyr ; for the person presiding in his time offers prayers and thanksgivings according to his ability ($ὅση\ δύναμις\ αὐτῷ$).[2] Even after a prescribed form began to be used there was liberty to vary from it (*Const. Eccles. Egypt*, ii. 34) ; and it was not till 633 that complete uniformity of worship was required, and free prayer forbidden by the Council of Toledo. It is also interesting to observe that the brief prayers recorded here are obviously modelled after the *Eulogiæ* or thanksgivings

Earliest examples of prescribed prayers.

---

[1] *Adv. Hær.*, B. IV. 18, 1.   [2] Justin, *Apol.*, i. 67.

of the Jewish Passover. The kinship between the two is manifest. As thanks are offered here for "the holy vine of David," so over the fourth cup of the Passover thanks are given "for the vine, and for the fruit of the vine." As thanks were offered in the Passover for the creation of the fruits of the earth, and for the good land given to the Hebrews, so here also thanks are rendered for creation, and for the food and drink supplied through the natural products of the earth. We know indeed that the bread and wine of the Eucharist were regarded not only as symbols of spiritual blessings, but also as tokens of the Divine goodness in the natural creation. We meet with this constantly in the early literature. For the purpose of comparison, I give the opening words of the Passover *Eulogia* over the fourth cup : "Blessed art Thou, O Lord our God, King of the Universe, for the vine, and for the fruit of the vine, and for the increase of the field, and for that desirable, good, and broad land wherein Thou hast pleasure, and which Thou hast given to our forefathers as an inheritance, to eat its fruit, and to be satisfied with its goodness," etc. The most recent investigations go to show that in a measure hardly realised before, not only the Jewish mode of government, but Jewish modes of worship, outside the Mosaic ceremonial, were adopted, without any breach of continuity, by the early Christians, who were themselves Jews. This was indeed inevitable in a religion which had its roots in Judaism, which in all its essential features was one with a system which our Lord Himself said He "came not to destroy but to fulfil" (Matt. v. 17).

(7) As to the conception of the *nature* of the

ordinance which our handbook indicates, it may be remarked that the deeper aspect of the service as a spiritual participation of Christ Himself is here distinctly recognised, as well as its significance as a symbol of the unity of Christians.

Nature and significance of Lord's Supper.

But probably what will have most struck the reader in the description of the Eucharist in the passage which I have given from the *Didaché*, is the use of the term "sacrifice" with reference to it. What does this mean? Some Roman Catholic and Anglican writers have hastily concluded that we have here the Romish and Ritualistic view of the Lord's Supper, as being a repetition of the great sacrifice of Calvary. There is no foundation for this belief. No one who has paid any adequate attention to the use of this word, and the meaning which it carries in the earlier patristic literature, could entertain such an idea. The word "sacrifice" employed here is applied habitually in the New Testament to the spiritual sacrifices offered up by Christians. Praise, and prayer, and almsgiving, and well doing, and the consecration of themselves to God by Christians are all described as "sacrifices" (Heb. xiii. 15; Phil. iv. 18; Heb. xiii. 16; Phil. ii. 17; Rom. xii. 1). Now the Lord's Supper, as we have just seen, was thought of pre-eminently as a *Eucharist* —a service of *thanksgiving;* and the prayers through which they gave utterance to their gratitude, the bread and wine and other offerings which the communicants were accustomed to bring and present for the Eucharist, for the *Agapé* and for the poor, and the offering and solemn dedication of themselves to

In what sense the term "sacrifice" applied to it originally.

God in the service, were all regarded as a spiritual sacrifice of thanksgiving. It is invariably in reference to this that the word "sacrifice" is employed in the earlier Christian writings when speaking of the Eucharist. The idea of the Lord's Supper being an actual repetition of the sacrifice of the cross never for a moment occurs to them. Clement of Rome speaks of praise, of a broken spirit, of the prayers and thanksgivings in the Eucharist, of the gifts brought by the people for the celebration of the ordinance and for the poor as "sacrifice."[1] Justin refers to the sacrifices which Christians, whom he calls "the true high-priestly race," offer through the name of Christ in the Eucharist, and adds that "prayers and giving of thanks when offered by worthy men are the only perfect and well pleasing sacrifices to God; for such alone Christians have undertaken to offer; and in the remembrance effected by their solid food whereby the suffering of the Son of God which He endured is brought to mind."[2] Irenæus describes the bread and wine presented by the people for the Eucharist as "the first-fruits of His own created things offered unto God," and quotes in reference to this the passage from Malachi about "a pure sacrifice," adding that what is needed to secure this is a right disposition in the person coming to the service.[3] "Those who have become acquainted with the second ordinances of the apostles," says the writer of the Pfaff Fragment, attributed to Irenæus, "are aware that the Lord

---

[1] See *Ep.* of Clem., i. c. 35, 41, 44, 52; cf. also *Ep.* of Barnabas, c. 2.
[2] *Dial. with Tryph.*, c. 117.
[3] *Against Heresies*, B. IV. 17, 18.

instituted a new oblation in the new covenant, according to Malachi the prophet. For 'from the rising of the sun even to the setting, My name has been glorified among the Gentiles, and in every place incense is offered to My name and a pure sacrifice,' as John also declares in the Apocalypse, 'the incense is the prayers of the saints.' Then again Paul exhorts us to 'present our bodies a living sacrifice, holy, acceptable unto God, which is your reasonable service.' And again, 'Let us offer the sacrifice of praise, that is the fruit of our lips.' Now those oblations are not according to the law, the handwriting of which the Lord took away from the midst by cancelling it; but they are according to the spirit, for we must 'worship God in spirit and in truth.' And therefore the oblation of the Eucharist is not a carnal one, but a spiritual; and in this respect is pure."[1] The fact is that the Christian literature of the second century knows nothing of the Romish and Ritualistic doctrine of the repetition of Christ's sacrifice in the Eucharist.

[1] Fragment discovered by Pfaff.

CHAPTER VI.

THE LORD'S DAY.

THE title which our book employs to designate this day is peculiar—"the Lord's day of the Lord." In the earlier apostolic times it is always spoken of as "the first day of the week" —μία τῶν σαββάτων—(John xx. 1, 19; Acts xx. 7; 1 Cor. xvi. 2.) The phrase, as the form of it will suggest to those acquainted with Hebrew, is a Hebraism. In Jewish writings the several days of the week are described as "the Sabbath," "the first of the Sabbath" (the Lord's day), "the second of the Sabbath" (Monday), "the third of the Sabbath" (Tuesday), etc. Of course the great event which signalized the first day of the week was the resurrection of our Lord from the dead—an event which would for ever after transfigure and glorify it in the thoughts of His followers; but in other ways besides He Himself put honour on it. He selected it as the day on which He appeared to His disciples after His resurrection. It was on the evening of this day that, as He sat at meat with two of His disciples at Emmaus, He "took bread and blessed it, and brake and gave to them" (see John xx. 1, 19, 26; Luke xxiv. 1, 13, 30). Nor is it without significance that the Evangelist records how

[margin: The Lord's day in the New Testament.]

"after eight days again" He appeared to Thomas (John xx. 26). In like manner it was the day singled out by Him for fulfilling "the promise of the Father" in the great outpouring of His Spirit; for the day of Pentecost fell that year on the first day of the week; and indeed already on that day, before the extraordinary baptism had taken place, and probably not without regard to the sanctity which the day had already acquired in connection with their Master the disciples had assembled together in one place. At all events, from this time forward we find this day distinguished and observed by the Christians assembling on it for the celebration of the Lord's Supper and the other exercises of worship. Thus, we are told (and it is characteristic of the way in which such matters are recorded that the reference seems a casual one) how Paul and his companions come to Troas "where they abode seven days. And upon the first day of the week, when the disciples came together to break bread, Paul preached unto them" (Acts xx. 7). Here then it appears that the assembling together of the Christians in a stated place on the first day of the week for the celebration of the Eucharist, and for other religious services, is already a recognised and established practice at Troas, on the shore of the Ægæan, on Paul's return from his third missionary journey. The reference to the "many lights," with which the upper chamber was supplied on the occasion, indicates the stated character of the meeting and the preparation that had been made for it, as well as the considerable congregation which assembled, and which came together on this first day of the week, it is expressly stated, not for the purpose of hearing Paul, but "to break bread," the Apostle simply embracing the opportunity to address them. That there is no mention of any formal institution of the Lord's day at any particular time; but that its observance grew up spontaneously, is thoroughly characteristic of Christian institutions generally, and makes it none the less an apostolic ordinance. The Apostle's "order" to the Churches of Corinth and Galatia (1 Cor. xvi. 1, 2), that "on the first day of the week every one of them should lay by him in store as God hath prospered him" is another notice of the day not less significant. So far, the day is spoken of as "the first day of the week"; but by the time the Apocalypse is written, which may not have been long after the last reference, it has come to be known as "the Lord's day" (ἡ κυριακὴ ἡμέρα) by pre-eminence (Rev. i. 10). Probably the next earliest testimony extant—the earliest post-apostolic reference which we possess—is that of the *Didaché* now before us. The peculiar designation here applied to it, "the Lord's (day) of the Lord" (κυριακὴ Κυρίου)—at once embraces and amplifies that of John in the Apocalypse. Dr. Taylor conceives the formula in the *Didaché* to be framed on an Old Testament model, but so as to depose the Jewish Sabbath. He says "the phrase 'Sabbaths of the Lord' is found in Lev. xxiii. 38, and a kindred phrase, cited by Barnabas as τὸ σάββατον Κυρίου, in Exod. xx. 10; but the Christian is to celebrate no longer a *Sabbath* of the Lord, but a *Lord's day* of the Lord." He adds that "what the Teaching hints at by its *Dominica Domini* is categorically expressed by

The Title in the Didaché —"Lord's day of the Lord."

Ignatius, when he describes those who have attained to newness of hope as *no longer sabbatizing, but living according to the Lord's day*, in which our life did arise through Him, and His death, which some deny " (*Magn.* 9). In the corresponding passage in the *Apostolical Constitutions* the day is called " the day of the resurrection of the Lord, that is, the Lord's day." This suggests a different explanation from that proposed by Dr. Taylor, namely, that the *Didaché* text may have suffered some mutilation, and that the apparent tautology may be due to the fact that some words have been dropped out by transcribers. At all events, we have here a very early and valuable testimony for the observance of the Lord's day by the Christians meeting on it for the celebration of their religious service—a testimony which is thoroughly in harmony with all the early literature on the subject. Pliny in his famous letter to Trajan relates how he had elicited from the Christians themselves who had come before him, that "their offence or crime was summed up in this, that they were accustomed to assemble together on a stated day before dawn [*ante lucem*], and to sing a hymn responsively or in turn with one another to Christ as unto God, and to bind themselves by a sacrament (or covenant) not for any wicked purpose, but never to commit fraud, robbery, or adultery, never to break their word, or to deny a trust when called on to deliver it up: after which it was their custom to separate, and to come together again, and to partake together a harmless feast." Pliny adds, " From this custom," however, " they desisted after the proclamation of my edict, by

<small>Pliny refers to it.</small>

which, according to your command, I forbade the meeting of any assemblies. In consequence of this declaration, I judged it necessary to try to get at the real truth by putting to the torture two female slaves, who were said to officiate in their religious rites [deaconesses doubtless], but all I could discover was evidence of an absurd and extravagant superstition. And so I adjourned all further proceedings in order to consult you. It seems to me a matter deserving your consideration, more especially as great numbers must be involved in the danger of these prosecutions, which have already extended, and are still likely to extend, to persons of all ranks, ages, and of both sexes. The contagion of the superstition is not confined to the cities, it has spread into the villages and the country."[1] These last sentences I have given from Pliny not because they are necessary for my present purpose, but because they are so interesting in themselves. There is no doubt that "the stated day" (*stato die*) of Pliny's epistle is none other than the Lord's day. We hear not a little in early times, especially in times of persecution, of these *ante-lucan* assemblies. The morning service began towards cockcrow; and was originally held at this early hour, partly because Christ's resurrection took place "very early in the morning" (Luke xxiv. 1), "when it was yet dark" (John xx. 1); and partly to escape observation in those perilous times when the Church was an *ecclesia pressa*; but, like so many other customs, the practice continued in later times, when at least the original necessity for it had ceased. We have

Why Christians met in the morning of the day.

[1] *Epist.* x. 97.

frequent references to it both in Christian and in heathen writers. Tertullian, for example, remonstrating with Christians for marrying with the heathen, asks "What (heathen) husband will be willing to permit his wife to rise from his side to go *to the nocturnal assemblies?*"[1] He says that the Christian people partook of the Eucharist in the *ante-lucan* meetings.[2] In Minucius (*de Idol. Vanit.*) the heathen cavils at the Christians for this reason, and calls them "a skulking generation, mute in public, but garrulous in dark corners," and Celsus (in Origen, *Cont. Cels.*) objects to these meetings of theirs held in secret.

But to return: Barnabas, after his spiritualizing method, explains away the fourth commandment by asserting that the six days mean six thousand years (a day being a thousand years), and by supposing the rest of the seventh day to point to the coming of the Son of man, when He shall judge the ungodly and truly rest. Then he goes on, "Ye perceive how He speaks: Your present sabbaths are not acceptable to Me, but that is which I have made, when giving rest to all things, I shall make a beginning of the eighth day, that is the beginning of another world; wherefore also we keep the eighth day with joyfulness, the day also on which Jesus rose again from the dead."[3]

The "eighth day" in Barnabas.

Ignatius (whose testimony we record for what it may be thought to be worth) says, "If, therefore,

---

[1] Tertull., *ad Uxor.*, lib. ii. cap. 4.
[2] Tertull., *de Coron. Mil.*, c. 3. *Ante lucanis cœtibus eucharistiam sumimus*, etc.
[3] Barnabas, *Ep.*, c. 15.

those who were brought up in the ancient order of things have come to the possession of a new hope, no longer observing the sabbath (μηκέτι σαββατίζοντες) but living conformably to the Lord's day (ἀλλὰ κατὰ Κυριακὴν ζωὴν ζῶντες), on which also our life has sprung up again through Him and His death. . . . how shall we be able to live apart from Him?"[1] He goes on to observe that "it is absurd to profess Christ and to Judaize," and urges his readers to lay aside the old leaven, and to be changed into the new leaven which is Jesus Christ. The writer of the Epistle to Diognetus speaks somewhat to the same effect.[2] Justin Martyr is very copious on this subject. He too speaks of the Jewish sabbath as having been imposed "as a sign," on account of the people's sins, and the hardness of their hearts.[3] He associates it with circumcision. It is, therefore, now done away, he says, and Christians do not observe it; but "the new law requires a perpetual sabbath," which he explains to be a cessation from sin; but he very distinctly and emphatically testifies to the observance of the Lord's day. "Sunday is the day on which we all hold our common assembly, because it is the first day on which God, when He changed the darkness and matter, made the world; and Jesus Christ our Saviour on the same day rose from the dead."[4] Dionysius of Corinth, about the middle of the second century, writing to Soter says, "To-day was the Lord's day kept holy, and we read

Ignatius mentions this day; and the Epistle to Diognetus; and Justin Martyr; and Dionysius of Corinth;

---

[1] *Ad Magnes.* 9. [2] *Ep. ad Diogn.*, c. 4.
[3] *Dial. c. Tryph.*, 18, 19, 21, 27. [4] *Apol.*, i. 67.

your letter, from the reading of which from time to time we shall be able to derive admonition, as we do from the former one written by the hand of Clement.[1] Irenæus gives a representation of the Jewish sabbath precisely similar to that of Justin Martyr.[2] Clement of Alexandria says, "We must honour and worship Him whom we believe to be the Word, the Saviour, the Master; and by Him we must worship the Father, not on certain chosen days only as some imagine, but in every possible manner, and through the whole course of life. The true Christian does not worship God in a consecrated place, nor on certain festival and appointed days, but always and in every place. He believes that God is everywhere, and not confined within certain enclosures. We who believe in His universal presence, and make our entire life a festival—we sing his praises as we work, as we sail on the sea, and go about our various occupations. All places, all times in which the thought of God occupies our minds, are alike sacred."[3] At the same time Clement distinctly recognises the peculiar sacredness of the Lord's day, and the obligation of Christians to observe it; and he enables us to understand the meaning of Ignatius when he calls on Christians to live according to the Lord's day. "He who observes the precept of the gospel," Clement says, "makes it to be the Lord's day whilst he casts away every evil thought, and takes to him the true Gnostic thoughts of wisdom and knowledge, thereby glorifying the resurrection of the Lord."[4] Similarly

[1] Euseb., *H.E.*, iv. 23. [2] *Adv. Hær.*, iv. 16.
[3] *Strom.*, vii. 7, 35, 36. [4] *Ibid.*

Tertullian says that for Christians the Jewish sabbath means, "that we ought to rest always from every servile work, and not only on each seventh day, but through all time."[1] It is remarkable how unanimous the early writers are in their sentiments on this point. The Ebionites were in fact condemned for joining the observance of the sabbath according to the law with that of the Lord's day according to the Christian manner.[2] But Tertullian also gives no uncertain sound with respect to the Lord's day. He speaks of it as a Christian institution kept in honour of Christ's resurrection, a day which he says, "we give to joy," and on which it is a duty to abstain from worldly labour and care—*omni anxietatis habitu et officio cavere debemus, differentes etiam negotia, ne quem diabolo locum demus.*[3] This is the earliest reference which we have observed to rest from secular business on the Lord's day.

and Tertullian, who is the first to speak of it as a day of rest from secular business.

Nor should we be surprised at this when we remember the difficult situation of the early Christians who, belonging as the great majority of them did to the humbler classes, the sons of toil, had not the disposal of their time in their own hands, but were at the mercy of their heathen masters, and exposed to their persecutions. It is manifest, however, long before Tertullian's time, that the sacredness which the Christians attached to the Lord's day would naturally and inevitably include cessation from secular employment, where that cessation was possible. Dionysius, who

---

[1] *Contra Jud.*, c. 4.
[2] Theod., *de Fabul. Hæret.*, lib. ii. c. 1.
[3] *De Orat.*, c. 23.

has been already quoted, writing about the middle of the second century calls the day " the Lord's holy day," or " the Lord's day which we keep holy,"—τὴν κυριακὴν ἁγίαν ἡμέραν. The reader will have noticed that Justin Martyr applies to it the designation " Sunday." Tertullian does the same.[1] But it ought to be remarked that it is only when they are writing in their apologies to the heathen that they so describe it. It is Tertullian's habit, when addressing Christians, to call it "the Lord's day."

From the *Apostolical Constitutions*[2] and from many other sources[3] we learn that the Eastern Church observed both the seventh and the first day of the week by holding similar services on both; the Council of Laodicea enjoining rest from labour not on the sabbath but on the Lord's day.[4] The seventh day was not kept after the Jewish manner but after the Christian by the celebration of the communion and other religious services. In the Latin Church the seventh day was observed as a fast day. Considering how the Jewish sabbath was regarded by the early Christians, how it was distinguished from the Lord's day, and yet still in a certain manner observed by them, remembering also how it was still strictly kept after the Jewish law by the Jews amongst whom they lived, we shall not think it strange that it is not till the fourth century that we find the term " Sabbath " applied to the Lord's day. The reader of patristic literature cannot but be struck with the fact that the

Marginal note: Both the sabbath and the first day observed in early Church.

---

[1] *Apol.*, c. 16.   [2] *Apol. Const.*, ii. 36 ; v. 20.
[3] Athanas., *Homil. de Semente*, Socrates, lib. v. c. 22 ; Cassian, *Inst.*, ii. 5 ; iii. 2.   [4] *Conc. Laodic.*, can. 29.

Lord's day is never associated with the Jewish sabbath except to be distinguished from it, nor even with the fourth commandment, nor with the rest on the seventh day at the creation, but with the resurrection of our Lord, and with the creation of light on the first day of the week. The deeper and truer view that the fourth commandment had something more in it than what was local, national, and temporary, that it reposed ultimately on a permanent necessity both in man's physical and moral constitution for a weekly rest, and was therefore most properly embodied in the brief code of moral laws summarized in the ten commandments was not realised by the early Church. In these circumstances it is not remarkable that it is not till after the time of Constantine, not till the fourth century, that we find the term "Sabbath" transferred to the first day of the week.

The Lord's day not called 'Sabbath' till after Constantine.

So much with reference to the Lord's day itself. Our next inquiry is as to the nature of the *service* held on it. And what strikes one here is, that our Directory confines the instruction which it offers to the Eucharist. "On each Lord's day of the Lord be ye gathered together, and break bread and give thanks, after confessing your transgressions, that our sacrifice may be pure" (*Did.* c. 14). It thus appears, as indeed we learn from other sources, that the Eucharist was celebrated every Lord's day; and it alone is mentioned because it was regarded as constituting the centre, crown and consummation of the Lord's-day worship, *Cor reipublicæ*. Hence, as Chrysostom informs us, the Lord's day was in ancient times called

The Lord's day services.

The Eucharist observed each Lord's day;

dies panis, the day of bread.[1] The fullest representation given us, in the early literature, of the Lord's day service is that contained in the first Apology of Justin Martyr, and which, for the sake of the reader who has not access to Justin's writings, may be here transcribed :—

Which was called dies panis.

"On the day which is called Sunday all who live in cities or in the country assemble together in one place, and the memoirs of the apostles or the writings of the prophets are read as long as we have time. Then, when the reader has concluded, the president verbally instructs, and exhorts to the imitation of these excellent things. Then we all rise together and pray; and, as I said before, when our prayer is concluded, bread is brought and wine and water, and the president in like manner offers prayers and thanksgiving so far as his ability enables him; and the people give their assent by saying Amen; and there is a distribution to each, and a participation of the Eucharistic elements, and to those who are not present they are sent by the hands of the deacons; and such as are in prosperous circumstances, and desire to do so, give what they will, each according to his choice; and what is collected is placed in the hands of the president, who assists the orphans and widows, and such as through sickness or any other cause are in want; and to those who are in bonds, and to strangers sojourning among us, and in a word to all who are in need, he is a protector. And Sunday is the day on which we all hold our common assembly, because it is the first day on which God, when He changed

The service as described by Justin Martyr.

---

[1] Chrys., *Hom.* 5 *de Resur*.

the darkness and matter, made the world ; and Jesus Christ our Saviour on the same day rose from the dead ; for on the day before that of Saturn He was crucified, and on the day after it, which is Sunday, He appeared to His apostles and disciples, and taught them these things, which we have given to you also for your consideration."[1]

In the foregoing account of the Lord's-day congregational service there is no mention of psalmody. It has been thence inferred by Vitringa and others that in those primitive times there was no service of song in the public worship of the Lord's day, that it was confined to the love-feasts, and to social life. The inference, however, is not warranted. There is abundant evidence that from the earliest times the worship of the Christians found utterance in song. Justin himself has in a previous chapter expressly stated that the Christians were accustomed to worship God by hymns; and it is for that reason perhaps that he does not find it necessary to repeat the fact again. Meeting the charge of Atheism, brought against the Christians by the heathen, he says : " That we are not Atheists, what sober minded person will not confess, from our worship of the Creator of this universe, whom we assert, as we have been taught, to have no need of sacrifices of blood, and libations, and incense, but whom we praise to the utmost of our power with the reasonable service of praise and thanksgiving for all things supplied to us, having been taught that the only service worthy of Him is, not to consume by fire what He has given us for our sustenance, but to apply it to our own

Psalmody.

---

[1] Justin, *Apol.*, i. 67.

benefit, and to that of those who are in need, and with gratitude to Him to offer thanks by solemn acts of worship and *hymns*, for our creation, for all our means of health, and for the various qualities of the different kinds of things, and for the changes of the seasons," etc.[1] It is probable, however, that in the description of chapter sixty-seven, Justin intends to include psalmody under the head of "prayers and thanksgivings," just as he associates prayer and praise in his thirteenth chapter. Indeed they were not broadly distinguished from one another by either the Jews or early Christians. The Psalms are called "prayers." One of the books closes with the words "the prayers of David the son of Jesse are ended." The ninetieth psalm is called "a prayer." Habakkuk's song is called "a prayer." In Jewish literature sacred song is treated of under the head of "prayer." Vitringa, in his book on the synagogue, following the Jewish custom, treats of psalmody under the head *de ritu precationis*. And Calvin, in the preface to his "Forms of Prayers and Church Songs," published in 1542, says: "As for public prayers, they are of two sorts, the one uttered in words only, the other accompanied with singing."[2] Nor in early times was there so marked a difference between singing and prayer as has since developed. The former had then little of the art which characterises sacred music in modern times, and was more like the measured, rhythmical, rising and falling, sing-song utterance which one sometimes hears in prayer. "Only tem-

Prayer and praise not broadly distinguished from each other in early times.

---

[1] Justin, *Apol.*, i. 13.
[2] *Opera*, vol. ii. pp. 168, 169.

perate harmonies are to be admitted," says Clement of Alexandria. "We are to banish as far as possible from our robust mind those soft liquid harmonies which, through pernicious arts in the modulations of tones, train to effeminacy and giddiness."[1] "The early Church," says Isidore of Seville, "sang in such a manner that the gentle modulations of the voice were more like reading than singing."[2]

If it be asked in what forms the voice of early Christian song expressed itself, it is certain that the primitive Church found to some extent a vehicle for its praise in Old Testament Psalms. But it is equally certain that from very early times distinctively Christian hymns constituted a large part of their psalmody. *Hymnology.* It is in the "new songs" and doxologies which abound in the Book of the Revelation that we see the best example both of the matter and spirit of early Christian praise. It is true that what appears in the Apocalypse seems at first sight to be a glowing picture of the praise-service of the redeemed in heaven ; but the early Christians took the representation given in the Revelation of the songs of the redeemed in heaven as an invitation to the Church on earth to conform her praise to the heavenly ideal ; nor, considering the indirect, incidental manner in which on this and on other matters the New Testament offers its instructions, can their having done so be thought unreasonable. Even in other parts of the New Testament traces of Christian hymnology have been observed. Both from the manner in which they are quoted, and from the symmetrical, and balanced, rhythmical struc-

[1] *Pæd.*, ii. 4.   [2] *De Eccles. Offic.*, i. 5.

ture of Eph. v. 14; 1 Tim. iii. 16 and 2 Tim. ii. 12, 13, these and other passages are regarded by such scholars as Bishop Lightfoot, Professor Plumptre and others as fragments of early Christian hymns, already in circulation, and familiar to the Church in apostolic times. However that may be, the Christian psalmody of the early centuries is largely an echo and reproduction both in spirit and in letter of the new songs and doxologies of the Apocalypse. I have already given the words of Pliny, the Roman proconsul of Bithynia, who reports to the emperor how he had been informed by the Christians who had been before him, that they were accustomed in their stated meetings to "sing alternately (or responsively) a hymn to Christ as to a divinity." One thing which cannot but strike the student of early Church history is the direct worship paid to Christ in prayer and song from the beginning. Among other titles applied to Christians they are described as "those who call upon the name of Christ" (Acts ix. 14, 21 ; 1 Cor. i. 2 ; 2 Tim. ii. 22). Not only in the doxologies of Paul, but in the doxologies and songs of the Apocalypse, we find praise offered to Christ "as unto God ;" and the worship of the sub-apostolic Church is a continuation of this practice. Eusebius quotes an early writer, now identified as Hippolytus (who was a disciple of Irenæus, who was a disciple of Polycarp, who was a disciple of the Apostle John), and Hippolytus, in writing against Artemon, an early denier of the divinity of our Lord, affirms in a book called "the Labyrinth," that "many psalms and hymns were composed by the brethren from the beginning, and transcribed

(margin: Testimony of Hippolytus.)

by the faithful, and that these celebrate the Word by asserting His divinity."[1] Socrates, another Church historian, says that "hymns were composed by Ignatius to set forth the divinity of Christ, and in praise of the Holy Trinity, to be sung alternatively."[2] It was, doubtless, some such hymn that Pliny speaks of, if it was not one of the new songs of the Apocalypse, or such a hymn as that of which 1 Tim. iii. 16 gives a fragment. Hippolytus himself wrote a book of odes and hymns, which seem to have been largely used, as they are often referred to in early times. Lucian, the heathen satirist, in one of his dialogues, describes his coming into a Christian assembly, and hearing the prayer which begins with "Father," and "the hymn of many names" (lit. the many-named ode—πολυώνυμον ᾠδὴν) "at the end." The hymn "Gloria Patri," which belongs to the very earliest age of the Christian Church, answers to Lucian's description. Clement of Alexandria, who belongs to the second century, has at the end of his book called the Pædagogue, a hymn entitled, "A Hymn to the Saviour." It begins thus: "Assemble thy simple children to praise holily, to hymn guilelessly with innocent mouths, Christ, who is the guide of children, . . . Let us sing together simple praises, true hymns to Christ our King. . . . O choir of Christ, O chaste people, let us sing together the God of peace." This hymn has been beautifully rendered into verse by the late Dr. Lindsay Alexander. Tertullian, in words already cited, says of the Christians that at their feasts

of Socrates,
of Pliny,
of Lucian,
of Clement of Alexandria.

---

[1] Euseb., *H.E.*, Book v. 28.   [2] Soc., lib. 6, cap. 8.

of charity after the Communion, "when they had washed their hands and brought in lights, every one was encouraged to sing something out of Scripture, or some hymn of his own composing." Athenogenes suffered martyrdom towards the end of the second century. Basil says he composed a hymn setting forth the glory of the Holy Ghost, and Basil speaks of another hymn so ancient that he knows not who is the author of it. For using a certain form of the hymn *Gloria Patri*, rather than the form used by the Arians, Basil vindicates himself by quoting the example of the Church Fathers from the apostolic times, and says he did no more than was done before him by Clement of Rome, the two Dionysii, Irenæus, Origen, and others whom he names, and done with the consent of all the Eastern and Western Churches.

<small>Athenogenes composed hymns.</small>

<small>Testimony of Basil.</small>

<small>of "The Contemplative Life."</small> A book on *The Contemplative Life* has been hitherto given among the works of Philo, a contemporary of Christ. A German writer, named Lucius, has endeavoured to show that it is not a work of Philo, but that it really gives an account of certain Christian communities who lived near Alexandria. In its description of these communities the book says, "that the president among them after he had made a sermon, first began to sing a hymn of praise to God, either such as he had composed himself, or one taken out of the prophets, in the close of which all, both men and women, joined in concert with him." Again, "In their vigils they divided themselves into two choirs, the one of men and the other of women, each of which had their precentor; and so they sang hymns to the glory of

God, composed in different sorts of metres. . . . Thus they not only pass their time in meditation, but compose songs and hymns to God." As we proceed in the history the evidence to the same effect accumulates, but it is needless here to pursue it further.

That sacred song would form a part of the Lord's-day worship might have been expected from the Eucharistical, buoyant, we might almost say, idyllic spirit which characterised it. *Joyous spirit of the Lord's-day service.* The early writers lay constant stress on the gladsome, exultant, and triumphant feeling appropriate to that day of Christ's victory over sin and death. The reader will have noticed this in the passages already given from Barnabas and others. No fasting was permitted on this day. Tertullian tells us it was considered a crime to fast on the Lord's day,[1] and, referring to the Montanists, he remarks that even they, who were so rigid in their fasting, omitted it both on the seventh day and on the Lord's day ; and this on account of the joyfulness with which it was fitting they should commemorate the resurrection.[2] For the same reason Christians were strictly enjoined, except in the case of penitents under discipline, to pray on that day not *kneeling* but in a *standing* posture ; and they were instructed to do this whether in their own homes or in their public meetings, in token of their Master's resurrection from the dead, of their risen and joyful life in Him, and of that elevation from the dust, and upright posture of their whole manhood, of which His resurrection is an earnest and an image. Irenæus traces the custom back to apostolic times.

[1] *De Coron. Mil.*, c. 3.   [2] *De Jejun.*, c. 15.

In the reference of the *Didaché* to the Lord's-day service there is no specific mention of exhortation or preaching as forming part of it. But that this did form a part of it is clearly enough implied in the instructions given respecting the apostles, prophets and teachers, and the bishops and deacons in chapters xi. and xv.; and in the passage quoted above from Justin, it is related how, when the reading from the memoirs of the apostles, or the writings of the prophets has concluded, "the president verbally instructs and exhorts us to the imitation of the excellent things" contained in them. Such exhortations were not necessarily restricted to officials. The ecclesiastical spirit, which has since developed more or less in all the Churches, was then unknown. "Even if a teacher be a layman," we read in the *Apostolical Constitutions*, "still, if he be skilled in the word and reverent in habit, let him teach, for Scripture says, They shall be all taught of God." As we shall see more fully afterwards, the same freedom which characterised the apostolic Church in this matter continued more or less into the following ages. Even in those primitive times the sermon was sometimes *read* to the congregation. What was formerly regarded as the second Epistle of Clement of Rome is now recognised to be a homily or sermon, which has internal evidence of having been read to the assembled Christians. In the body of the discourse these words occur: "Therefore, brothers and sisters, after the God of truth hath been heard, I read to you an exhortation, to the end that ye may give heed to the things which are written, so that ye may save both yourselves and him that readeth in the midst of you." This particular homily is interesting as being the earliest post-apostolic sermon on record. As a rule, the sermon does not seem to have been at all elaborate, or even very carefully premeditated, but in a great degree extemporaneous—a simple and practical exhortation, based on the portion of Scripture which had been read. It is curious also to find that, even at this early date, in the case of such speakers as Origen, who, by the way, was not even a presbyter, the discourse was taken down by shorthand writers—for shorthand was an art cultivated even in those days—and afterwards revised by the preacher. Nor is it less interesting, though contrary to our modern notions, to learn that, in the East at least, as a general rule the preacher sat, while the auditors stood during the discourse. Eusebius reports that when he himself preached before Constantine, the Emperor insisted on standing through the whole service. If it served no other purpose, the consequence of falling asleep under such circumstances was well calculated to keep the hearers awake!

It is significant that in the *Didaché* there is no reference to the *place* of meeting. This silence regarding the building in which the Christians assembled is characteristic of the early Christian literature generally. The place where they assembled was at this period to the Christian thought relatively a minor matter. They would meet wherever it was convenient—in an apartment in some dwelling placed at their disposal by one of their number,[1] in the *schola* or club-room of some associa-

The place of meeting.

---

[1] Thus Euprepia, a pious Roman matron, assigned the title of her house over to the Church for holding divine service in.

tion, or it might be in some subterranean chamber in the catacombs. Church buildings, expressly designed and erected for Christian worship, are institutions of a later date. It was as friendly societies, and particularly as burial clubs, that Christian congregations were first recognised by the civil power in the first and second centuries. The *schola* or club-house, and the *cella* or chapel in the cemetery, were, in all probability, the earliest example of real property owned by Christian Churches, and in these also we behold the first germs of Christian church architecture. How little stress is laid on the place where the Christians assemble we have already learned from Clement. "*Wherever* two or three are gathered together in My name, I am in the midst of them," said Christ. From these words, and from the principles enunciated by our Lord in His conversation with the woman of Samaria, the primitive Church inferred that the place of meeting was a matter of indifference, if it was only sufficiently commodious. To them worship had no more sanctity in one place than in another. The idea that worship which is legitimate in one place is evil in another, is as foreign to their notions as to the New Testament itself. "It is not the place, but the congregation of the elect I call the Church," says Clement of Alexandria; and "where two or three Christians are, though they be laymen, there is a Church there," says Tertullian. "Where do you assemble?" the Roman proconsul asked Justin; and his reply was, "Where each one will and can. You believe doubtless that we all meet in the very same place. Not so; for the God of the Christians is not confined to one spot; but being invisible, fills heaven and earth, and everywhere is worshipped and glorified by the faithful." The prefect said again, "Tell me where you assemble, or into what place do you collect your followers?" Justin said, "I live above one Martinus, at the Tirniotinian Bath; and during the whole time (and I am now living in Rome for the second time), I am unaware of any other meeting than his."[1] When Celsus makes it a reproach against Christianity that it has no sanctuary, Origen admits the fact, but replies that the true temple is the man who bears God's image. The word "sanctuary," as a name for the Christian place of worship, does not appear till later, and comes in with the consecration of the church building (a thing unknown till the fourth century), the development of the hierarchy and ceremonial religion.

Our handbook contains the earliest extant notice of another custom which may be referred to in this connection—an observance, however, which, unlike that of the Lord's day, is purely ecclesiastical, carrying no apostolic authority—the *Wednesday and Friday fasts*. "Let not your fasts be with the hypocrites" (says the *Didaché*, c. 8); "for they fast on the second day of the week and on the fifth; but ye shall fast on the fourth day and the preparation,"—*i.e.* on Wednesday and Friday. The reference to this custom in our manual suggests how early the "doctrines and commandments of men," began to be superadded to the simple apostolic rule of Christian living. The reason for fasting on the days specified is given in the

The Wednesday and Friday Fasts.

---

[1] "Martyrdom of Justin and Others," chap. ii.

Apostolical Constitutions thus: "because on the *fourth* day the judgment went forth against the Lord, Judas then promising His betrayal for money; and on the *preparation* (fast) because the Lord suffered on that day the death of the Cross."[1] These days were called "station days"—*dies stationum*.

Dies stationum.

Christians were thought of as Christ's soldiers. Tertullian compares the Church to a camp in presence of the enemy, and represents Christians as always standing on guard against the dark demoniac powers—a race ready for death. The baptismal vow was *sacramentum militiæ christianæ*. And just as the Roman soldier had his *dies stationum* —his station-days when he stood on sentry; so it was thought not inappropriate that the Christian soldier should have his station-days or vigils also— days to be spent in fasting, in watching and in prayer —days which were connected with the Passion of our Lord, and with His command, "watch and pray." "Why have you come hither so early in the morning?" the Shepherd asks Hermas; and he answers— "Because, sir, I have a station." "What is a station?" he enquired. "'I am fasting, sir,' I replied. 'What is this fasting,' he continued, 'which you observe?' 'As I have been accustomed, sir, so I fast,' I reply. 'You do not know how to fast unto the Lord,' he said. 'This useless fasting you observe is of no value. . . . God desires not such empty fasts; for, fasting to God in this way, you will do nothing for a righteous life. But offer to God a fasting like the following: Do no evil in your life, and serve the

---

[1] *Apostol. Const.*, vii. c. 23.

Lord with a pure heart. Keep His commandments, walking in His precepts, and let no evil arise in your heart; and believe in God. If you do these things, and fear Him, and abstain from every evil thing, you will keep a great fast, and are acceptable unto God.'" Then the Shepherd goes on to tell him, when he fasts, to reckon up the cost of the dishes he would have eaten, and to give it to a widow or an orphan, or to some one in want.[1] These "stations" or "vigils" were soon extended to the night-season, and whole nights were spent in watching and prayer in the place of meeting. John Wesley, when his watch-night services were challenged on one occasion by an Irish rector, appealed to this practice of the primitive Church in their justification.

Such sacred days as those just referred to soon began to multiply in the early Church, nor was it content to find occasions for them only in the life and passion of our Lord. Already in the course of the second century the festivals of martyrs began to be celebrated. In the account of the martyrdom of Polycarp in the Epistle of the Church of Smyrna, there is distinct reference to such commemorations. After referring to the spot where his ashes had been deposited, the narrative goes on to say: "There also, as far as we can, the Lord will grant us to assemble, and to celebrate the natal day of his martyrdom in joy and gladness, both in commemoration of those who have finished their contest before, and to exercise and prepare those that shall be hereafter."[2] One cannot but be struck here with

Festivals of Martyrs.

---
[1] The *Pastor* of Hermas, B. iii. Sim. 1, 2, 3.
[2] Eusebius, *H. E.*, Book iv. c. 15.

the fact, so full of meaning and suggestiveness, that those early Christians thought of the day of martyrdom, not as the day of death for those who underwent it, not as the termination of their career, but as their *natal* day, the day of their birth, through which they issued into a higher condition of existence in another and a better world ; and that, in accordance with that conception, they celebrated the day not with the funereal symbols of sorrow and gloom, but with joy and gladness. Tertullian, Cyprian and others mention these aniversary festivals of the martyrs, which were observed with religious services and commemorative addresses, and which had become so numerous in the time of Chrysostom that every week brought with it its festival of some martyr, and often more than one.

About the same time that the martyr festivals originated, or a little earlier, we begin first to hear of the Easter commemoration. It was with regard to the day on which it should be kept that the great Quarto-deciman controversy, which so disturbed the primitive Church, arose, and to consult about which appears to have been one object of Polycarp's visit to Rome about the middle of the second century. The Churches of Asia, Eusebius informs us, thought that they were bound to keep it on "the fourteenth day of the moon," which might fall on any day of the week—a custom which led them to be called "Quarto-decimanians"—whereas the Roman Church commemorated the death of Christ always on a Friday, the day of the week on which the event actually occurred. It is a mark of the early date of our manual that it is silent with

<small>Easter.</small>

respect to this and other observances which arose about this period, and which it could hardly have failed to mention had they been prevalent at the time when it was written.

CHAPTER VII.

CHURCH ORGANIZATION.

ON this subject our Directory is particularly full, luminous, and interesting. Its statements enable us to understand better than ever before many of the New Testament allusions to the Christian ministry; they supply an important link of connection between the apostolic and post-apostolic Churches in the matter of Church order; they touch closely the various questions involved in the organisation of the early Church; and already they have given a great impulse to the further investigation of this question. Not to speak of the discussions they have originated in Germany, they have chiefly furnished the occasion for a series of interesting articles in the pages of *The Expositor*, in which Dr. Harnack, Dr. Sanday, and others have taken part.

It will be best to set out here in full what the *Didaché* has to say on the different orders of the Christian ministry:—

<small>The *Didaché* on the Christian ministry.</small>

"But allow the prophets to give thanks in such way as they please."

Chapter xi. "Whosoever therefore cometh and teacheth you all these things aforesaid, him receive. But if he that teacheth, himself perverted, teach other doctrine to the undoing thereof, do not hear him;

but if to the advancement of righteousness and knowledge of the Lord, receive him as the Lord.

"And concerning the apostles and prophets, according to the ordinance of the gospel, so do ye. And let every apostle that cometh to you be received as the Lord. And he shall not remain (beyond) one day, but, if there be need, the next also ; but, if he remain three days, he is a false prophet. And let the apostle, when going away, take nothing but bread to last him till he be lodged ; but if he ask for money he is a false prophet. And every prophet that speaketh in the Spirit ye shall not try nor judge ; for every sin shall be forgiven, but this sin shall not be forgiven Yet not every one that speaketh in the Spirit is a prophet, but only if he have the ways of the Lord. From their ways therefore shall the false prophet and the prophet be known. And no prophet that appointeth a table in the Spirit shall eat of it, but if he do so he is a false prophet. And every prophet that teacheth the truth, if he doeth not what he teacheth, is a false prophet. And no prophet, approved and true, that doth anything with a view to a worldly mystery of the Church, but teacheth not others to do as he doeth, shall be judged by you, for his judgment is with God ; for in like manner also did the ancient prophets. And should any one say in the Spirit, Give me money or some other thing, ye shall not hear him ; but if he tells you to give in behalf of others that are in want let no one judge him."

Chapter xiii. " But every true prophet who wishes to take up his abode among you is worthy of his food. In like manner a true teacher is also worthy, like the workman, of his food. All the first-fruit then of the produce of wine-vat and threshing floor, oxen and sheep, shalt thou take and give to the prophets; for they are your chief priests. And, if ye have not a prophet, give to the poor. If thou makest a batch of bread take the first-fruits, and give them according to the commandment. In like manner when thou hast opened a jar of wine or oil, take the first-fruits and give to the prophets. And of money and raiment and every possession, take the first-fruits, as may seem good to thee, and give according to the commandment.

Chapter xv. "Elect (by vote) therefore for yourselves bishops and deacons worthy of the Lord, men meek and free from avarice, and true and approved: for they too minister to you the ministry (λειτουργοῦσι τὴν λειτουργίαν) of the prophets and teachers. Despise them not therefore; for they are those that are held in honour among you with the prophets and teachers."

Two different sorts of functionaries are mentioned in the foregoing passage — first, the "teachers," "apostles," and "prophets," who for the most part itinerate from place to place, belong to the whole Church, and are not elected by the people, but receive their gifts and appointment directly from the Church's Head. These may be called the extraordinary offices, which soon came to an end. Secondly, there are the "bishops" and "deacons." These are the local office-bearers of the congregation, elected by the congregation, and responsible for conducting the worship and administering the affairs of the congregation, except in so far as these duties are discharged by the itinerant ministry.

Two classes of ministers—the itinerant and the local.

A.—THE UNATTACHED OR ITINERANT MINISTRY.

The "teachers," "apostles," and "prophets" are neither in the New Testament, nor in the *Didaché*, nor in the other early literature, sharply distinguished from one another. The same person is sometimes called by each of the three titles, according to the aspect of his work prominent at the moment. Thus in the New Testament, Barnabas and Paul are called "teachers," "prophets," and "apostles" (Acts xiii. 1; xiv. 4, 14; Gal. ii. 9). Silas is called both "prophet" and "apostle" (Acts xv. 32; 1 Thess. i. 1; ii. 6). Similarly in our document the "apostle" is also called a "prophet" (c. xi. 5, 6); but on the other hand there are "teachers" who are neither "prophets" nor "apostles" (compare c. xi. 1, 2, with xi. 3 and xiii. 1, 2). Let us look at each separately.

(i.) *Teachers.*

Among the varied gifts bestowed so abundantly upon the early Church was that of *teaching* (Rom. xii. 6, 7). This gift and its exercise were by no means confined to the office-bearers of the Church (Acts viii. 4; xi. 19, 21; xiii. 1; xviii. 26, 28; 1 Cor. xiv. 5, 26, 31; Jas. iii. 1). There seems to have been the same freedom in this matter of teaching or preaching in the apostolic Church as there was in the Jewish synagogue (Luke iv. 17; Acts xiii. 15; xvii. 2). For the sake of order, and to secure the more regular and efficient discharge of the function of teaching, a

The gift of teaching not confined to office-bearers.

permanent local ministry was instituted, but not to the exclusion of its exercise by non-official members of the Church on whom the gift had been bestowed. Even so late as in the *Apostolical Constitutions* it is laid down that "though a man be a layman, if experienced in the delivery of instruction, and reverent in habit, he may teach; for the Scripture says 'They shall be all taught of God.'"[1] It was Pope Leo I. who first forbad lay preaching in the interest of ecclesiastical order. But the result of the wide bestowment of the charism of teaching and of its extensive exercise in the early Church, was the emergence of a considerable number of persons in the Churches who were known as "teachers," and who were not necessarily either apostles, or prophets, or presbyters. Thus in 1 Cor. xii. 28, "teachers" are named as a group by themselves, and distinguished from apostles and prophets on the one hand, and from governments on the other. So also in the *Didaché* (as we have just seen) and in the Pastor of Hermas, "teachers" are mentioned as a class distinct from apostles, prophets, and bishops.[2] And the words of 2 John 10, "If there come any unto you, and bring not this teaching, receive him not into your house, neither bid him God speed," seem to contemplate just the same sort of itinerant teachers as are implied in the *Didaché* when it says, "Whosoever then cometh and teacheth you all the things aforesaid, receive him. But if he that teacheth, himself perverted, teaches other doctrine to the undoing of this, do not hear him." In such men as Justin Martyr, Tatian, and Pantænus,

---

[1] *Apostol. Const.*, viii. 31.
[2] *Pastor*, Vis. iii. 5; Sim. ix. 15, 16, 25.

Harnack, with good reason, sees representatives of the "teachers" of the early time.

(ii.) *Apostles.*

It should not surprise us to find this term applied to others besides the twelve apostles. There is nothing clearer than that it is applied in the New Testament to certain ministers outside the circle of the twelve. Thus Barnabas as well as Paul is styled an apostle. Referring to these brethren, the writer of the Acts says, "part held with the apostles," and, again, "when the apostles Barnabas and Paul heard this they rent their clothes" (Acts xiv. 4, 14). Again in 1 Cor. xv. 5, 7, we read, "And after that he was seen of Cephas, then of the twelve . . . then of all the apostles." James, the Lord's brother, who was not one of the twelve, is called an apostle (Gal. i. 19; Acts xv. 7); Paul describes Timothy and Silas as apostles along with himself (1 Thess. i. 1; ii. 6); and according to the most natural sense of the words in Rom. xvi. 7, Andronicus and Junias are also represented as apostles. So here in the *Didaché*, in the *Pastor* of Hermas, in Irenæus, Tertullian, Origen, and the *Ancient Syriac Documents* edited by Cureton, the term is extended to others besides the twelve.

The designation "apostle" not confined to the twelve.

It is of course an inferior and secondary sense which the title bears as thus applied to others than the original apostolate, for some of them at all events had not seen Christ, nor were, what Paul calls "the signs" of an original apostle, wrought by them. It has been contended even by some that the term "apostle" in such cases is not employed as a title, but simply as a literal description to convey that the persons so called were *sent forth*. Of course that is always implied in the word, but that in the passages above cited or referred to it is employed not simply as a literal indication of the fact that those described by it were *sent forth*, but as a *title*, we do not see how any candid and competent judge can deny.

What was distinctive in the "apostle"? The question is—what was the position occupied by those who in this inferior secondary sense were called apostles? What was *distinctive* about them? Let us see if we cannot ascertain this.

Eusebius, in his chapter "Concerning Distinguished Evangelists" of the sub-apostolic age, has a statement which will throw some light on the enquiry. He says:—

Statement of Eusebius as to the early evangelists. "Of those who flourished in these times was Quadratus also, whom, along with the daughters of Philip, history holds distinguished for his prophetical gift. And along with these, others also were signalized in these times, occupying the first place of the succession to the apostles. And these as being the distinguished disciples of such men, also built up in every place the foundations of the Churches which had been laid by the apostles, advancing the Gospel more and more, and spreading the salvation seeds of the kingdom of heaven far and wide throughout the world. For most of the disciples at that time, animated with an ardent love for the Divine word, had first fulfilled the precept of the Saviour by distributing their substance to the needy. Afterwards, leaving their own country, they performed the work of evangelists to those who had not yet heard the faith, whilst, with a noble ambition to proclaim Christ, they also delivered to them the writing of the Divine Gospels. And these, having laid the foundations of the faith in foreign parts (that only being their business), and having appointed pastors over others, and committing to them the care of those who had been recently brought in, they departed again to other regions and nations."[1]

These evangelists were itinerant missionaries whose one business ($a\dot{v}\tau\grave{o}$ $\mu\acute{o}\nu o\nu$) it was to preach the gospel, and lay the foundations of the faith in foreign parts, and appoint pastors, and then depart to other regions not yet evangelized. This office of appointing pastors was (as we shall see afterwards) no exclusive prerogative of theirs, but was discharged by others as well, as for example by presbyters; but it was one necessary to their position as missionary pioneers, as it is necessary still to missionaries in heathen countries.

But is there anything to show that the term "apostle" was sometimes applied to such evangelists? Tertullian supplies the link. He asks, "Who are false prophets unless false preachers? Who are false apostles unless spurious evangelists?"[2] And it is very noteworthy that the office of the evangelist described above by Eusebius was just the position occupied by Timothy and Titus, and that Timothy is not only called an apostle, but is exhorted to "do the work of an evangelist" (2 Tim. iv. 5). They were itinerant missionaries sent forth to evangelize and to

---

[1] Euseb., *H.E.*, iii. 37. [2] Tertullian, *De Præscr.*, iv.

organize congregations. But in the times to which our document belongs, as well as in earlier times, there were many "false apostles" who sought to impose themselves on the Churches, and, to enable them to distinguish the true from the false, certain tests are suggested in the *Didaché* by which to prove any who would come. If they wished to remain longer than two days in one place, or if they asked for money, they might be regarded as false apostles.

(iii.) *Prophets.*

What differentiated the "prophet," properly so called, from the "apostle" and the "teacher," appears to have been his speaking in the Spirit" (ἐν πνεύματι), though not every one who spoke in the Spirit was a true prophet, for it might be an evil spirit (*Did.* xi. 8). A false prophet would be known by his not having the ways of the Lord, his ordering a table or love-feast for his own personal gratification, or his taking money for himself. We cannot refrain from quoting here, on account of its illustrative value, a parallel passage from the *Shepherd* of Hermas :—

<small>The "difference" of the prophet.</small>

"Hear then in regard to the spirit which is earthly and empty and powerless and foolish. First, the man who seems to have the spirit exalts himself and wishes to have the first seat, and is bold and impudent and talkative, and lives in the midst of many luxuries, and many other delusions, and takes rewards for his prophecy; and if he does not receive rewards he does not prophecy. Can, then, the Divine Spirit take rewards and prophecy? It is not possible that the prophet of God should do this, and prophets of this character are possessed by an earthly spirit. Then it never approaches an assembly of righteous men, but shuns them. And it associates with doubters and the vain, and prophesies to them in a corner, and deceives them, speaking to them according to their desires, mere empty words; for they are empty to whom it gives its answers. For the empty vessel when placed along with the empty is not crushed, but they correspond to each other. When, therefore it comes into an assembly of righteous men who have a Divine Spirit, and they offer up prayer, that man is made empty, and the earthly spirit flees from him through fear, and that man is made dumb and is entirely crushed, being unable to speak. For if you pack closely a storehouse with wine and oil, and put an empty jar in the midst of the vessels of wine or oil, you will find that jar empty as when you placed it, if you should wish to clear the storehouse. So also the empty prophets, when they come to the spirits of the righteous are found to be such as they were when they came. This, then, is the mode of life of both prophets. Try by his deeds and his life the man who says that he is inspired."[1]

The prophet of the *Didaché* might settle in a particular locality, in which case he is worthy of support. According to our manual, very special honour was conferred upon the prophets. They might give thanks as they desired in the public worship, and were not tied down to any forms of prayer. All the first-fruit was to be given to them: "for," it is added, "they are your

The "prophet" of the Didaché specially honoured.

[1] *Pastor*, Com. xi.

chief priests." They are so called, not at all in the spirit of a later sacerdotalism, for there is none of this in our document, but partly on account of the high honour in which they are held, and partly because, like the Jewish priesthood, they had no personal means of support, but were dependent on the Christian community.

B.—THE LOCAL MINISTRY.

Immediately following a paragraph on the Lord's-day service, and in express connection with it, our manual has the words already quoted : " Elect there- Bishops and fore for yourselves bishops and deacons deacons. worthy of the Lord, men meek and free from avarice, and true and approved ; for they too conduct the service ($\lambda\epsilon\iota\tau o\nu\rho\gamma o\hat{\upsilon}\sigma\iota$ $\tau\grave{\eta}\nu$ $\lambda\epsilon\iota\tau o\upsilon\rho\gamma\acute{\iota}a\nu$) of the prophets and teachers. Despise them not, therefore; for they are those that are held in honour among you, with the prophets and teachers" (*Did.* c. xv.). Bishop Lightfoot expresses the most generally prevalent opinion in saying that "when our author wrote, 'bishop' still remained a synonym for 'presbyter,' and the episcopal office, properly so called, had not been constituted in the district in which he lived."[1] But the discussion of the whole question of the local ministry is at present so unsettled ; theories quite divergent from that of Bishop Lightfoot have been recently put forward and supported with such learning by specialists in this department of study, like Drs. Hatch, Harnack, and Weizsäcker ; and

[1] *Expositor*, January, 1885.

Bishop Lightfoot's own view seems to us at some points so wide of the real facts of the case; that, for the proper elucidation of the subject, it will be necessary to examine it with some detail.

I.

THE NATURAL HISTORY OF THE LOCAL OFFICE-BEARERS.

The first question which arises has reference to what may be called the natural history of the local Church officers, or, in other words, to the source whence, both as to name and idea, they were derived. And here it is necessary to notice the view advocated with so much erudition by Dr. Hatch in his Bampton Lecture on "The Organization of the Early Christian Churches," and whose treatise has been generally accepted as the most weighty utterance on the subject since the appearance of Bishop Lightfoot's *Dissertation on the Christian Ministry*, in his Commentary on the Epistle to the Philippians. The case presented by Vice-Principal Hatch is briefly as follows.

In all parts of the Roman empire there were associations for all sorts of purposes—trade guilds, dramatic guilds, athletic clubs, burial clubs, friendly, literary, and financial societies, and religious associations, each with its lodge-room or guildhall (*schola*). The members of each association contributed to a common fund, and partook together of a common meal; and the same names—"synagogue," "ecclesia," "synod"—were applied to their meetings as to those of the Christian commu-

Dr. Hatch's theory:

nities. Government by a council or committee was almost universal, not only in Palestine, but in the organizations over the empire. Every association had its committee, every municipality its curia or senate. Διάκονος was not only a common name for those who served at table, but for those who at a religious festival distributed the meat of the sacrifices among the festival company. Πρεσβύτερος was the name not only of those who constituted the Jewish synedrion or local court, which in every place sat side by side with, though distinct from, the synagogue, and exercised administrative and disciplinary functions; the members of the Greek γερούσιαι (or municipal councils) were also called πρεσβύτεροι, and the professor in the philosophical schools was described sometimes by the same title. Ἐπίσκοποι appears also to have been used to describe the committee of an association, especially when entrusted with funds for any purpose. It occurs as the title of the financial officer of an association and of a temple. Dr. Hatch thinks that the early Churches simply adopted the order and nomenclature which they found existing in the societies around them; that they grew up spontaneously in different places, and varied with the locality, and that the development was much slower than is usually believed.

that the early Churches adopted the organization of the heathen societies around them.

Now that in its main outlines and nomenclature the organization adopted in the Christian Church existed already in Jewish institutions, has been always recognised. What is peculiar to Dr. Hatch's view is the extent to which he supposes it to have been shaped by the secular societies of the empire, and to have grown up spontaneously under their influence. The proof which he offers in support of his theory seems to us, however, to be altogether inadequate. As Dr. Sanday has pointed out, the few allusions that are found to ἐπίσκοποι in connection with associations or temples are insufficient to prove that such use of the term was anything but occasional and rare ; and M. Waddington infers from a study of the inscriptions that the Christian use of the term was derived not from Greek associations, but from its occurrence in Syria or Palestine.

Proof of the theory insufficient.

But what strikes one most is that Dr. Hatch's theory is completely at variance with the history which the Acts of the Apostles gives us of the development of the ecclesiastical organization. We are not quite sure, indeed, what Dr. Hatch includes in the authentic historical sources from which he draws his facts. If one begins, like Dr. Harnack, by denying the authenticity of the Acts and of the Pastoral Epistles as apostolic documents, and by relegating them to the second century, and finds thus the earliest trace of an official ministry in Philippians i. 1, we may expect from him a theory to suit the facts which he admits. But Dr. Hatch's position in relation to these books is somewhat undefined. We understand him to have given up the Pastoral Epistles ; but as to the Acts, so far as we can gather, he differs from Harnack. In an article in the *Encyclopædia Britannica* he says of the Acts : "What colouring of a later time, derived from later controversies, has been spread over the original outline of

The theory quite at variance with the Acts of the Apostles.

the history cannot now be told. While, on the one hand, the difficulty of the narrative as it stands cannot be overlooked, yet on the other hand no faithful historian will undertake, in the absence of all collateral evidence, the task of discriminating that which belongs to a contemporary testimony, and that which belongs to a subsequent recension." We are thus not sure whether Dr. Hatch may not regard the references to Church order in the Acts as "the colouring of a later time," and as due to "a subsequent recension." At any rate, feeling satisfied as we do with such arguments as those so ably presented by Dr. Salmon in his *Historical Introduction to the Study of the Books of the New Testament*, that the history of the Acts is thoroughly trustworthy, it is to us a sufficient condemnation of Dr. Hatch's view that it is irreconcilable with the narrative which that book contains. Let us trace rapidly the rise and spread of the Presbyterate and Episcopate as indicated by the writer of the Acts.

(*a.*) *The Rise of the Eldership.*

With regard to the origin of the Eldership there is substantial unanimity. It is generally admitted that The Christian Eldership formed after the model of the Jewish. it was a copy of the mode of government by a council of elders which already from ancient times obtained among the Jews. From the time of Moses onwards we hear of elders as rulers of the people, each town having in later times its bench of elders (Deut. xix. 2 ; Judges xi. 5, 7 ; Ruth iv. 2 ; 1 Kings xxi. 8 ; 2 Kings xi. 1). Dr. Hatch has pointed out that the synedrion or local court of elders was distinct from the synagogue, though side by side with it, and that their duties were administrative and disciplinary. When, then, at an early stage in the history of the Christian Church, and without any previous notice of the institution of the office, we find "elders" in the Church at Jerusasalem, as a definite body of office-bearers, established in a Jewish-Christian community, by Jewish-Christian leaders who have never been out of Palestine; "elders" who are known and recognised at a distance as a representative and responsible body of officers, to whom relief for the poor Christians in Judæa is sent by the disciples of Antioch through the hands of Barnabas and Saul (Acts xi. 30); and when immediately after the visit of these apostles to the elders at Jerusalem, we read of their missionary journey through Asia Minor, and of their having elders *appointed by election*, and with a solemn religious service, in all the congregations planted by Paul and his companion over that region (Acts xiv. 23); we cannot doubt that the government by elders thus instituted in the Churches of Judea and Asia Minor was in its main features simply a continuance of the Jewish system of government by elders. True, it is maintained by Harnack that in the early Church the term "elders" does not, till after the time of Paul, imply officials, but persons so called from age and experience, and who on this account solely, and not by virtue of appointment to office, exercised authority. But no one who accepts the history of the Acts of the Apostles as trustworthy can doubt the official character of the elders named in it; for we are distinctly informed with respect to the Churches of Proconsular

Asia planted by Paul and Barnabas, that they "ordained" (lit., had elected by vote) "elders in every Church" (Acts xiv. 28).

(b.) *The Rise of the Episcopate.*

It is here strongly urged by Dr. Hatch that the organization adopted in the Gentile Churches had "a spontaneous origin; for the members of the governing council had various names, and the names in use for the Jewish officers did not at once prevail."[1] The name which prevailed here, he thinks, was not "elder" but "bishop"—a name which was applied to the financial officer of an association and of a temple, and to the committee of the governing body, or a committee of it when entrusted with funds for any purpose. It was after such a model that (as he supposes) the council of bishops, who in the first instance had to do chiefly with finance, arose in the Gentile Churches.

<small>Hatch thinks the Episcopate arose spontaneously in Gentile Churches.</small>

The chief objection to this theory is that it ignores the history of the early episcopate as we have it in the New Testament and in the sub-apostolic writings, and that it is based on an exaggerated view of the importance of a few isolated inscriptions in which the term ἐπίσκοπος occurs; but which do not prove even that the persons so described were permanent officers, or that their duties were confined to finance.[2] Dr. Hatch's view

<small>This view contradicted by the evidence.</small>

---

[1] *Bampton Lecture*, Lect. III.
[2] See Dr. Sanday's Criticism in the *Expositor*, Feb., 1887, pp. 98, 99.

of the origin of the episcopate is in fact quite at variance with the evidence which the early literature supplies. When the term "bishop" first comes into use it is certainly not as the title of an officer whose primary and most prominent duties are financial. The word "bishop," when it first occurs (Acts xx. 28), is used as a synonym for "presbyter," and neither there, nor in the Pastoral Epistles, nor in the sub-apostolic literature, do his financial duties appear as his primary ones. On the other hand, the writer of the Acts (xi. 30), Clement of Rome, and Polycarp, exhibit the presbyters as being in charge of the offerings; and in the *Didaché* it is the prophets, and not the bishops, who are represented as the primary and chief almoners of the Church. Again, the statement that the Jewish term "elders," as well as the office which it designated, did not at once prevail among the Gentile Churches, is flatly contradicted by the narrative in the Acts of the Apostles. The Churches established throughout Proconsular Asia were as much Gentile Churches (including Greek Christians among their members) as those organized in Greece (see Acts xiii. 48; xiv. 1); and, on the other hand, in the chief centres of Greece, as in those of Asia Minor, it was as a rule Jews and Jewish proselytes who formed the nucleus of the Christian community. Now let us trace the history of the rise of organized government in the Church over all these regions, so far as the Acts of the Apostles and the other records enable us to do so. Even at the expense of a little repetition of what has been said already, it will be important to

"Bishop" first used as a synonym for "presbyter."

The term "elder" did prevail in Gentile Churches.

have a connected and complete view of its development over these countries.

First of all, as has just been pointed out, we find at an early date a definite, well-known, and responsible body of "elders" at Jerusalem, taking charge of the funds handed to them by Barnabas and Saul for the poor Christians in Judæa (Acts xi. 30)—a recognised and authorised organ of administration. With these "elders" Paul and Barnabas are, on the occasion of their visit, brought into close personal intercourse, and made familiar with them as a governing body in the mother Church at Jerusalem. What immediately follows in the history? On returning to Antioch, Paul and Barnabas are sent forth on their first missionary journey, during the course of which they found Churches in Perga, in Antioch of Pisidia, in Iconium, Lystra and Derbe, and "the region round about,"—a wide district of Asia Minor. Having reached Derbe, and made many disciples there, they return through the Churches they had planted, confirming the souls of the disciples, exhorting them to continue in the faith, and having elders elected and appointed, with fasting and prayer, "in every Church" hitherto founded by them; evidently guided in this matter by the example which they found set them by the mother Church. Coming back to Antioch (in Syria), and finding the Church there deeply agitated over the question of circumcising the Gentile converts, Paul and Barnabas and others are deputed to go to Jerusalem "unto the apostles and *elders* about this question." In the account which Luke gives of the conference which

[marginal note: History of the rise of organized government as given in Acts contradicts Dr. Hatch.*]*

ensued, "the elders" are always associated with the apostles, and the decree issued is said to have been "ordained by the apostles and elders" (Acts xv. 2, 4, 6, 22; xvi. 4). Returning once more to Antioch, Paul, accompanied this time by Silas, sets out on his second missionary journey. Visiting on their way the Churches organized in the previous tour, they come to Troas, whence they cross to Greece, founding Churches at Philippi, Thessalonica, Berœa, Athens, and Corinth; in all which places they find Jews or Jewish proselytes, and make numerous Jewish converts. After a stay of a year and a half at Corinth the apostle goes up to Jerusalem again; and coming down to Antioch, sets out on his third journey through the Churches of Asia Minor, "stablishing all the disciples." For more than two years he remains at Ephesus, then visits Greece, and, after a brief stay here, sets out again for Syria. Now it is true that the historian does not mention the setting up of the eldership in the Churches planted in the more western parts of Asia Minor, or in Greece. He is content with giving us an example of Paul's method of organization in his first journey. This is not because a similar course of appointing elders was not pursued in the other Churches; for we learn casually that as a matter of fact elders had been ordained in other Churches, though the writer of the Acts does not think it necessary to record their appointment. As has been well remarked by Professor Lumby in his Introduction to his Commentary on the Acts, we fail to appreciate the peculiar character of the history which this book records, unless we recollect that it is "a history of *beginnings* only." After pointing this out in detail, Professor Lumby adds that "through the whole of what is related concerning the labours of the apostle, we learn only of the *founding* of Churches and societies, and of the *initial steps* of the Christian work in the places which he visited." The book, he says again, "is a description of the *beginnings* of Christianity. And with this in mind we can see that the matters on which he dwells are exactly those which we should have expected him to notice."[1] But that office-bearers were appointed in the Churches referred to, though the historian does not, after the typical example of the apostle's mode of action recorded by him, think it necessary to chronicle the fact, we learn afterwards in an incidental way. We had not been told that the presbyterate had been set up at Ephesus; but now when, on his way to Syria, the apostle comes to Miletus, he sends to Ephesus for "the elders of the Church" there, to whom also, be it noted, he applies the designation "bishops" (Acts xx. 17, 28). Again, we hear nothing of the appointment of Church officers at Thessalonica, at Philippi, or Corinth. The Church was founded at Thessalonica on the apostle's second missionary journey, in the year 52; and yet already in his first epistle to this Church, the earliest of his epistles, written about the beginning of 53 A.D., he exhorts the Christians there to "know them which labour among them, and are over them in the Lord, and admonish them, and to esteem them highly in love for their work's sake" (1 Thess.

<small>Rulers at Thessalonica;</small>

---

[1] See "The Acts of the Apostles," by Professor Lumby, in the Cambridge Bible Series, Introduction, pp. x.-xv., xviii.

v. 12). From the Epistle to the Philippians we learn that there were Church officers at Philippi described as "bishops and deacons" (Phil. i. 1), the same sort of officers whom Polycarp at a later date, in his epistle to the same Church, calls "presbyters and deacons." Similarly, we hear nothing in the Acts or Epistles of any organized ministry at Corinth, but even if we had no means of knowing, who could believe, in view of the facts I have recited, that a Church so large and important, and where Paul himself, on his second journey, stayed for a year and six months, would be left by him unorganized, and without any form of government? But the early history is not silent about the fact whether a ministry had been instituted at Corinth. Clement of Rome writes to this Church in the year 95 or 96 A.D., not forty years after Paul had written to them, and not much more than thirty years since Paul's death. When Clement wrote there must have been many still alive at Corinth who had known the apostle, and who, as Clement must have been well aware, could judge of the accuracy of what he said respecting that earlier time. Yet Clement reminds the Corinthians how the apostles had appointed certain officers whom he describes as "presbyters," and had given instructions that when these should fall asleep other approved men should succeed them; adding (with reference to the sedition which had been raised against the presbyters at Corinth) that those appointed by the apostles, or afterwards with the consent of the whole Church, and "who had *for a long time* possessed the good opinion of all, could not be justly dismissed

at Philippi;

at Corinth, though not named in Acts.

from the ministry.¹ From all which it is manifest that the Churches both of Asia and of Greece, though it did not consist with the plan of the historian of the Acts to record each case fully, were duly organized, and had office-bearers appointed in them soon after they were founded. Nor can any one who closely follows the history believe that the organization sprang up independently and spontaneously in the Gentile Churches, after the analogy of the Gentile associations and their modes of government, and not after the pattern of the Jewish eldership.

Clearly, the organization in the Churches of the western part of Asia Minor and of Greece was simply a continuation of the presbyterate at Jerusalem, and which Paul himself had instituted in many Asiatic Churches on his first missionary tour. And as to the term "bishop," we first meet with its use in Christian nomenclature, not in Greece, but in reference to the elders of Ephesus. And here we learn how the word came originally to be applied to the elders. It is used by Paul as a synonym for elders, or rather to describe the functions to be performed by these office-bearers. He invites the elders of Ephesus to meet him at Miletus, and exhorts them to tend (lit. *to shepherd*) the Church over which the Holy Ghost has made them bishops, their duties being analogous to those of the shepherd's calling. So also Peter exhorts the "elders" to "tend" or "feed ($\pi o \iota \mu \acute{a} \nu a \tau \epsilon$) the flock, taking the oversight (or episcopate) thereof" ($\grave{\epsilon} \pi \iota \sigma \kappa o \pi o \hat{v} \nu \tau \epsilon \varsigma$), 1 Peter v. 1, 2. Nor to account for the employment

Earliest use of the term "bishop."

¹ 1 *Ep.*, c. xliv.

of this term by Paul and Peter is it necessary to prove by laborious erudition that the financial officer of a heathen association or of a temple was called ἐπίσκοπος. We doubt if the knowledge of such a fact would have greatly encouraged its use by them. It was evidently employed as the word in common use to describe *oversight*—a sense in which it occurs repeatedly in the Septuagint. It is the term that would naturally occur to the apostle to describe the function of the presbyters as having oversight of the Church; and it is important to bear in mind that the word first occurs as *a description of the work performed by elders.* And indeed, on Dr. Hatch's own showing, the Gentile Christians would be as familiar with the term "elder" as with that of "bishop." Not only were there, in all those centres where Churches were established, the "elders" of the Jewish Synedrion, but, as Dr. Hatch himself points out, the members of the *gerousiai* were called *elders*, as were professors in the philosophical schools.

On the whole, then, we must pronounce Dr. Hatch's attempt to show that the organization of the Gentile Church was an independent and spontaneous growth a complete failure.

The question remains—how were the apostles led to adopt the particular organization which they hit upon, namely, a council of elders chosen by the Christian people? It is part of Dr. Hatch's theory that no extraordinary action of the Holy Spirit was needed to direct them in the choice of a form of government; that the organization grew and took shape under the impulse of forces acting naturally, so

[margin: Were the apostles guided by the Spirit in adopting this organization?]

that no supernatural guidance was required. He holds, accordingly, that there is no form of Church government which can be said to have a monopoly of "Divine right"; that when the sacred books were written the polity was still in a fluid state, capable of becoming a monarchy, an oligarchy, or a democracy, according to the element which would become dominant; and that it is right and proper, and indeed inevitable, that the ecclesiastical polity should be moulded by the age, and by the existing forms of government in society.

As to Hatch's view that the mode of government continued fluid, unformed, and inchoate throughout the apostolic age, it is impossible to any one who accepts of the Acts and the Pastoral Epistles. I have shown that from a very early date in the history of the Church, the polity had taken a fixed and definite shape—that of a council of elders or bishops chosen by the Christian people; and we shall see farther on that this continued till towards the middle of the second century, when monarchical episcopacy began to lift its head. And as to the idea that it is permissible to adopt whatever form of Church polity is best suited to the age, I have to remark that it is not contended that anything more than the broad outlines and great fundamental principles of Church government are indicated in Scripture. We do hold, however, that these are most clearly legible in its pages; that, as I hope to show, they are eminently in harmony with, and a suitable vehicle of, the Christian spirit; that they are demonstrably applicable to any age or land; though, no doubt, in applying them practically in different ages and in different countries and circumstances, there is room for great variety of detail.

(1) The apostolic form of Church polity—government by a council or committee chosen by the free suffrages of the Christian community— seems admirably adapted to the spirit and genius of Christianity itself. It is surely a matter of some importance that the outward framework of the Christian society should be in harmony with the Christian spirit—a home and not a prison for the Church; not a strait jacket, but an easy, comfortable garment in which its free, spontaneous life and movement would have room for play. Christianity is essentially and fundamentally a spiritual religion, emancipating and not enslaving and oppressing men's consciences; for, "where the spirit of the Lord is there is liberty." It may be surely accepted as axiomatic that, whatever form the organization may assume, it must be adapted to and in unison with Christianity itself. Now an autocratic, despotic rule, which imposes its authority on the Church and allows no adequate expression to its mind and spirit, cannot be a suitable organ of government, and must necessarily cramp and injure the Church's life and action. We now begin to see why the original founders of the Church singled out the form of government they adopted—a council or committee of presbyters, chosen by the free vote of the Christian people—and preferred it to any other. It was not simply because it was a Jewish institution; for Jewish institutions were passed over by the apostles when they found them unsuitable to their ends, and incongruous with the religion which they

margin note: 1. The form adopted by them specially adapted to the spirit of Christianity.

taught. Much less was it because they found that government by a council or committee obtained among certain heathen societies around them. They found the monarchical, autocratic principle—that which concentrated power in the individual—in operation as well, and recommended by the halo of imperial splendour which surrounded it; and yet they deliberately put it aside; and in preference to any other they selected for their purpose the principle of government by a council elected by the governed as manifestly the organization best suited to the genius of Christianity, its spirituality and freedom; as the one best fitted to secure order and effectiveness on the one hand, and yet simplicity and expansiveness on the other—a system which, in the language of a great man, secures "superiority without tyranny, parity without disorder, and subjection without slavery."

(2) For another peculiarity of this principle is its suitability to the most varying circumstances. It is the mode of government chosen in all ages and all the world over in all free societies for managing their affairs, the one which commends itself to the common sense of mankind as at once the most simple, and the most effective. It existed, as we have seen, among the Jews from a remote period of their history, showing its applicability to a primitive Oriental people. It is the method of local government in operation at this moment, and has been from time immemorial, in the towns and communities throughout the Chinese empire, the governing council bearing the very name of "elders," or at least its Chinese equivalent. It

2. Suitable to the most varying circumstances.

was the form of government, as Hatch himself shows, adopted by the municipalities and associations over the Roman empire in the opening centuries of our era; and, without apparently perceiving the significance of the concession, Dr. Hatch admits its applicability to our own democratic age. He says that "under the impulse of the vast secular revolution now going on, all organizations, civil or ecclesiastical, must be, *as the early Churches were*, more or less democratical." What the Church of the present democratic age needs is, he thinks, a return to the more or less democratical constitution of the early Church. If it was suited to that early age, and if it is also capable of being adapted to the changed conditions of this nineteenth century, if it is alike indigenous to ancient Judæa and to modern China, it is hard to imagine any time or circumstances to which it is not applicable, or why it should not have been intended by the Spirit of God to be the permanent mode of government in His Church. That a few simple Galilean fishermen fixed upon a polity so much in keeping with Christianity itself, so suitable to any circumstances that Dr. Hatch thinks a return to something like it would fit our democratic age, a polity which still commends itself to the most civilized communities as the one most effective for their purpose, was surely no accident, but due to the light and leading of that Divine Spirit by whom they were animated and guided. We see no good reason why we should accept apostolic teaching as authoritative on other matters and reject it on this.

(3) The institution of the pastorate and the government of the Church is in Scripture expressly

attributed to Christ Himself. He is represented as having "given" along with other functionaries "pastors and teachers" for the perfecting of the saints and for the work of the ministry (Eph. iv. 11); and "teachers," "helps" and "governments" are stated to have been "set in the Church" by God (1 Cor. xii. 28); while the apostle thinks it necessary to give specific and detailed instructions respecting the qualifications required in bishops or presbyters and deacons (1 Tim. iii. 1–13; Tit. i. 5–9).

3. Expressly attributed to God in Scripture.

II.

WERE "PRESBYTER" AND "BISHOP" NAMES OF THE SAME OFFICE-BEARERS?

A more important question than the origin of the local ministry and of its nomenclature, though one intimately connected with it, has now to be considered, namely, were "presbyter" and "bishop" originally names of the same officers, or did they designate two different classes of ministers? It has been generally held by scholars, among whom Bishop Lightfoot may be named as the most eminent, that during the greater part of the apostolic period, if not during the whole of it, these names were applied indifferently to the same officials. Till very recently this has been accepted as an established fact needing no further proof. Dr. Hatch, however, as has been seen, endeavoured to show in his Bampton Lecture that the two names were distinct in their origin, and also that whereas the "presbyter" was

Lightfoot and others affirm that "bishop" and "presbyter" were originally identical.

primarily concerned with discipline, the "bishop" acquired his name and attained to his eminence as chief almoner in the Church. Dr. Hatch, indeed, did not very clearly and distinctly define his view of the relation between "presbyters" and "bishops," though he seemed to accept of Bishop Lightfoot's conclusion that they were names of the same office-bearers. Harnack, however, starting from Hatch's premises, carries them out to what he regards as their logical issues. He maintains that "presbyters" and "bishops" were not only distinct in their origin, but all along different in their functions; that they were never at any time identical; that "presbyters" were responsible for discipline, but had nothing to do as such with the public worship; and that "bishops" had to do primarily and chiefly with finance, and that as having been concerned with the offerings, they came to preside over the worship of the congregation. His chief argument is that while bishops and deacons are habitually associated, we find no such association of the presbyters and deacons. He refers to Phil. i. 1, and to 1 *Clem. ad Cor.* c. xlii., in proof of this, and to the *Pastor* of Hermas, where, he says, bishops and deacons are kept distinct from presbyters. In 1 Tim. iii. 1–13, instructions are given with regard to bishops and deacons, but presbyters are mentioned in a different connection at chap. v. 17–19. His contention is that the "elders" of the early Church were not official persons, the πρεσβύτεροι and νεότεροι having been simply the old and the young, the former having been persons whose age and experience qualified them for advising and governing, and entitled them to honour and obedience. As-

This denied by Harnack.

signing the composition of the Acts of the Apostles and the Pastoral Epistles to the second century he says that it is in that century that we first meet with chosen or appointed presbyters. Bishops and deacons, he affirms, are named for the first time in the Epistle to the Philippians, which belongs to the year 63 A.D.; but he thinks that as yet the terms do not point to any ecclesiastical office of authority over the Church. It is in the Epistle of Clement of Rome that for the first time we meet with bishops and deacons as regular officers elected in the Church. Weizsäcker, who previously regarded the presbyters and bishops as identical, now accepts of Harnack's view, and says, "the theory is wrong that the same persons are sometimes called presbyters and sometimes bishops, though often this is apparently so." And Dr. Sanday and other writers of a series of articles in *The Expositor*, though not prepared to go the whole length with Harnack in these conclusions, do go a considerable way with him, Dr. Sanday suggesting that the bishops may have been so called because they exercised supervision over the deacons.

Harnack's view examined. On the theory thus developed by Harnack, we have to offer the following remarks.

1. In relegating to the second century such passages as Acts xx. 17, 28, and Titus i. 5-7, wherein the terms "bishops" and "elders" are treated interchangeably, Harnack is referring them to the very period when such identification of "bishops" and "elders" as they contain was least possible. It was towards the middle of this century that, according to

Does not get rid of the passages by referring them to second century.

all the evidence, the terms "bishop" and "presbyter" ceased to be used interchangeably, and that the term "bishop" began to be confined to and monopolised by one individual officer. From that time such a representation as that in Acts xx. 17, 28, which, be it observed, describes *the presbyters as bishops*, and not the bishops as presbyters (a very different thing), became impossible. Does Dr. Harnack refer the passages to an earlier period, say to the end of the first, or beginning of the second century? In that case they constitute a powerful proof that at that time the terms were used indiscriminately, and they thus upset Dr. Harnack's theory; which indeed he does not help, but only embarrasses and makes more improbable by his vain endeavour to get rid of these inconvenient passages by fathering them on the second century. The only alternative to such absurdity is to explain the statements away, which is the natural and handy way for the theorizer, and which Dr. Harnack has recourse to in the case of the statements of Clement of Rome and of Polycarp.

2. For let it be remarked further that Dr. Harnack's theory is not even justified by a fair treatment of his own premises, and of the records which he accepts. Take for example the case of the Epistle of Clement of Rome. The persons against whom the revolt at Corinth took place are over and over again called by Clement "the presbyters." "It is shameful, dearly beloved, yes, utterly shameful and unworthy of your conduct in Christ, that it should be reported that the very steadfast and ancient Church of the Corinthians, for the sake of one or two persons, maketh sedition against

Not justified by his own data.

What Clement of Rome says.

its presbyters" (chap. xlvii.). "Let the flock of Christ be at peace with its duly appointed presbyters" (chap. liv.). "Ye, therefore, that laid the foundation of the sedition, submit yourselves unto the presbyters" (chap. lvii.). Now the question is, were these "presbyters" unofficial persons of age and experience, from among whom, as Dr. Harnack imagines, the bishops had been selected; or were they presbyters in the official sense, presbyters who had been regularly appointed to office? It seems to me beyond question that, according to the conception and representation of Clement (and it is what *his* testimony is we want to learn), they were duly appointed office-bearers. Dr. Harnack's theory, as we understand it, is, that the persons who have been thrust out of office are *now*, when Clement writes, and have been for a considerable time, bishops, who previous to their appointment to the episcopate had been persons of age and experience, and had on that account borne the unofficial name of "presbyters." But they are described by Clement as being *now*, at the very time of his writing, presbyters. This is their *present* title throughout the epistle. Look at the language in which he describes them, as given a few sentences back. Is that the way one would expect them to be designated, if Dr. Harnack's theory were the true one? If they are persons who were formerly called "presbyters" on account of their age and experience, but who have been duly appointed bishops, and have for a length of time held that office, would not Clement call them "bishops"? Would he not in that case call upon the Church at Corinth to "live on terms of peace with their appointed bishops"; and reprove them for "making sedition against their bishops"? Nor is this all. As if to put the matter beyond doubt, *their appointment as presbyters* is particularly and expressly noted. The Church is exhorted to live on terms of peace " with the duly appointed presbyters" (μετὰ τῶν καθισταμένων πρεσβυτέρων). Is this the language it would be natural to use if they were persons who had been appointed not presbyters, but *bishops*; though at a former time they had belonged to the unofficial class of presbyters? Would any one, without a theory to support, ever think of putting such a violent construction on plain language? Nor is this the whole case. With special reference to the ejected ministers, who are thus called "presbyters duly appointed," and by way of remonstrance with the Church of Corinth for ejecting them, Clement says : " Those therefore who were appointed (τοὺς οὖν κατασταθέντας) by them, or afterwards by other men of repute, with the consent of the whole Church, and have ministered unblameably to the flock of Christ in holiness of mind, peacefully, and with all modesty, and for long time have borne a good report of all, these men we consider to be unjustly thrust out from their ministration" (chap. xliv.). Clearly, then, the persons against whom the revolt has taken place are not only presbyters, but presbyters who have been regularly appointed to office.

And that these presbyters are conceived by Clement as bishops, and as having filled the office of the episcopate, is equally clear ; for the effect of the sedition has been *to eject these presbyters from the episcopate.* Immediately after the last sentence quoted above, Clement proceeds: " For it will be no light sin for us, if we thrust out from the episcopate those who have unblameably and holily offered the gifts." And, if possible, to make it still more certain that those who held the bishop's office were none other than official presbyters, he goes on: "Blessed are those presbyters who have gone before, seeing that their departure was fruitful and ripe; for they have no fear lest any should remove them from their appointed place." He supposes that, had they been still alive, they might have feared such removal from "their appointed place," and implies that *as presbyters* they had held such a place. The presbyters who have been removed were, therefore, *in the episcopate*, were bishops, and in the conception of Clement, as indeed his whole argument against their ejection shows, correspond to the bishops of c. xlii.; for c. xlii. is a part of his remonstrance in behalf of the ejected presbyters. For Clement the presbyterate and episcopate are one —the presbyters are bishops.

As to the association of bishops and deacons in Phil. i. 1 and in 1 Tim. iii., on the supposition that "presbyters" and "bishops" are names for the same officers, there is nothing extraordinary in the fact that in one or two cases the term "bishop" occurs rather than "presbyters," nothing to show that the use of that term rather than this was more than accidental. In Clement of Rome the collocation in a single instance (c. xlii.) is evidently employed to enable Clement to show that such officers had been mentioned by Isaiah, and had therefore the sanction of ancient prophecy. But it is not even a fact that "bishops" and "deacons" are always associated, and that "presbyters" and "deacons" are not similarly grouped. "Presbyters" and "deacons" are grouped together in the Epistle of Polycarp in precisely the same manner that "bishops" and "deacons" are in Phil. i. 1;[1] and it should be remembered that Polycarp too, like Paul, is describing the office-bearers of the Church at Philippi; the "presbyters" and "deacons" of Polycarp's epistle corresponding exactly to the "bishops" and "deacons" of Paul's epistle; a fact which Harnack sweeps away majestically with a wave of his hand thus: "the presbyters here named, to whom detailed exhortations are addressed in chap. vi., are in reality bishops. But Polycarp does not so name them because he, as belonging to Asia Minor, is willing to acknowledge and name only *one* bishop in each congregation"— an acknowledgment, however, of which his epistle is entirely innocent! No wonder Mr. Matthew Arnold laughs so scornfully at the "vigorous and rigorous" methods by which German theologians construct their theories, bending the facts to suit their theories, or, when they will not bend, breaking them! A theory which compels one to deal, as Harnack thus deals with plain facts, awakens suspicion of its soundness. No doubt, after the middle of the second century, when the bishop has concentrated in himself the power which had previously belonged to all the presbyters, and when the deacon has become a mere appendage to the bishop, we do find the two constantly associated, but that makes nothing for the hypothesis in question as applying to an earlier age.

(margin: What Polycarp says.)

3. So far I have assumed Dr. Harnack's premises

---

[1] *Ep.* of Polycarp, c. v.: "Being subject to the presbyters and deacons as unto God and Christ."

to be sound and unexceptionable. They are, however, it appears to me, very far from being so. I cannot agree to consign the Acts and the Pastoral Epistles in their present form to the middle of the second century. For reasons which cannot be stated here I take them to be genuine products of the apostolic age—of Luke and of Paul. I have referred already to the series of articles on the Christian Ministry in *The Expositor*. One serious defect in many of those articles, as it seemed to me, was a lack of clear understanding in them as to the witnesses whose testimony was admissible on this subject. Few, if any, of the writers went with Dr. Harnack in throwing over the Acts and the Pastoral Epistles, or even with Dr. Hatch in parting with the latter. And yet they seemed in many cases to accept of a representation of the facts which was only possible on the supposition that Harnack's position in relation to these writings is a just one. Holding as I do, however, the historicity of these books, I must now direct the notice of the reader to the evidence which they as well as the sub-apostolic writings furnish that "presbyter" and "bishop" were, in the age to which those documents belong, but names for the same officials.

(a) It is noteworthy that these officials have other significant *titles* in common besides those of "bishop" and "elder." Every student of early Church history knows that when, after the middle of the second century, the monarchical bishop has concentrated in himself the functions which before that time belonged to the

<small>Dr. Harnack's premises not granted: historicity of the Acts accepted.</small>

<small>Evidence of identity of "bishop" and elder."</small>

<small>1. They have other titles in common;</small>

presbyters generally, he appears as pre-eminently "the shepherd" (ὁ ποιμήν) of his flock. (See the *Apostolic Ordinances*, 18; *Apostolical Constitutions*, B. iii. 5; ii. 1). But before this monopoly took place the term is applied habitually to the presbyters. It is remarkable, indeed, that even the members of the Jewish synedrion are called not only "elders" but also "overseers" or "bishops" (*Mishna*, Taamid, v. 1), and "shepherds"—*parnasim* (*Jerusalem Pea*, viii.; *Babylon Chagiga*, 60; *Sabbath*, 17 a). In the apostolic and early patristic period the presbyters are as constantly called "shepherds" as are the monarchical bishops of a later time. See Acts xx. 28; 1 Pet. v. 2; Eph. iv. 11 (where the "pastors" or shepherds (ποιμένας) are no doubt, like those of Peter, elders or bishops); Clement of Rome, cc. xliv., liv. "Let the flock of Christ (ποίμνιον) live on terms of peace with the presbyters set over it" (μετὰ τῶν καθεσταμένων πρεσβυτέρων) says Clement; whereas in the *Apostolical Constitutions* (ii. 1) "the shepherd set over" the flock (τὸν ποιμένα τὸν καθιστάμενον) is the bishop.

as "shepherd;" which like "bishop" was also applied to the Jewish elder.

(*b*) So far as the facts enable us to judge, precisely the *same qualifications* were required in elders as in bishops. See Tit. i. 5–9, and cf. 1 Tim. iii. 2–7. It goes to confirm one's conviction of the identity of the elder and bishop that the qualifications here distinctly required of both are strikingly similar to those which were requisite in the Jewish elder. It was required of the member of the synedrion that he should be blameless, the husband of one wife, that his children

2. The same qualifications required in them.

should be in subjection under him, just as also his election depended upon the suffrages of the members of the synagogue (*Berachoth*, 55*a* ; Maimonides, *Jad-Ha-Chezaka, Kilchoth Sanhedrin*, ii. 8 ; *Menachoth*, 5 *a* ; *Sanhedrin*, 17 *a*, 36 *b* ; *Mishna Horajoth*, i. 4). The qualifications prescribed by Paul as necessary in the case of the Christian elder or bishop are almost verbatim similar to those required in the Jewish elder. We have here another evidence not only of the identity of the "presbyter" and "bishop," but of the Jewish elder having been the prototype of both.

(*c*) As is more or less implied in their requiring the same qualifications, and bearing the same names, just the *same functions* are attributed to both.

3. The same *functions attributed to them;*

It is admitted that *ruling*, and especially the administration of *discipline*, was a primary function of the elders. By Hatch and Harnack it is regarded as indeed their only proper function. In Acts xv. the elders are represented as taking part with the apostles in the decision arrived at. In 1 Tim. v. 17, in Hermas *Vis.*, ii. 4, 3, in Clement of Rome, in Polycarp, and elsewhere the presbyters are those who *rule* or *preside* over the Church (οἱ προστάντες τῆς ἐκκλησίας) or those to whom the Church is to be subject. In Polycarp (*Ep.* vi.) they are counselled not to be "severe in judgment." But this function also is attributed to the bishops. It is implied in the "*shepherding*" of Acts xx. 28 ; and in 1 Tim. iii. 4 it is stipulated that the bishop should be "one that ruleth well his own house, having his children in subjection with all gravity. For if a man

as ruling,

know not how to rule his own house, how shall he take care of the Church of God?"

Both Hatch and Harnack lay special stress on the circumstance that the bishops presided over the public *worship* of the Church. According to the former, it was as the chief almoner of the congregation, and as having charge of the offerings, that the bishop came to be so closely associated with the worship. And Harnack says, "Bishops are originally the directors of the worship, the offerers κατ' ἐξοχήν. They are called overseers insomuch as they direct or superintend the assembly met for worship. Out of this function all others have necessarily developed."[1] Again, "beyond a doubt the προσφέρειν δῶρα τῷ Θεῷ in the sense of the offering of the sacrifice appears as the most important function of the episcopus."[2] It is quite true the *Didaché* informs us respecting the bishops and deacons that they too perform the service (τὴν λειτουργίαν) of the prophets and teachers, though it is to be noted that this service is represented in the *Didaché* as being primarily in the hands of the prophets and teachers. In Justin Martyr "the president of the brethren" (ὁ προεστὼς τῶν ἀδελφῶν) offers prayers and thankofferings (*Apol.* i. 65, 67). Now what of the presbyters? I pass by James v. 14, where we learn that it is the part of the presbyters to *pray* over the sick—a *liturgical* office. And I do not assume, as Bishop Lightfoot does, that the bishops of the *Didaché* are none other than presbyters. I am content to rest the case on testimony which

[margin: presiding over *public worship*.]

---

[1] *Expositor*, May, 1887, p. 342.
[2] *Ibid*, June, 1887, p. 413.

expressly sets the presbyters before us as having charge of this part of the service, and such testimony I find in Clement of Rome. The object of his epistle is to quell a sedition against the rulers of the Church at Corinth. The apostles knew, he says, there would be "strife on account of the name of the episcopate." For this reason they appointed those already mentioned, and gave instruction that when they should fall asleep other approved men should succeed them in the ministry ($\tau \grave{\eta} \nu$ $\lambda \epsilon \iota \tau o \upsilon \rho \gamma \acute{\iota} a \nu$). He thinks, therefore, that those appointed by them or afterward, by other men of repute, with the consent of the whole Church, and who have blamelessly served ($\lambda \epsilon \iota \tau o \upsilon \rho \gamma \acute{\eta} \sigma a \nu \tau \epsilon \varsigma$) the flock, cannot be justly dismissed from the ministry ($\tau \hat{\eta} \varsigma$ $\lambda \epsilon \iota \tau o \upsilon \rho \gamma \acute{\iota} a \varsigma$). For he says, "Our sin will not be small, if we eject from the episcopate those who have blamelessly and holily presented the offerings ($\pi \rho o \sigma \epsilon \nu \epsilon \gamma \kappa o \nu \tau a \varsigma$ $\tau \grave{a}$ $\delta \hat{\omega} \rho a$). Blessed are those presbyters who having finished their course before now . . have no fear lest any one deprive them of the place now appointed them." And to leave no room for doubt that the persons ejected are none other than the presbyters, he describes it as disgraceful that this ancient Church should "engage in sedition against its presbyters," and exhorts those who "have laid the foundation of this sedition to submit themselves to the presbyters," and to "live on terms of peace with the presbyters set over them" (see Clement's Epistle, cc. xliv., xlvii., liv.). But observe their function is described as a $\lambda \epsilon \iota \tau o \upsilon \rho \gamma \acute{\iota} a$. It is $\pi \rho o \sigma \phi \acute{\epsilon} \rho \epsilon \iota \nu$ $\tau \grave{a}$ $\delta \hat{\omega} \rho a$, which included the Eucharistic service, and the whole worship of the congregation; and from the charge of this service the presbyters of Corinth have been ejected by the mutineers. Why, even after the bishop becomes separated from, and raised over the presbyters, the latter still take part with him in the service. In the *Apostolic Ordinances* the presbyters are συμμυσταί with the bishop. And yet Dr. Hatch ventures to affirm that "presbyters as such had no part in the Eucharistic service."[1]

Again, it is a strong point with Dr. Hatch that the bishop was originally the chief almoner of the Church, and that he was primarily concerned with *finance* and with *the poor*. "He received," he says, "and distributed the alms and the offerings of the people, which were made at the Eucharistic service at which the bishop presided. Hence the bishop's association with the central rite, and its being soon definitely assigned to him," and hence too the close connection between the bishop and the deacons. It is worthy of note in passing that the Jewish elders attended to the *charities* of the synagogue.[2] At all events from the very first mention of Christian elders in the history we find them concerned prominently with such matters. The relief contributed at Antioch for "the poor brethren in Judæa" is sent to the elders at Jerusalem. We have just learned from Clement of Rome how in his time they had charge of the gifts and offerings of the Christian people. In the Epistle of Polycarp (c. v.), the presbyters are not only associated with the deacons as bishops are elsewhere, but they are exhorted to be " compassionate and merciful to all . . . visiting all the sick, and not neglecting

Both concerned with finance;

---

[1] *Bampton Lecture*, p. 78.
[2] See Geikie's *Life and Words of Christ*, vol. ii. c. xxxix. (note *b*).

the widow, the orphan, or the poor" (c. vi.); and Polycarp grieves over Valens, a presbyter, who has embezzled the money of the poor (c. xi.). He makes no reference to bishops, but exhorts the Philippians to be "subject to the presbyters and deacons."

Once more, from a very early date the office of *teaching* is equally associated with both the bishop and the presbyter. It is evident,

and with public teaching.

both from the general sense of the word and from the context, that the "shepherding" of the flock in Acts xx. 28 includes instruction, or spiritual feeding; the word as applied to Peter certainly includes this meaning (see John xxi. 17, 18, where the word βοσκεῖν is employed to indicate what is included in the shepherd's office). "Aptness to teach" is required in bishops (1 Tim. iii. 2); and in the *Didaché* the bishops and deacons fulfil the ministry of the prophets and teachers. In the *Coptic Church Order* it is demanded of the bishop, who is called "the shepherd," that he should be "able to explain the Scriptures well" (cf. 16 and 18). In Justin Martyr the president gives instruction (*Apol.*, i. c. 67). Now as regards elders, it is doubtless true that, like the elders of the Jewish synedrion, they were primarily concerned with administration and discipline. When the gift of teaching was so largely bestowed upon the Church, and when prophets and teachers were so numerous, it was less necessary that the elders should be prominent in this work. Still at a comparatively early time the elders are expected to engage in it, and those of them who "labour in the word and doctrine" are to be specially honoured (1 Tim. v. 17). In Titus the elders, who are also called bishops (cf.

Tit. i. 5 with v. 7), are exhorted to "hold fast the faithful word as they have been taught, that they may be able by sound doctrine both to exhort and to convince the gainsayers" (v. 9). Other terms of a more general kind are applied to the rulers, such as "those who preside over the Church" ($προϊστάμενοι$), and "those who rule, or lead" the Church ($ἡγούμενοι$); and yet these are represented as engaged in the work of teaching. The Thessalonians are instructed to "know them that labour among them, and are over them ($προϊσταμένους\ ὑμῶν$) in the Lord and admonish them" (1 Thess. v. 12). The article occurs only with the first of the participles, showing that not three classes of ministers are referred to, but that those who are "over them" are the same as those who "labour among them and admonish them." And this association of the teaching function with the rulers is brought out still more clearly in Heb. xiii. Those who have the rule over the Hebrew Christians ($ἡγούμενοι$) whom they are exhorted to "obey" and "submit to" are those who "have spoken unto them the word of God" (*vv.* 7, 17). These are none other than the presbyters who are similarly described by Clement of Rome and by Hermas. Harnack endeavours to make out that they are not officials at all; but it is by pushing back the statements in Acts and the Pastoral Epistles to the second century, and even apart from that his arguments are unsatisfactory. I have already given reasons for believing that the Church of Thessalonica, as well as the Churches generally in Asia and Greece, was fully organized before this time.

It would be somewhat strange then if Dr. Hatch's

very positive assertion that "in the numerous references to presbyters in sub-apostolic literature there is not one to their being teachers, even when a reference might have been expected," were well founded. But though by more than one writer it has been quoted as an oracle, we are bound to say that it is at variance with the plainest facts. From the part which the presbyters are described by Clement of Rome as taking in the public service of the congregation it would be a legitimate inference that that service embraced instruction ; but we are not left to inference. In the so-called Second Epistle of Clement to the Corinthians, which is now regarded as a homily probably addressed originally to that Church, and for that reason connected with the Epistle of Clement, the exhortation occurs: " Let us not think to give heed and believe now only [*i.e.* in the congregation] *while we are admonished by the presbyters*, but, likewise, when we have departed home let us remember the commandments of the Lord . . . and the unbelievers shall see His glory and His might; and they shall be amazed when they see the kingdom of the world given to Jesus, saying, Woe unto us, for Thou wast, and we knew it not and believed not, and we obeyed not the presbyters *when they told us of our salvation.*" Here the presbyters appear as not only admonishing the Christian congregation, but as preaching to the unbelieving. But this is not all. In the *Pastor* of Hermas the presbyters are described as "those who preside over the Church" ($\pi\rho o \ddot{\iota} \sigma \tau a \mu \acute{\epsilon} \nu o \iota$) and as those who rule or lead ($\pi \rho o \eta \gamma o \acute{\upsilon} \mu \epsilon \nu o \iota$). See *Vis.* ii. 4 ; ii. 2 ; iii. 9. And to the presbyters who thus " preside over the Church," Hermas says, " Be not like drug-mixers. For the drug-mixers carry their drugs in boxes, but ye carry your drug and poison in your heart. . . . How will you *instruct the elect of the Lord, if you yourselves have not instruction?*" (*Vis.* iii. 9). Surely in view of such unequivocal testimony, Dr. Hatch is not justified in saying that "in the numerous references to presbyters in the sub-apostolic literature there is not one to their being teachers." Even Dr. Hatch himself shows that the professors in the philosophical schools were sometimes called presbyters; while the widows or presbyteresses referred to in 1 Tim. v. 10, and whom we so often meet with in the early history, Origen informs us, presided over and instructed the other women of the Church. Origen interprets the statement in 1 Tim. v. 10, as to their washing the saints' feet, as referring figuratively to doctrine. At all events the office ascribed by Origen to the presbyteresses points to the presbyters having been invested with a corresponding one.

If Harnack's theory be the true one we have thus two sets of officers in each congregation having several names in common, requiring precisely the same qualifications, performing the same functions, taking the same part with regard to finance, general oversight, ruling and instruction and the public service of the congregation; two sets of officers strictly co-ordinate and yet distinct from one another; and we have this both in large Churches like Rome and Corinth and in small ones. Even Harnack himself has to admit that his view implies a sort of *dyrarchy*. But the theory is clumsy and preposterous on the face of it; and the facts adduced already, even if we possessed no other point clearly and emphatically to the identity of the presbyterate and episcopate, and to the conclusion that the two terms describe but two different aspects of the same officials.

(*d*) But there is evidence not yet brought forward which proves as clearly as anything of the kind could be proved that "presbyter" and "bishop" are names of the same office-bearers: there are passages clear and numerous wherein *these terms are used interchangeably.*

The terms "presbyter" and "bishop" used interchangeably.

They are so employed in the passage often adverted to already (Acts xx. 17, 28), concerning which Harnack remarks that "it says only that the bishops appointed by the Holy Ghost were at the same time presbyters, which I have never denied." That, however, is not what it says. What it says is that *the presbyters of Ephesus were bishops*—a very different thing, and, taken along with the admitted fact that *all bishops were presbyters*, a very clear demonstration of the identity of the presbyters and bishops.

As to 1 Tim. iii. 1–7 and v. 17, it should be borne in mind that Timothy who is here addressed by Paul is labouring at Ephesus, that the "bishops" and "elders" referred to in this epistle are officials at Ephesus, and that in Acts xx. 17, 28 we have these identified as one set of office-bearers under two names. And the pastors or "shepherds" of Eph. iv. 11 are doubtless none other than the Ephesian presbyter-bishops of Acts xx. 28 who are told to "shepherd" ($\pi o\iota\mu a\iota\nu\epsilon\iota\nu$) the Church, and the same as the Ephesian presbyter-bishops of First Timothy.

Nowhere is the identity of the elders and bishops

more clearly taught than in Titus i. 5–7. Paul reminds Titus how he left him in Crete to "ordain *elders* in every city as I had appointed thee. If any be blameless, the husband of one wife, having faithful children, not accused of riot or unruly. For a *bishop* must be blameless," etc. The apostle interchanges the two words as names of the same officers, using them indiscriminately. Harnack has a handy way of surmounting the difficulty, and one which in Mr. Matthew Arnold's phrase is at once "vigorous and rigorous." He is not content with saying that he regards "the Pastoral Epistles as writings which in their present form were composed in the middle of the second century:" he informs us "Tit. i. 5–7 I cannot accept as a valid proof because I believe that i. 7–9 was interpolated into the received text by the redactor." A short and easy method of removing a difficulty! But when was this interpolation inserted? We gather from his statement already quoted that it was "in the middle of the second century." At any rate, let it belong to whatever date it may, it regards elders as official persons, and as identical with bishops. In assigning it to the second century Dr Harnack is not getting rid of the testimony which it bears to that identity, nor has he explained how such a deliberate assertion of identity could be made at so late a period. In connecting it with a time when we know that a separation took place between the presbyterate and the episcopate, when the bishop was distinguished from and elevated above the presbyters, he is doing great violence to probability, and making a heavy draft on our credulity.

1 Pet. v. 1, 2 is equally unambiguous: "The elders

which are among you I exhort, who am also an elder. . . . Feed (lit. *shepherd*) the flock of God which is among you, taking the episcopate thereof" (ἐπισκοποῦντες). Dr. Harnack says, "the reading ἐπισκοποῦντες has not been established." It is omitted by B and the Sinaitic MS., but given in the others, and appears in all the versions. It is, therefore, retained by the English Revisers, and is, in any case, a second century reading, and was inserted by a writer who regarded the presbyters as exercising the bishop's office, supplying thus important evidence of the identity of the presbyters and bishops of the early age. The very fact that after the middle of the second century presbyters were not regarded as filling the bishop's office shows that the reading must have been a very early one.

The identity of the presbyters and bishops in the Epistle of Clement of Rome has been already demonstrated.

In view of all the facts and considerations which have been presented, I do not see how to avoid the conclusion that Dr. Harnack's position is untenable, and that presbyters and bishops were in the early Church names of the same office-bearers. The evidence which points to this seems irresistible.

III.

Was Monarchical Episcopacy Set Up by the Apostles?

Another question of hardly less moment than that just discussed now presses for an answer. Supposing the identity of "presbyters" and "bishops" throughout the Apostolic age, at what time did monarchical episcopacy arise? At what period did the name "bishop" come to be appropriated to one of the presbyters, who had risen to superiority over the rest? Did this development take place while some of the apostles were still alive, and with their express sanction? or did it occur later? This, which involves the question—Did monarchical episcopacy obtain the seal of apostolic sanction?—is a matter of considerable importance on this subject of Church order, and deserves close attention. It is a question on which we find ourselves confronted with the high authority of Bishop Lightfoot. While granting that in the New Testament writings "presbyters" and "bishops" are names of the same officials, he maintains that "there is satisfactory evidence of the development of a localized episcopate in the later years of the apostolic age; that this development was not simultaneous and equal in all parts of Christendom: that it is more especially connected with the name of St. John; and that in the early years of the second century the episcopate was widely spread and had taken firm root, more especially in Asia Minor and Syria."[1] He says again, "If the writer of these letters [the Ignatian Epistles] had represented the Churches of Asia Minor as under presbyterial government, he would have contradicted all the evidence, which, without one dissentient voice, points to episcopacy as the established form of Church government from the close of the first

Bishop Lightfoot's view;

---

[1] *The Apostolic Fathers*, Part II. S. Ignatius and S. Polycarp, vol. i. p. 377.

century." The result of his investigation into the origin of the Christian ministry, he says in his preface to the sixth edition of his Commentary on the Epistles to the Philippians, "has been a confirmation of the statement in the English Ordinal: 'It is evident unto all men diligently reading the Holy Scripture and ancient authors that from the apostles' time there have been three orders of ministry in Christ's Church, Bishops, Priests and Deacons.'" He affirms that it is "vain to deny that early in the second century the episcopal office was firmly and widely established"; and maintains that "during the last three decades of the first century, and consequently during the lifetime of the latest surviving apostle, this change must have been brought about"; that "in the mysterious period which comprises the last thirty years of the first century—episcopacy must have been mainly developed"; that "during the historical blank which extends over half a century after the fall of Jerusalem, episcopacy was matured and the Catholic Church consolidated."[1]

liable to same objection which he urges against Rothe's. Now it might be pointed out that the very same argument which Bishop Lightfoot urges so effectually against Rothe's hypothesis tells with equal force against his own. Bishop Lightfoot argues that if episcopacy had been established, as Rothe imagines, by a council of the apostles after the fall of Jerusalem, it would have been immediately and generally adopted, whereas we know that as a matter of fact it was slow and gradual in coming into operation, and in maturing. In like manner, considering the constant intercourse

[1] *Commentary on Philippians*, pp. 201, 205, 207.

that went on among the Churches it is inconceivable that, had episcopacy been established by the Apostle John, it would have been so tardy in coming into effect in large and important Churches not far away from the scene of John's labours. The slow and gradual development of diocesan episcopacy, admitted and emphasised by Lightfoot, is a powerful argument against its having been established with apostolic sanction. But we do not propose to rest satisfied with general considerations. Let us fairly and without prejudice look at the facts, and see if they justify the position so emphatically taken up by Bishop Lightfoot.

He admits, let it be borne in mind, that in the New Testament references the terms "bishops" and "elders" are interchangeable. Nor does he attempt to make much of the cases of James, Timothy and Titus.

As to James, there is no evidence that he did more than hold the position and exercise the influence which would naturally belong to one so nearly related to our Lord—"the Lord's brother"—and one of such energy and lofty character. There is not a particle of evidence in the Acts that he claimed and exercised specially episcopal prerogatives farther than they are possessed by any minister of a congregation. Stress has been sometimes laid on the part taken by him in the conference at Jerusalem, and especially on his words in Acts xv. 19, "Wherefore my sentence is," etc. (lit. *I judge*). Lumby, for example, says "the pronoun is emphatic, and indicates that the speaker is deciding with authority;" but evidently the emphatic position of

The cases of James,

R

the pronoun signifies: "The other speakers have given their judgment, *I* give mine." And this accords with the fact that the decree is always spoken of, not as that of James, but as that of "the apostles and elders" (see Acts xv. 22-29; xvi. 4). But even supposing that the New Testament had invested him with still higher and more authoritative prerogatives, it might be answered that these belonged to the apostolic status expressly assigned to him. In Acts ix. 27 we are informed that Barnabas brought Saul of Tarsus "to the apostles" at Jerusalem, while Paul himself says (Gal. i. 18, 19) he went up to see Peter, and that "other of the apostles saw he none save James, the Lord's brother." See also 1 Cor. xv. 7. Nor does it seem to have been in the secondary sense that he was recognised as an apostle. After the death of his namesake, the son of Zebedee, "James the Lord's brother" appears to have taken his place among the twelve. It is a strong confirmation of this when we find him so often associated with the other apostles, and on a perfect level with them, as when Paul himself, naming James first, speaks of him and Peter and John as "pillars"—a term which Clement of Rome applies to Peter and Paul (*Ep.* v.). If, as is very probable, he was regarded as holding the apostolic status among the twelve after the death of the other James, nothing is gained for episcopacy, any more than from Paul's recognition as an apostle; and on the other hand, if he did not occupy that status, his near relationship to Christ (a matter to which Orientals attach great importance), and his high personal character are quite sufficient to account for his place and influence at Jerusalem, and make nothing for an office which has no existence in history till well on in the second century.

With respect to Timothy and Titus I have already pointed out that their position was in no way different from that of an organizing missionary or evangelist (as Timothy indeed is called), like Quadratus in Eusebius, or such as non-episcopal Churches constantly avail themselves of in heathen countries. Bishop Lightfoot indeed admits that "it is the conception of a later age which represents Timothy as Bishop of Ephesus, and Titus as Bishop of Crete. St. Paul's own language implies that the position they held was temporary. In both cases their term of office is drawing to a close when the apostle writes (see 1 Tim. ii. 3; iii. 14; 2 Tim. iv. 9–21; Tit. 1–5; iii. 12)."

Timothy and Titus.

When Dr. Salmon affirms that Timothy was "not a mere delegate of Paul," that he had been ordained to office by the laying on of the hands of the presbytery, and that his office was that of an evangelist (2 Tim. iv. 5) or preaching and organizing missionary,[1] we are, therefore, not disposed to differ from him. But Dr. Salmon overlooks the fact that, besides being an evangelist, and ordained to office by the presbytery, Timothy was "charged" or delegated by the apostle to do a special work, and, in the two epistles which bear his name, received from the apostle express written instructions how to perform it. He was acting in short as Paul's Special Commissioner and substitute until he should be able to come himself (1 Tim. iii. 14, 15). Nor was this all. Over and above this, Timothy had had bestowed on him a

[1] See *Expositor* for July, 1887, p. 26.

"charism," which was not a natural gift merely, but a supernatural gift of the Spirit, imparted to him through the laying on of the Apostle's hands (2 Tim. i. 6). If, therefore, he did exercise extraordinary authority, we are not entitled to conclude that it was other than exceptional, exercised in pursuance of special apostolic appointment and instruction, and also by virtue of the supernatural gift conferred on him. Dr. Salmon alleges that his office was higher than that of the presbyters, and that he exercised authority over them. Armed as he was with a special apostolic commission and authority, and having a gift of the Spirit, that might well be without involving any warrant for the constitution of a permanent monarchical authority in the Church after the apostles were withdrawn, and when supernatural gifts had ceased. But I see no valid proof that he did exercise such individual authority over regularly organized presbyters. True, in his first letter the apostle writes: "Against an elder receive not an accusation, except at the mouth of two or three witnesses" (1 Tim. v. 19). But it should be borne in mind that many of the instructions sent to Timothy were intended not for his own personal guidance alone, but for the office-bearers and members of the Church generally, that they might know how to behave themselves in the house of God, the Church of the living God (1 Tim. iii. 15). There might be cases where the organization was still imperfect, and where examination and decision would devolve on Timothy himself, as Paul's Commissioner. But we are not warranted to conclude from this that where Timothy found a Council of Elders already in existence, and where a charge was made against one of them, he would supersede the others, and take the trial into his own hands. That interpretation certainly is not required. It is a perfectly natural construction of the words to take them as a direction how he and the presbyters should act in such a case. If even Peter, James, and John associated the elders with themselves in the decision at the Conference at Jerusalem (Acts xv.), it would be rash to infer that Timothy himself alone was to sit in judgment on the presbyters. In any case, in view of the fact that Timothy was acting as the Commissioner and substitute of the apostle, we have no right to argue from this the institution of a permanent individual rule and authority in the Church. All the early history is against it.

We may now pass, then, to the sub-apostolic evidence.

At the close of the three decades during which, according to Lightfoot, the change initiated by John has been going on, Clement writes from Rome to the Church of Corinth. Now suppose that three decades, or even one decade, or half a decade before his death John had established monarchical episcopacy, the fact must have speedily become known in such great centres as Rome and Corinth, and must have had its natural effect in these Churches. And yet Clement's epistle knows nothing of a bishop presiding over presbyters: his statements are, as we have seen, exactly in a line with the New Testament references on the subject. Bishop Lightfoot himself admits that "though Clement has occasion to speak of the ministry as an institution

Sub-apostolic evidence.

Monarchical episcopacy unknown at Rome and Corinth in Clement's time.

of the apostles, he mentions only two orders, and is silent about the episcopal office. He still uses the word bishop in the older sense as a synonym for presbyter." He concludes that Clement knew nothing of episcopacy in the later sense, and that he was himself simply "the chief among the presbyters." If the establishment of the later episcopacy has been going on under the Apostle John at Ephesus, and over Asia Minor, for a period of thirty years, and if, as Dr. Lightfoot well shows in reply to the writer of "Supernatural Religion," there was at that time close and constant intercourse among the Churches, and, as a consequence, a remarkable unity and solidarity amongst them, both in doctrine and practice, so that any differences that existed were insignificant, it is surely passing strange that about the time of John's death, *thirty years after the process is supposed to have begun*, there is not a trace of the later episcopacy in the old, large, central, long-established Churches of Rome and Corinth; and equally strange that Clement has evidently never heard of it, nor of John's action with regard to it!

Dr. Salmon, referring to Clement, concedes that we are "not to suppose that the name bishop was then distinctively used to denote the head of the Church; or that the line of separation between him and the other presbyters was so marked as it became in later times"; but asks "if episcopacy had not arisen before the end of the first century, and if Linus, Cletus, Clement were but names of leading presbyters, how comes it that the letter of the Roman Church should be universally known as the letter of Clement, whose name is not once mentioned in it?"

Dr. Salmon on Clement.

The point is so trivial as to be unworthy of Dr. Salmon. We see no greater difficulty in the way of the letter becoming known as Clement's, supposing him to have been a leading and distinguished presbyter, than in the case supposed by Dr. Salmon, which differs extremely little from the other alternative suggested. There is every probability that, if Clement was not (as Harnack thinks possible) the consul Flavius Clemens, Domitian's cousin, who was put to death by the Emperor for his Christianity, he was at all events closely related to the imperial house. This alone would give him great prominence and distinction. Nor was this all. The old woman who appears in vision to Hermas says, "You will write therefore two books, and you will send the one to Clemens, and the other to Grapte. And Clemens will send his to foreign countries, for *to him that office has been committed.* And Grapte will admonish the widows and orphans. But you will read the words in this city [Rome] *along with the presbyters who preside over the Church.*"[1] Dr. Salmon admits that it is Clement of Rome who is here described as one to whom has been committed the office of communicating with foreign countries. All this, which would soon become known in the Churches, with the circumstance that Clement would, no doubt, in communicating with Corinth, make known his name as the writer, would be quite enough to connect his name with the epistle. Indeed one thing that cannot but strike the student of early Church history is the slow development of episcopacy at Rome. Hatch remarks (Lecture IV.) that "so late as the third century the extant epitaphs

[1] *Pastor, Vis.* ii. 4.

of Roman bishops do not give the title episcopus";
and Salmon reminds us how "Epiphanius, evidently
drawing from an older writer, represents Marcion's
dealings as having been with the Roman presbyters."

As to Hermas, we have just seen how he represents
not Clement, but *the presbyters* as presiding
over the Roman Church. When in another
connection he mentions bishops, it is in the
plural; devoting one chapter to the deacons, and the next to the bishops, but here silent as
to presbyters, evidently treating the bishops as identical with the presbyters of a previous vision. Had
Hermas known anything of a "bishop" different
from and over the presbyters, he could not have
omitted reference to him.

Monarchical episcopacy unknown to Hermas,

Then again the bishops of the *Didaché* are, as Dr.
Lightfoot himself holds, presbyters. "The
episcopal office, properly so called," he says,
"had not been constituted in the district in which
the author lived." Dr. Salmon, indeed, attempts to
show that its circulation was limited; but I have
given reasons in favour of a very different view. I
have shown that it was used by Barnabas, by Hermas,
by Clement of Alexandria; that by the latter it is
quoted as Scripture, showing that it held somewhat
the same place in the early Church as Hermas and
Barnabas, who are similarly quoted, and that it
manifestly had similar wide acceptance. When Dr.
Salmon refers to the fact that it is apparently not
known to Tertullian, it is enough to point out, as I
have done already, that neither does Tertullian cite
nor refer to the Epistle of Barnabas—a fact which

and the Didaché.

should make us chary of building much as to the circulation of a book on the circumstance of its not being mentioned by a particular writer. It is now generally supposed that the *Didaché* originated in Palestine or Syria. At all events, monarchical episcopacy was unknown in the region to which it belonged. It was thus manifestly quite unknown both in the West and in the East at the end of the first century.

But Dr. Lightfoot says: "The maturer forms of episcopacy are first seen in the regions where the latest surviving apostles (more especially St. John) fixed their abode, and at a time when its prevalence cannot be dissociated from their influence and sanction." Let us now, then, carefully scrutinize the evidence which that region offers to us. It so happens that of the state of things there in the first part of the second century we have a most competent and opportune witness in John's disciple, Polycarp. The date of Polycarp's letter is not absolutely certain. Lightfoot supposes it to have been written not later than A.D. 118. Harnack, on what seem good grounds, combats Lightfoot's date, and assigns the epistle to the period 130–140 A.D. For my present purpose, however, the exact date is not important. What deserves the reader's attention is, that if monarchical episcopacy was established by John in this very region, and if it has been in existence there for some half-a-century before Polycarp writes, we ought to find some clear trace of it in the epistle of John's disciple, written forty or fifty years after Lightfoot supposes the system to have originated, an epistle which refers

No trace of it even in Polycarp.

expressly to the Christian ministry, and to Church order. What, then, is Polycarp's testimony on the subject? In his opening sentence Polycarp classes himself with the presbyters thus: "Polycarp and the presbyters with him" (or "those who with him are presbyters"). He exhorts the Philippians to be "subject to the presbyters and deacons," but says nothing of the bishop. Supposing the thirteenth chapter to be genuine, he mentions Ignatius four times, but never calls him bishop. As Dr. Lightfoot says: "Though two or three chapters are devoted to injunctions respecting the ministry of the Church, there is not an allusion to episcopacy from beginning to end. . . . He speaks at length about the duties of the presbyters, of the deacons, of the widows and others, but the bishop is entirely ignored." How does Bishop Lightfoot account for this? He accounts for it by saying, "it is probable the ecclesiastical organization was not yet developed there!" And arguing for the genuineness of Polycarp's letter against the writer of "Supernatural Religion," and forgetting his strong statements elsewhere about the development of episcopacy in Polycarp's region at this time, he actually uses the absence of any reference to the episcopacy as a proof of its early date! "The absence of all such language" [as that of Irenæus about episcopacy in its developed form] "is a strong testimony to its early date"! And he asks, "Can anything be more unlike the ecclesiastical literature of this later generation [that of Irenæus] whether we regard the use of the New Testament, or *the notices of ecclesiastical order*"? Now if the title "bishop" had come to be confined to the

Bishop Lightfoot quoted against himself.

presiding elder when Polycarp wrote (as Dr. Lightfoot says it had), the absence of any recognition of this in the letter could hardly be a testimony to its early date! For in that case there is no difference between Polycarp's age and that of Irenæus. But to infer that, because Polycarp ignores episcopacy at Philippi, it must have been less developed there than at Smyrna, is to make too great a demand on our credulity. "The ecclesiastical organization not yet developed" in that old Church, planted at the beginning of Paul's ministry, and having its bishops and deacons in his time! "The ecclesiastical organziation not yet developed" at a centre "commanding," as Lightfoot himself well says, "the great high-road between Europe and Asia," which made Philippi, as he says, "a thoroughfare for the traffic of nations," "the confluence of the streams of European and Asiatic life"; "not yet developed there," though the maturing process has now been going on for some fifty years just on the other side of the Ægean Sea, and though, as this very letter of Polycarp proves, intercourse between the Churches of Smyrna and Philippi was close and intimate, and, on Dr. Lightfoot's own showing in reply to "Supernatural Religion," the unity and solidarity between the Churches of the time were remarkable! The thing is preposterous; and the only reasonable inference is that Smyrna was like Philippi, and that the ecclesiastical organization was not yet developed there either into its later form.

True, Ignatius in his Epistle to Polycarp styles the latter "Bishop of the Church of Smyrna"; but, without raising any question here about the genuineness of the letter or of the in- Ignatius on Polycarp.

scription, we may remark with Hatch that "the absence of the definite article [before 'bishop'] and the inscription of Polycarp's own letter are inconsistent with the hypothesis that the word was already specially appropriated to the head of the community" (Lecture IV.). At all events it is quite consistent with Polycarp's having been one of a number of presbyter-bishops at Smyrna. The same may be said of the word as used in the Epistle of the Church of Smyrna with regard to Polycarp's martyrdom. The trustworthiness of the whole Martyrium is indeed denied by some, while most scholars, with Zahn and Funk, look upon it as having considerable additions and interpolations.

Indeed the state of things at Smyrna to which Polycarp thus indirectly but significantly testifies, *Even after* seems to have continued for some time *Polycarp's* after his death. There is a fragment of *time the bishop* Hippolytus "Against the Heresy of Noetus," *is ignored:* thought to be a part of his work "Against Thirty-two Heresies." In this fragment he describes Noetus as representing that the Father Himself was *case of* born, and suffered and died, and relates *Noetus;* how Noetus was dealt with by "the blessed presbyters." He says: "When the blessed presbyters heard this they summoned him before the Church, and examined him. But he denied at first that he held such opinions. Afterwards, however, taking shelter amongst some, and having gathered round him some others who had embraced the same error, he wished thereafter to uphold his dogma openly as correct. And the blessed presbyters called him again before them and examined him. . . .

Then, after examining him, they expelled him from the Church." Hippolytus describes Noetus as a native of Smyrna, and says, "he lived not long ago." The presbyters named were no doubt the presbyters of Smyrna, or of some Church in that region; yet we hear only of the presbyters—not a word of "the bishop," without whom, according to Ignatius, nothing could be done. The work of Hippolytus, "Against Thirty-two Heresies," is characterized by Photius as a synopsis of lectures which he heard from Irenæus, and is supposed to have been written by him in early life, before the close of the second century. Noetus appears to have been dead at the time he wrote, for he speaks of him as having "lived not very long ago."

Nor is this a solitary instance of the kind. Eusebius quotes a writer against the Cataphrygians or Montanists, who relates how lately he had been at Ancyra, a city of Galatia, and had discoursed many days in the Church against the heresy, so that (he says) "the presbyters of the place requested that we should leave some comment of those things that we said, in opposition to the opponents of the truth, Zoticus Otrenus also being present, who was our fellow-presbyter." This Zoticus, here called a presbyter, and others, he afterwards calls bishops.[1] It is singular also that Justin Martyr, who was a contemporary of Polycarp, when giving an account of how public worship was observed, and having occasion within the space of two or three short chapters to mention some four or five times the person who took the lead in it, never calls him

case of Montanists.

---

[1] Eusebius, *H. E.*, v. 16.

"the bishop," but simply "that one of the brethren who presided," or "the president of the brethren" (ὁ προεστὼς τῶν ἀδελφῶν). And another most important testimony points in the same direction. The Peshito or old Syriac version of the New Testament, which Westcott supposes to have been made "within the first half of the second century," gives *kashisho* (presbyter) as the rendering for ἐπίσκοπος in every case except in Acts xx. 28, where *episcopus* is preserved. To those who made the version the terms "bishop" and "presbyter" were still interchangeable.[1]

I have thus examined all the evidence which we possess before the middle of the second century, with the one exception of Ignatius, with whose case, as an exceptional one, I propose to deal separately. And yet, in the face of such evidence as we have reviewed, Dr. Lightfoot says, "If the writer of these letters [of Ignatius] had represented the Churches of Asia Minor as under presbyterial government, he would have contradicted all the evidence, which without one dissentient voice points to episcopacy as the established form of Church government in those districts from the close of the first century." (!) The reader will, I think, grant that Harnack is much nearer the truth when he says in reply that "Apart from the Epistles of Ignatius we do not possess a single witness to the existence of the monarchical episcopate so early as the time of Trajan and Hadrian."

How does Bishop Lightfoot propose to nullify the

[1] See Westcott, *On the Canon of the New Testament*, Part I., chap. iii. pp. 235-40.

evidence of the period itself, and to prove in the teeth of that evidence that the later epis-copacy was instituted by the Apostle John, and had been really maturing through the last thirty years of the first century? Demonstration of a very cogent sort would be required. What sort of demonstration does he offer? *Lightfoot meets this evidence by testimony of writers at close of 2nd century!* Why the testimony of a few writers towards the close of the second century, writing at a time when monarchical episcopacy had been admittedly in operation for thirty or forty years, and who naturally do not distinguish between the episcopacy known to them and that of an earlier time. Let us for a moment consider the real value of their testimony.

Irenæus says, "the blessed apostles, having founded and built up the Church, committed into the hands of Linus the office of the episcopate. . . . To him succeeded Anacletus; and after him, in the third place from the apostles, Clement was allotted the bishopric." *Irenæus.* He goes on to mention how Evaristus succeeded Clement, and Alexander came after Evaristus, and after him Sixtus, and then Telesphorus, and then Hyginus, etc. He then states how Polycarp "was by apostles in Asia appointed bishop of the Church in Smyrna, whom I also saw in my early youth, for he tarried a very long time,"[1] etc. We are able to test the value of this evidence by the case of Clement of Rome, who knows nothing of monarchical episcopacy. Indeed Lightfoot himself attaches no weight to it as regards Linus and his successors. But the fact that Irenæus knew Polycarp

[1] Irenæus, *Contra Hær.*, iii. 3.

personally may be thought to impart special value to the testimony in his case. Let it be observed, however, that it was "in early youth" Irenæus says he saw Polycarp. Supposing Irenæus to mean that Polycarp was appointed a monarchical bishop by the apostles (he does not use the article, and therefore leaves the sense ambiguous), how can we be certain that Irenæus was not mistaking the *mono*-episcopacy of his own time for the *plural* episcopacy of an earlier time, especially when we know that he makes this mistake in the case of Clement? The mere fact that he saw Polycarp in early youth would certainly be no sufficient guarantee against such an error, than which nothing could be more natural in the circumstances.

The same remark applies with still greater force to Polycrates, who wrote about the year 195. The very fact mentioned by him, that seven of his relatives had been bishops, makes it likely that they were bishops of the earlier type, of whom there were several in a congregation.

<small>Polycrates.</small>

The legend repeated by Clement of Alexandria at the end of the second century (*Quis. Div. Salv.*, 42), about the Apostle John committing the young man to the care of the bishop or presbyter, is of still less value as a proof of monarchical as opposed to plural episcopacy. Clement himself gives it as a legend or story ($\mu\tilde{v}\theta ov$), which however he says has truth in it, a story of which he implies that there were several versions. Now every one knows how such a story gets fresh colouring unconsciously from every new relator. And even as the narrative stands it is easy to see how the bishop in question (who is also called a presbyter)

<small>Clement of Alexandria.</small>

was in all probability in the real occurrence a presbyter bishop. We read in the narrative of "the presbyters" sending for John. The fact that in such a "legend" such an exact and candid scholar as Bishop Lightfoot should see a proof that the later episcopacy was established by John seems to indicate that real proof of this must be scarce. When the Muratorian fragment, referring to John, speaks of "his fellow disciples and his bishops," the words are also so worthless as an evidence that monarchical episcopacy was introduced by the apostle that we wonder how Bishop Lightfoot could attach the slightest value to them. If the story has any foundation in fact the persons called John's bishops were no doubt (as Harnack points out) the council of presbyters or bishops at Ephesus. Such then are the facts and circumstances in view of which Bishop Lightfoot affirms that "during the last three decades of the first century, and consequently during the lifetime of the latest surviving apostle, the episcopal office was firmly and widely established"; and that if Ignatius had represented the Churches of Asia Minor as under presbyterial government, he would have contradicted all the evidence. We have now to look at the testimony of Ignatius himself.

The Ignatian Testimony.

For so far I have left out of consideration the testimony of Ignatius. I have done so for several reasons: partly, because of the doubt which rests upon its genuineness; partly, because in Lightfoot's opinion it is not necessary to establish his case; but chiefly because, owing to its character, it requires separate consideration. We have now, however, reached a point in our investigation when it may be conveniently examined.

In briefly glancing at it it is not my purpose to enter into the large and difficult question of the genuineness of these epistles—"the most perplexing" (Bishop Lightfoot says) "which confronts the student of earlier Church history." It would be impossible to do this satisfactorily in the parenthetical way possible in the midst of a discussion upon Church order. There are, however, a few points to which I desire to direct attention, because if kept in view they would, I think, contribute greatly to lighten and relieve the controversy on this subject.

1. It ought to be carefully remembered that, properly speaking, no particular Church has any denominational interest in either supporting or assailing the genuineness of these epistles. The bishop of the Ignatian epistles is a quite different official from the modern diocesan bishop. As Harnack truly says, Ignatius "knows nothing yet of applying the name of bishop beyond the realm of the local congregation."[1] The Ignatian bishop finds his modern equivalent, not in the bishop of a diocese, but in the incumbent of a parish, in a Methodist or Presbyterian minister. It is singular indeed how nearly the position of the latter corresponds to that of the bishop of the Ignatian letters. Of course, neither a diocesan bishop nor a Presbyterian minister would apply to himself the extravagant and almost blasphemous glorification

No denominational interest involved in the decision of the question.

[1] *Expositor*, January, 1886, p. 16.

which Ignatius heaps upon his bishop. But apart from this, his position is remarkably similar to that of a Presbyterian minister. There can be no regular meeting of the elders without "the minister" as moderator, or chairman; and no administration of the sacraments but by him—none by the other presbyters. In short, he is, just like the bishop of Ignatius, the chief officer of the congregation, and indispensable to the orderly celebration of Christian ordinances. Modern diocesan episcopacy, therefore, has nothing to gain and other forms of Church order nothing to lose by the establishment of the genuineness of the Ignatian epistles; for the monarchical episcopacy which they advocate is still *congregational* episcopacy. The chief thing which they note is the monopolization by the presiding presbyter of a congregation of the title bishop, and of certain spiritual prerogatives: just as now the Methodist or Presbyterian official monopolizes the title "minister" and certain ministerial functions. Historically, no doubt, this monopolization was the first step in the development which soon issued in diocesan episcopacy; but the fact that the Presbyterian minister (or congregational bishop) has never developed into the diocesan bishop proves that there is no inherent tendency in congregational episcopacy to develop into diocesan episcopacy. It is worthy of note, too, that the district where (if we accept the Ignatian testimony on Church order as genuine) we first find this monarchico-congregational episcopacy flourishing is not Asia Minor, is not the district of the Apostle John, but Antioch. The Epistle of Polycarp, and the other evidence to which I have referred, raise a strong presumption against the development having as yet gone so far in Asia Minor and in the adjacent regions. Of course Bishop Lightfoot is well aware of the fact that the Ignatian bishop is simply a congregational official, with his congregational elders and deacons around him ; but it would have eased the controversy a good deal, and prevented much confusion of thought and denominational bias in this matter if he had made it more prominent, and even kept it before his own mind more steadily. All, then, that is gained by the proof of the genuineness of the epistles is the assurance that the development of the presiding presbyter into the permanent congregational bishop had taken place over a limited area a few years earlier than would be otherwise apparent.

2. Again, granting the genuineness of these epistles, and supposing their declarations on Church order not to be interpolations of a later age, it is also clear that even this monarchico-congregational episcopacy was, so far as the history enables us to judge, a comparatively isolated phenomenon in say A.D. 116. *The Ignatian episcopacy an isolated phenomenon, if genuine, when he wrote.* We find nothing like it in the region to which the *Didaché* pertained. We discover nothing like it in the great central Churches of Rome and Corinth in the time of Clement and Hermas. There is no trace of it at Philippi on the other side of the Ægean Sea, and on the high road of communication between the East and the West—no trace of it when Polycarp writes, after Ignatius has passed on his way to Rome, in that old Church, already well organized, with its bishops and deacons before the death of

Paul; and in Polycarp's epistle no trace of it even at Smyrna, but rather a presumption against its development having as yet gone so far in that region. In fact the utmost we can be sure of from the statements of Ignatius, supposing them to be genuine, is that the form of episcopacy which they advocate had already taken shape at Antioch, and perhaps in the adjacent districts. His assertion as to there being at the time when he wrote "bishops settled everywhere to the utmost bounds of the world," we know to be incorrect, taking bishops in his sense. Harnack recognises the isolated and exceptional character of the Ignatian testimony with regard to episcopacy, and regards it as an unsolved enigma, although in his case the difficulty is a good deal lessened by his bringing down the date of it to 130-140, a date for which he seems to make out a better case than Lightfoot does for his date of 116. But even this postponement of date is very far from removing the enormous difficulties which beset the Ignatian references to Church order. Let me assist the reader to realise to himself the true state of the case.

3. It is a simple matter of fact, not to be blinked by the historian, that the Ignatian representation of the bishop is a great anachronism, not only out of unison with all we know of his own time, but in some respects far in advance of anything we find on the subject towards the close of the second century, and to discover a complete parallel to which we must go forward to the times of Cyprian, and to the *Apostolical Constitutions*. At the cost of going a little into detail, I must make this clear

The Ignatian bishop an anachronism: proof of this.

(*a*) In Irenæus, at the close of the second century the bishop, though over the presbyters, is (to use the language of Bishop Lightfoot) "still regarded as in some sense one of them"; and is as often called "presbyter" as "bishop."[1] In the same way Clement of Alexandria speaks sometimes of two orders— presbyters and deacons—and sometimes of three, bishops, presbyters, and deacons.[2] At Alexandria, too, the bishop is nominated and ordained by twelve presbyters out of their own number.[3] The development, even at the period referred to, is still going on, not yet completed. But in Ignatius, seventy or eighty years earlier, according to Lightfoot's date, the separation of the bishop from the presbyters is complete, and the nomenclature has become thoroughly fixed and stereotyped. He never calls the bishop a presbyter. In his pages the distinction between the bishop and the presbyters has become wider, and the position of the bishop higher and more autocratic than they are even at the end of the second century in the other literature.

(*b*) In the Ignatian letters the bishop is invested with prerogatives to parallel which we must go forward to the times of Tertullian, Cyprian, and even of the *Apostolical Constitutions*.

With Cyprian, to be without the bishop is to be outside the Church, and his principle is, no bishop no Church. "You ought to know that the bishop is in the Church, and the Church in the bishop, and that

---

[1] Iren., *Against Heresies*, iii. 2, 2 ; 3. 2, 3 ; iv. 26. 2, 3, 4, 5. Euseb., *H. E.*, v. 24.
[2] *Strom.*, vi. 13 ; vii. 1.
[3] Jerome, *Epist.* cxlvi., *ad Evangel.*

if any one is not with the bishop he is not in the Church."¹ Ignatius says: "Apart from these [the bishop, etc.] there is no Church."² "As many as are of God and of Jesus Christ are also with the bishop."³ "Continue in intimate union with Jesus Christ our God and the bishop. He that is within the altar is pure, but he that is without is not pure ; that is, he that does anything apart from the bishop and presbyters and deacons, such a man is not pure in his conscience."⁴

Tertullian lays it down that there is no power to baptize, nor to perform any other act in the Church, without the bishop.⁵ The same rule is enacted in the 56th Canon of the Council of Laodicea. So Ignatius: " It is therefore necessary that without the bishop ye should do nothing ";⁶ "Do nothing without the bishop."⁷ "Let no man do anything connected with the Church without the bishop. Let that be deemed a proper Eucharist which is administered either by the bishop, or by one to whom he has entrusted it. . . . It is not lawful without the bishop either to baptize or to celebrate a love-feast ; but whatever he shall approve of, that is also pleasing to God, so that everything that is done may be secure and valid."⁸

Cyprian argues that, " as there is one Church, there must be one altar and one episcopate " ;⁹ and Ignatius that "there is one flesh of our Lord Jesus Christ, and one cup into the unity of His blood ; one altar as there is one bishop."¹⁰

¹ Cyprian, *Ep.* 66.
² *Trall.* iii.
³ *Philad.* iii.
⁴ *Trall.* vii.
⁵ Tertull., *De Bapt.*, 17.
⁶ *Trall.* iii.
⁷ *Phil.* vii.
⁸ *Smyrn.* viii.
⁹ Cyp., *Ep.* 43, 46, 55, 67.
¹⁰ *Phil.* iv.

Cyprian traces all evils to want of union with the bishop: "All heresies and schemes take their original from hence, that men do not submit to God's priest, and consider that there ought to be but one bishop in a Church, and one judge as the vicar of Christ."[1] So Ignatius: "He that is without the altar is impure; that is, he that does anything apart from the bishop" (see above). "It is a fearful thing to contradict any such person as the bishop";[2] "it is well to reverence both God and the bishop. He who honours the bishop has been honoured by God; he who does anything without the knowledge of the bishop serves the devil."[3]

The fact cannot and must not be ignored, that in the time intervening between 116 A.D. and the time of Tertullian and Cyprian—in Polycarp, in Irenæus, in Clement of Alexandria, and elsewhere—we have no such representation of the bishop as thus appears in Ignatius.

(c) Then again in Ignatius the bishop is in place of God Himself, while the presbyters are successors of the apostles: "Your bishop presides in the place of God, and your presbyters in the place of the assembly of the apostles along with your deacons."[4] "Let all reverence the deacons as an appointment of Jesus Christ, and the bishop as Jesus Christ, who is the Son of the Father, and the presbyters as the sanhedrim of God and assembly of apostles."[5] Whereas in Irenæus, Cyprian and others, the bishop is the successor of the apostles, we must pass on to the *Apostolical Constitutions* to find an exact parallel

---

[1] *Ep.* 55 al. 59 *ad. Cornel.* [2] *Magnes.* iii. [3] *Smyrn.* ix.
[4] *Magnes.* vi. [5] *Trall.* iii.

with Ignatius in this matter, and here the parallel is remarkable. In the *Apostolical Constitutions* the bishop is described as "one sustaining the character of God among men, as being set over all men, over priests, kings, rulers, fathers, children, teachers" (ii. 11). "Next after God, he is your father. . . . He is your ruler and governor; your king and potentate; he is next after God your earthly god who has a right to be honoured by you. . . . For let the bishop preside over you with the authority of God. But let deacons minister to him as Christ does to the Father. . . . Let also the deaconess be honoured by you in place of the Holy Ghost. . . . Let the presbyters be esteemed by you to represent the apostles. . . . Let the widows and orphans be esteemed as representing the altar of God" (*Ap. Const.*, ii. 26).

The Ignatian picture of the bishop is thus without doubt a huge anachronism, out of harmony with anything even in the second century; and it is difficult to resist the conclusion that, even granting the genuineness of the body of the epistles, there has been interpolation by later hands in the references to Church order.

In pleading for the genuineness of Polycarp's epistle against "Supernatural Religion," Dr. Lightfoot asks, "Can anything be more unlike the ecclesiastical literature of this later generation [that of Irenæus] whether we regard the use of the New Testament, or the notices of Church order?" We ask, Can anything be more unlike the ecclesiastical literature of Polycarp's generation, and more like that of the generation of Tertullian and Cyprian, and of the *Apostolical Constitutions* than the notices of ecclesi-

astical order in Ignatius? If the dissimilarity of
Polycarp's epistle to anything in Irenæus proves it
to belong to an earlier time, the dissimilarity of the
statements quoted from the Ignatian epistle to anything in Polycarp, and their resemblance to those in
Cyprian and the *Apostolical Constitutions* prove them
to belong to a later age than Polycarp's. As Harnack
says, "Ignatius' conception of the position and significance of the bishop has its earliest parallel in the
conception of the author of the *Apostolical Constitutions;* and the epistles show the monarchical episcopate so firmly rooted, so highly elevated above all
other offices, so completely beyond dispute, that on
the ground of what we know from other sources
of early Church history no single investigator would
assign the statements under consideration to the
second, but at the earliest to the third century."[1]

IV. APOSTOLICAL SUCCESSION.

We have now to catechise the *Didaché* and the
other early documents with respect to another matter
relating to the ministry, that of Apostolical Succession.
Do they teach, or lend any countenance to, the High
Church view on this subject? Before proceeding to
examine them, it is necessary to understand clearly
what this theory is; and the best way to do this is
to take it as it is conceived and shaped by one of its
most distinguished advocates. It is thus
put by Canon Liddon in a sermon entitled
"A Father in Christ," preached in St.
Paul's Cathedral, at the consecration of the

The theory stated by Canon Liddon.

---

[1] Dr. Harnack in *Expositor* of January, 1886, p. 16.

Bishops of Lincoln and Exeter: our Lord, he says, deposited ministerial authority in its fulness in the college of the apostles, and he bases the statement on the texts: "All power is given unto Me in heaven and in earth; go ye therefore and make disciples of all nations:" "As My Father hath sent Me, even so send I you." He then proceeds, "The apostles thus invested with the plenitude of ministerial power, detached from themselves in the form of distinct grades or orders of ministry, so much as was needed, at successive epochs, for building up and supporting the Church. First, they created an order which was charged with the care of the poor and with the administration of Church funds, although also specially empowered to preach and to administer the sacrament of baptism. Next, they bestowed on the Church a large separate instalment of ministerial power—that of the presbyters or bishops—as in those first days the second order was called indifferently. To this order full ministerial capacity was committed, excepting the faculty of transmitting the ministry. Lastly, St. Clement of Rome tells us that desiring to avoid controversy which they foresaw, the apostles ordained certain men, to the end that when they should have fallen asleep in death others of approved character might succeed to their special office. Such were Timothy and Titus; not yet exclusively called bishops, but certainly bishops in the sense of the sub-apostolic and of our own age; men who in addition to the fulness of ministerial capacity had also the power of transmitting it."[1] Canon Liddon says, 'Upon a true episcopal succession depends the

[1] "A Father in Christ," etc., pp. 9, 10.

validity of the Eucharist—one chief means of communion with our Lord." As to the power of transmission, he remarks that as it is the prerogative of the father to transmit the gift of physical life, so "the bishop alone can transmit ministerial power to others"; and this prerogative is not shared by the presbyters. As the father is the natural teacher of his children, so, as the father of his diocese, the bishop is "the one teacher within its limits. In the eye of the Church all the clergy are his substitutes." Again, as the father of his diocese, the bishop "is its ruler." Canon Liddon grants that "since lay baptism is of undoubted validity," "non-episcopal bodies may have a true baptism, supposing the matter and words of that sacrament to be duly administered." But he adds, "that which in our belief and to our sorrow, the non-episcopal communities lack, is participation in those privileges which depend upon a ministry duly authorized by Christ our Lord, and in particular the precious sacrament of His Body and Blood."[1] Canon Liddon not only sees, but defends the justice of, the insuperable barrier thus raised between the English Church and all non-episcopal Churches both here and on the Continent. There is no reason but the pressure of facts why he should make an exception in favour of the non-episcopal Churches in the matter of baptism; for, according to this theory, baptism by a layman is not lawful except as authorized by the bishop. We have already seen that the position taken by Tertullian and others on this point is the same as that of Ignatius. "The right of giving baptism belongs to the chief priest, that

[1] "A Father in Christ," 2nd Edition, pp. 16–21, and xxxviii. *sq.*

is the bishop."[1] It is only where there is no bench of clergy, according to Tertullian, that laymen may baptize and present the eucharistic offerings.[2] And the same rule is laid down in the 56th Canon of the Council of Laodicea. Further, the act of baptism was not regarded as completed or consummated till after the bishop's hands had been laid on those baptized, this consummation of the act having been called the σφραγίς or *signaculum*.[3] If then the administration of baptism by non-episcopal Churches may be recognised, there is no reason why Canon Liddon should refuse to allow the lawfulness of their celebration of the Eucharist, but his own caprice. In its essence, and as it has been generally held, the theory is, that Christ gave the Holy Spirit to the apostles to be by them transmitted by the laying on of hands to their successors, and through them to presbyters, conveying to them grace and supernatural power; and the grace needed to constitute either a bishop or a presbyter, and to enable him to discharge his functions efficaciously, is derived solely from the hands of a bishop.

Is there any trace of this doctrine either in Scripture, or in early Church literature? Let us see, but let us take care that we carry with us the real point at issue. The question is not whether a ministry has been appointed in the Church, and whether directions have been given for its continuance, and for a succession of duly constituted ministers, who receive their authority from Christ and act in His name. We hold this as strongly

The question at issue defined.

---

[1] Tertullian, *de Baptismo*, 17.   [2] *De Exh. Cast.*, 7.
[3] See Euseb., *H. E.*, vi. 43, and Cyprian, *Ep.* 72, *ad Stephan.*

as Canon Liddon. And the question is not whether
any one of his own motion may ordinarily assume the
office, and discharge its functions without appointment
by the constituted authorities. Just as in the State
there is a regular and prescribed method of appointing
magistrates, and as they do not assume office of
themselves, so is it in the Church. "While the
ministry flourishes in the Church, it (the Church)
ought indeed to use it (the ministry) in the calling
of pastors, nor can pastors be ordinarily instituted
except by a ministry already constituted" (says
Turrettin). And the question is not, whether as a
matter of fact the first ministers, appointed at the
instance of the apostles, were succeeded by others
duly constituted. This is not denied. The simple
question is, *Is there anything in the New Testament,
or even in the sub-apostolic literature, restricting this
power of transmitting office to bishops as distinct from
presbyters, and as alone successors of the apostles, and
is there anything conditioning the validity of orders
and the administration of ordinances on that transmission, and* ipso facto *unchurching every Christian
community which does not enjoy the advantage of this
manual propagation through diocesan bishops?*

1. In determining this question, one fundamental
historical fact to be noted is the great

<small>Arguments against Canon Liddon's theory:
1. Christianity a spiritual system.</small>

truth so much insisted on by our Lord
and His apostles, that Christianity is a
system of the spirit rather than of the
letter, of substance rather than of form—
a system which reduces to a minimum the
external and the formal, and magnifies the real, the
moral and the spiritual; which teaches that "it is the

spirit that quickeneth, the flesh profiteth nothing;" that Christian ministers are "ministers of the New Covenant, not of the letter, but of the spirit;" that we are now under "the ministration of the Spirit," and that "where the Spirit of the Lord is there is liberty." But the doctrine under consideration inverts this principle. According to it, it is not faith and love and holiness and every Christian excellence in men, and the scrupulous observance of Christ's commands, that constitute a Church. A Christian society may prove that they are united to Christ by the indwelling of His Spirit as evidenced by His fruit in holy living, that they have the faith of the apostles, and that in Christian love they are united with all His people; they may be a model to all the Churches in their missionary ardour, and in their success in extending Christ's kingdom at home and abroad; but unless they can prove by an unbroken line of succession the propagation to them through the laying on of the hands of prelates of some sort of power and virtue, they cannot be recognised as a Church of Christ at all. In searching for the true Church I am not to search for evidence of faith in Christ, and of union with Him, and possession of His Spirit in likeness to Him, in holiness and good works: I have nothing to do but to find a community having a ministry constituted in a particular mechanical fashion —by the laying on of the hands of prelates—only that, inasmuch as one broken link may vitiate the process, I must remain uncertain whether I have the true Church or no until I have been able to trace the succession back, link by link, through 1800 years of history, to apostolic hands. This is not only to subordinate substance to form, to make what is external and mechanical more important than the real and the spiritual: it is to put in imminent jeopardy the very existence of the true Church altogether; for that succession, in the dark and obscure periods of history, may have been broken at many points. There is in fact not a Church on earth that could prove that it possesses beyond question such an unbroken succession; for not to mention the confusion of the middle ages, we shall see in a moment how in the early Church the succession was through presbyters and not prelates. The Church which takes such a position, thereby cutting herself off from all other Churches, and unchurching them, is, in our opinion, committing a deep sin, and is profoundly guilty of what she is so ready to charge on others, the evil of schism. Assuredly she is contravening a fundamental Christian principle—a principle of reason and common sense—which puts the spirit before the letter, the reality above the form. It is more in accordance with the teaching of the New Testament to say with Irenæus, *ubi spiritus Dei, illic ecclesia,* and with Jerome, *ecclesia ibi est ubi vera fides est.* When Canon Liddon and Mr. Gladstone represent the Church of England in thus "unchurching" other Churches, as simply following the example of "the genuine Puritans and the whole Presbyterian body from Cartright downwards," when these latter pleaded that the constitution of the Church, as defined in the word of God, was Presbyterian, they are doing great injustice to the Puritans and Presbyterians. Though Cart-

[margin notes: The position jeopardizes the very existence of a Church. Mr. Gladstone and Canon Liddon misrepresent Puritans and Presbyterians.]

right and his successors held the constitution of the Church as defined in Scripture to have been Presbyterian, they did not begin by denying that that is a true Church of Christ which did not possess this constitution. On the contrary, laying primary and capital stress on the real and spiritual as opposed to the external, they and all the great Churches of the Reformation had it as their foundation principle respecting the Church, that it is not in its essential nature a society organized in one particular way, but the body of Christ, the company of believers, the *cœtus sanctorum*. In his book against the Anabaptists, Calvin says, "This honour is meet to be given to the word of God, and to His sacraments, that wherever we see the word duly preached, and God according to the same duly worshipped, and the sacraments without superstition administered, there we may without all controversy conclude the Church of God to be." *[Calvin quoted.]* The Reformation and Puritan principle is that adopted by the Westminster divines, than which nothing could be more broad and spiritual, or less calculated to "unchurch" other communities: *[Westminster divines.]* "The visible Church which is also catholic or universal under the gospel, consists of *all those throughout the world that profess the true religion*, together with their children; and is the kingdom of the Lord Jesus Christ, the house and family of God." . . . "This Catholic Church hath been sometimes more, sometimes less visible. And particular Churches which are members thereof, are more or less pure, according as the doctrine of the gospel is taught and embraced ordinances administered, and public worship per-

T

formed more or less purely in them."[1] The Reformation and Puritan principle was that every community professing the true religion, associated for the worship of God and the extension of His kingdom, however organized, was part of the visible Church. It might of course be more or less near to the New Testament ideal.

2. Another fundamental New Testament truth, and one which has a most important bearing on this question is—the *universal priesthood of believers*. All Christians are priests. There is not a syllable in the New Testament restricting this priesthood to a class. The New Testament recognises no priestly order different from the Christian people, who are all both *priests* (1 Pet. ii. 5) and *clergy* (κλῆροι, 1 Pet. v. 3). Basing themselves on New Testament teaching, the Reformers taught that the Holy Spirit, who is the fountain of all Church power, was not given to the bishops as a class, but to the Church as a whole. He dwells in all Christians and unites them to the body of Christ, which is the Church, and divides gifts to every man as He will. Hence in the Apostolic Church every Christian who had the gift of teaching or any other gift was encouraged to exercise it, if he only did so decently and in order. The only Church members forbidden to preach or pray in the Church were women. Since this was so, and since all Christians are priests, it was not originally a matter of principle that the celebration of the ordinances of Divine worship should be confined to a special class of office-bearers; but a permanent ministry responsible for

Marginal note: 2. Universal priesthood of believers.

[1] *Confession of Faith*, etc., c. xxv.

ruling and teaching was instituted by the apostles for the sake of order, and to secure the more efficient discharge of these functions, though not to the exclusion of their orderly exercise by those who had the gifts. It was, therefore, a fundamental principle with the Reformers that "all the power and authority necessary for the Church executing its functions, and attaining its objects lay radically and fundamentally in the Church itself—in the company of believers; so that, when necessity required, Churches might provide and establish office-bearers for themselves, and do whatever might be needful for securing all the objects connected with their own welfare, and the enjoyment of all the ordinances which Christ appointed."[1] *Principle of the Reformers stated by Dr. Cunningham.* In the articles of Smalcald, Luther says, *Ubicunque est ecclesia, ibi est jus administrandi evangelii, quare necesse est ecclesiam retinere jus vocandis eligendi et ordinandi ministros.* *Luther's view.* Calvin teaches the same thing, remarking that the Church is under obligation to have ministers and other office-bearers *ex necessitate precepti*, though not *ex necessitate medii;* *Calvin's view* and Turrettin lays it down that "the pastors exercise the right which belongs to the body, as representing it, and in such a way that that right always belongs radically to the body;" *Turrettin's view.* and again, "when a ministry is wanting or miserably corrupt, the Church, can elect for itself ministers for its edification even without the intervention of a ministry; as well both because this right it has from God, as because always and everywhere it is bound to preserve a ministry"—*tenetur mini-*

[1] Cunningham's *Historical Theology*, c. xxvi. sec. ii. p. 536.

sterium conservare. Canon Liddon appeals to Hooker, but fails to give Hooker's complete views on the subject, views which are broader and more spiritual than would suit Canon Liddon's purpose:

<small>Hooker's view.</small> "There may be sometimes," says Hooker, "very just and sufficient reasons to allow ordination made without a bishop. The whole Church visible being the true original subject of all power, it hath not ordinarily allowed any other than bishops alone to ordain; howbeit as the ordinary cause is ordinarily in all things to be observed, so it may be in some cases not unnecessary that we decline from the ordinary ways. Men may be extraordinarily, yet allowably, two ways admitted unto spiritual functions in the Church. One is when God Himself doth of Himself raise up any . . . Another . . . when the exigence of necessity doth constrain to leave the usual ways of the Church, which otherwise we would willingly keep."[1] Again: "Let them" (the bishops) "continually bear in mind that it is rather the force of custom, whereby the Church, having so long found it good to continue the regiment of her virtuous bishops, doth still uphold, maintain and honour them, in that respect, than that any true and heavenly law can be showed by the evidence, whereof it may of truth appear, that the Lord Himself hath appointed presbyters for ever to be under the regiment of bishops." Hooker adds that "their authority is a sword which the Church hath power to take from them."[2] In speaking thus, the more modern writers are reiterating a principle laid down long ago even

---

[1] *Ecclesiastical Polity*, vii. 14. See also iii. 11.
[2] *Ibid.*, vii. 5. See also i. 14; iii. 10.

by such a high Churchman as Tertullian, who, however, had deep spiritual tendencies: "Are not we laymen also priests?" he asks. "It is written 'He hath also made us a kingdom of priests to God and the Father.' It is the authority of the Church which makes a difference between the order (the clergy) and the people—this authority and the consecration of their rank by the assignment of special benches to the clergy. Thus where there is no bench of clergy you present the Eucharistic offerings, and baptize, and are your own sole priests. For where three are gathered together there is a Church, even though they be laymen."[1] *Tertullian's view.*

3. Some very clear and express enactment would be required to set aside principles which I have thus shown to lie at the heart of Christianity. Do we find in the New Testament any such enactment? On the contrary, all the facts both in the apostolic and sub-apostolic age point quite in the opposite direction, and lie exactly in a line with the great central principles which I have indicated. It was of course to be expected, and entirely consistent with those principles, that the apostles should take care that there would be a succession of regularly appointed ministers in the Church, but the point is, was the power of transmitting office confined to bishops as distinguished from presbyters, and was the validity of orders made to depend upon this transmission? And if it was so, *where?* If the matter is one so vital that this prelatical succession is necessary to constitute a Church, and to make Christian ordinances *3. History, both apostolic and sub-apostolic, opposed to Canon Liddon*

[1] *De Exh. Cast.*, 7

valid, the apostles would not surely leave it in ambiguity, but would take care to emphasise it; and we might expect to find it clearly recognised in the sub-apostolic literature. *Where* do we so find it? On Canon Liddon's own showing in the citation made from him above, presbyters and deacons are just as much successors of the apostles as prelatical bishops are. He says "the apostles detached from themselves in the form of distinct grades or orders of ministry so much as was needed for building up and supporting the Church"—first deacons, next presbyters (called also bishops), to whom "full ministerial capacity was committed, excepting the faculty of transmitting the ministry," and lastly bishops. Where is the evidence that "bishops" and not "presbyters" are successors of the apostles? Where is the proof that "the faculty of transmitting the ministry" was not given to the presbyter-bishops of the early Church, but confined to the class represented by the modern bishop? In the Churches planted by Paul, as we have seen, elders (or bishops) were appointed. In the Churches addressed by Peter we find elder-bishops, and no higher officers. In like manner, at the instance of Timothy and Titus, elders are appointed in Crete and elsewhere; just as at a later time, according to the testimony of Eusebius,[1] Quadratus and other "disciples of the apostles," also called "evangelists," acting as itinerant missionaries had similar appointments made in the regions where they preached. But by whom were *the next successors* of these presbyter-bishops appointed? Clearly by these presbyter-bishops themselves, on

That the transmission was through presbyter-bishops

[1] *H.E.*, iii. 37.

their successors being duly elected by the people. No other agency whatever is hinted at in the New Testament, or in the early sub-apostolic literature. The *Didaché* attaches so little value to the point that it says nothing of the agency by which the appointment is made, nothing of ordination, but says to the people, "Elect for yourselves bishops and deacons worthy of the Lord." Clement of Rome, who is specially appealed to by Canon Liddon, only makes it certain that the transmission of office was through presbyter-bishops, while he lends no countenance to the other high features of the theory. Referring to the apostles, Clement says (c. xli.) that "preaching everywhere through countries and cities, they appointed the first fruits, having first proved them by the spirit, to be bishops and deacons of those who should afterwards believe." "Our apostles knew," he says (c. xliv.), "through our Lord Jesus Christ, that there would be strife on account of the name of the episcopate. For this reason, therefore, having perfect knowledge beforehand, they appointed those already mentioned, and afterwards gave instruction that when they should fall asleep other approved men should succeed them in their ministry. Those, therefore, appointed by them, or afterwards by other men of repute with the consent of the whole Church, and who have blamelessly served the flock, and who have for a long time possessed the good opinion of all, cannot be justly dismissed from the ministry. For our sin will not be small if we eject from the episcopate those who have blamelessly and holily presented the offerings. Blessed are those presbyters who, having finished their course before now, . . . have no fear lest any one deprive them of the place now appointed them." Observe here that Clement regards "those presbyters who, having already finished their course" cannot be deprived of their place, as the predecessors of those now in danger of being ejected from the episcopate, and as having held the same position as they. And that those now ejected or threatened with ejection from the episcopate were *presbyters* is made absolutely clear by what follows. Still remonstrating with the insubordination at Corinth, Clement says it is disgraceful that that ancient Church "should on account of one or two persons engage in sedition against its presbyters" (c. xlvii.). Again, he says, "Submit yourselves to the presbyters.' "Let the flock of Christ live on terms of peace with the presbyters set over it" (cc. liv. lvii.). Lightfoot, Funk, Harnack, Haddan, and almost all scholars take the words "when *they* should fall asleep," and "*their* ministry," as pointing to "those already mentioned"—the first fruits who had been appointed bishops and deacons. But Canon Liddon argues that both phrases refer back to the apostles, and that what Clement affirms is that the apostles appointed those already mentioned, and directed that if they (the apostles) should fall asleep, other approved men should succeed them (the apostles) in their ministry. He adduces two arguments in favour of this exegesis. (1) The first is that ἐάν is used before κοιμηθῶσιν. If Clement meant to say the apostles appointed A B C as presbyters, and provided that when A B C died D E F should succeed them as presbyters, why did he say "*if* they should fall asleep"?—why not "when"? The answer is that ἐάν is often used in a sense equivalent to "when," or *in case of* an event, when the event is certain. See, for example, Zenophon's *Œconomicus*, xvii., and Plato's *Apology of Socrates*, xxxi. To take it thus is far more natural than the strained and clumsy method resorted to by Canon Liddon of putting in a phrase of his own in order to connect the pronoun with the apostles; "if they (the apostles) should fall asleep *before the presbyter-bishops*." But this is not what Clement says; it is an arbitrary addition by Canon Liddon, and shows how he must alter and amend the passage to get this meaning out of it. (2) As to Canon Liddon's second point, we quite agree with him in supposing "other men of repute" and "other approved men" to refer to the same class of persons. Who, then, are they? The answer is as clear as the text and context can make it. They are office-bearers who are called indifferently bishops or presbyters. They are called bishops in c. xlii. They are in danger of being ejected from the episcopate (c. xliv.). They are "the presbyters set over" the Church in cc. xlvii., liv., lvii. So that even granting Canon Liddon's exegesis it is far from establishing his case. The one thing certain is that the ministers of Clement's epistle, who are in danger of being thrust out from the episcopate, and the ministers who having died already are in no such danger, are *presbyters*, called indifferently bishops, and that the first fruits appointed by the apostles, or, for example, those mentioned in Phil. i. 1, were the same; and there is not a particle of evidence that the intervening ministers, described as "other men of repute," "other approved men," by whom the ejected ministers were appointed, were anything but presbyter-bishops likewise. The succession spoken of by Clement, whatever value it carries, is unquestionably through presbyters (also called bishops) just as in the New Testament Timothy is appointed to office by the laying on of the hands of the presbyters (1 Tim. iv. 14). So that when Liddon says, "To this order [that of presbyters or bishops, as in those first days the second order was called indifferently] full ministerial capacity was committed *excepting the faculty of transmitting the ministry*," he is, in making this exception, directly contradicting the testimony of Clement (to which he himself appeals), and all the early testimony we possess. For example, in the Church of Alexandria on till the third century, the presbyters, we are told, nominated and appointed the bishop out of their own body.[1]

But, now, why did the apostles, according to Clement, provide for the regular succession of ministers? Because otherwise the Church will be without a ministry? and because otherwise there can be no valid administration of the Lord's Supper? He never hints at such a thing. The simple reason he assigns is—to avoid disorder, and because the apostles foresaw that there would be such strife as has arisen at Corinth. Liddon represents Clement as saying that the apostles "made provision that others should succeed to *their own power of ordaining presbyters*." But, with all respect to Dr. Liddon, Clement says no such thing. What he says they made provision for was, that other approved men should succeed them in their ministry ($\lambda\epsilon\iota\tau o\upsilon\rho\gamma\iota\alpha$); and the reason for

[1] Jerome, *Epist.* cxlvi. *ad Evang.*; Ambrosiast. on Eph. iv. 12

making this provision was to *avoid disorder and contention.* He points out the sin and shame of this disorder, of the insubordination at Corinth; but he does not hint that in thrusting out their regularly appointed office-bearers, and substituting others, they will cease to be a Church, and that their ordinances will be invalid. His one plea is, that the apostles provided for a regular succession of ministers in the interests of order.

Irenæus refers at length to this succession, describing it sometimes as a succession of "presbyters," sometimes as a succession of "bishops." He attaches much value to the fact that this succession of presbyters or bishops can be traced down from the apostles; but the value he sets on it is very different from that of Dr. Liddon. To Irenæus it is important to be able to trace this succession, not because he thinks of it as indispensable for the transmission of ministerial power, or for the validity of the Lord's Supper —such an idea never occurs to him—but because he is able by means of this succession to trace the truths and doctrines which he holds back to the apostles. The heretics affirm that the Gospels of Matthew and the other evangelists are not correct nor authoritative, and that the truth cannot be extracted from them by those ignorant of tradition; for the truth was not delivered by written documents, but *viva voce.* "We refer them," says Irenæus, "to that tradition which issues from the apostles, and which is preserved by means of the succession of presbyters in the Churches. "It is within the power of all, in every Church, who may wish to see the truth, to contemplate clearly

margin: Liddon's theory finds no support in Irenæus.

the tradition of the apostles manifested throughout the world; and we are in a position to reckon up those who were by the apostles instituted bishops in the Churches, and the successions of these men to our own times; those who neither taught nor knew any thing like what these rave about. For if the apostles had known hidden mysteries, which they were in the habit of imparting to the 'perfect,' apart and privily from the rest, they would have delivered them especially to those to whom they were also committing the Churches themselves." He then goes on to give the succession at Rome, and to show how the apostolical tradition had been handed down through it. "In this order and by this succession the ecclesiastical tradition from the apostles, and the preaching of the truth, have come down to us. And this is most abundant evidence that there is one and the same vivifying faith, which has been preserved in the Church from the apostles until now, and handed down in truth."[1]

The idea begins to develop in third century under Cyprian. It is only when we come to Cyprian, only when we reach the period when sacerdotalism begins to flourish, that we begin to find some trace of Canon Liddon's doctrine. With Cyprian the bishop is (to use Bishop Lightfoot's language), "the indispensable bond of Christian brotherhood." "You ought to know," says Cyprian, "that the bishop is in the Church, and the Church is in the bishop, and if any one is not with the bishop, he is not in the Church."[2] "Such an one," he says, "is not a Christian."[3]

---

[1] Iren., *Against Heresies*, B. iii. cc. 1, 2, 3.
[2] Cyprian, *Epist.* 66.   [3] *Ep.* 55, 20.

Nor should it be overlooked that the thing chiefly emphasised in the early literature, in connection with the appointment of the ministry, is their election by the people, or the consent of the people to their appointment. We have already seen this in the *Didaché*, and in the Epistle of Clement of Rome. Even Cyprian calls this "an apostolic and almost universal regulation."[1]

<small>Great importance attached to the consent, or election, by the people in early Church.</small>

I have thus shown that the doctrine of apostolical succession, so strenuously advocated by Canon Liddon and the school which he represents, though the greatest of all obstacles to union between episcopal and non-episcopal Churches in the present day, grossly violates some of the first and most vital principles of Christianity, and has no countenance either in the New Testament or in sub-apostolic Christian literature. The idea is essentially a pagan one, derived from pagan sources, excusable, or at least intelligible, in men like Cyprian, who brought with them into Christianity many of the materialistic, heathenish superstitions in which their youth had been nurtured, and which pervaded the air which they breathed from day to day; but it is unworthy of those who have never laboured under their disadvantage, and who are familiar with the spiritual teaching of our Lord and His apostles.

V. Sacerdotalism.

It is quite true that a certain class of Christian ministers are called "chief priests" in the *Didaché*

[1] *Ep.* 60.

(c. xiii.). But it ought to be observed that it is the prophets who are so called, and that they are thus designated not because of any exclusive sacerdotal functions attaching to them, not certainly because they enjoy the prerogative of atoning for sin by the offering of sacrifice, but because of certain points of analogy between them and the Jewish priesthood, which are clearly enough indicated in the *Didaché*. They are, in the conception of the writer, the ministers who have the highest gifts. They might give thanks in the celebration of the Eucharist as they pleased, and they are mentioned with exceptional honour and prominence. But there was one feature which they had in common with the Jewish priesthood. They had no worldly occupation or means of livelihood; and were, therefore, dependent on the Church for support. This seems to be the chief point of analogy in the writer's mind in applying to them the title of priests. "Every first-fruit, therefore, of the produce of press and floor, of oxen and sheep, thou shalt take and give to the prophets; for they are your chief priests" (c. xiii.). Cf. Deut. xviii. 2, 3, 4, to which there is manifest reference in the *Didaché*. A strikingly similar comparison occurs in Irenæus, who says, "All the righteous possess the sacerdotal rank . . Who are they that have left father and mother, and have said adieu to all their neighbours, on account of the Word of God and His covenant, unless the disciples of our Lord? Of whom Moses says, 'They shall have no inheritance, for the Lord Himself is their inheritance.'" Here the same language is applied to all Christians, all of whom, as we have seen,

[margin: Why the prophets called "chief priests" in the Didaché.]

are in the New Testament represented as "a holy priesthood." In no other sense are ministers of any sort so called. It is indeed remarkable that never in a single instance in the New Testament writings is the term applied to them. They are called ministers, elders, bishops, teachers, shepherds, rulers, stewards, leaders, but never priests. Nor have we what is now regarded as the distinguishing characteristic of sacerdotalism—atonement for sin by the offering of sacrifice—ever connected with them in the sub-apostolic literature, But the growth of sacerdotalism advances and matures so quickly, and goes on so manifestly before the eyes of the student of the early literature, that a brief and rapid sketch of it may be interesting, as well as needful to complete our view of this subject.

Ministers never called "priests" in New Testament.

There is no taint of sacerdotalism in the earliest of the Apostolic Fathers, Clement of Rome, but he employs language which may have contributed to the development. The great object of his epistle is to put an end to the insubordination which has arisen against the rulers, and to restore order at Corinth. In pleading for this he refers to the case of an army, and to the order, obedience and submissiveness with which the soldiers serve under their generals. "All are not prefects, nor commanders of a thousand, nor of a hundred, nor of fifty, but each in his own rank performs the things commanded by the king and his generals" (c. xxxvii.). He points to the example of the human body, showing how the members are subject to one another, and work harmoniously together, and are under one common rule for the preservation of

No sacerdotalism in Clement of Rome;

the body (c. xxxviii). He then adduces the analogy of the Jewish priesthood. " His own peculiar services are assigned to the high-priest, and their own proper place is assigned to the priests, and their own special ministrations devolve on the Levites. The layman is bound by the laws that pertain to laymen." He is evidently referring here to the Jewish people, and describing them as laymen as distinguished from the priesthood. Then applying this analogy he adds: " Let every one of you give thanks to God in his own order. . . ." And he goes on to mention how the apostles sent forth by Christ appointed their first-fruits to be bishops and deacons. And what wonder is it, he asks, that the apostles appointed those ministers, considering that Moses noted down in the sacred books all the injunctions given him, and that when jealousy arose concerning the priesthood, and the tribes were contending among themselves which of them should be adorned with that glorious title, he commanded the twelve tribes to bring him their rods, and arranged that the tribe whose rod should blossom was the one chosen to the priesthood; just as the apostles, knowing that there would be strife on account of the name (or title) of the Episcopate, appointed their first-fruits to be bishops and deacons, and afterwards gave instructions that, when they should fall asleep, other approved men should succeed them in the service. The ministry is described as a $\lambda\epsilon\iota\tau o\upsilon\rho\gamma\iota a$ and the ministers are represented as having " presented the offerings " ($\pi\rho o\sigma\epsilon\nu\epsilon\gamma\acute{o}\nu\tau a\varsigma$ $\tau\grave{a}$ $\delta\hat{\omega}\rho a$); but these are the gifts brought by the people, and the sacrifice of praise and thanksgiving. There is no remotest hint of the offering of an atoning sacrifice, and Christ is "the High-priest of all their offerings."

Even Ignatius (as Lightfoot has shown) never conceives the ministry as a priesthood, nor does Hermas, nor Barnabas, nor Polycarp, nor Justin Martyr, who describes Christians generally as "the true high-priestly race of God, as God Himself also beareth witness, saying that in every place among the Gentiles are men offering sacrifices well pleasing unto Him and pure (Mal. i. 11). Yet God doth not receive sacrifices from any one except through His priests. Therefore, God anticipating all sacrifices through His name which Jesus Christ ordained to be offered, I mean those offered by the Christians in every region of the earth with the Eucharist of the bread and of the cup, beareth witness that they are well pleasing to Him."[1] I have already given the words of Irenæus embodying the same view. No doubt Polycrates, at the end of the second century, speaks of the Apostle John as having been made a priest, and "wearing the mitre," but, as Lightfoot points out, the language is doubtless figurative, and is explained by that of the apostle himself, who regards the body of believers as high priests (Rev. ii. 27).

<small>nor in Hermas, Barnabas, Polycarp, or Justin Martyr.</small>

Clement of Alexandria is at the opposite pole from sacerdotalism. "It is possible for men even now," he says, "by exercising themselves in the commandments of the Lord, and by living a perfect gnostic life in obedience to the gospel, to be inscribed in the roll of the apostles. Such men are genuine presbyters and true deacons

<small>None in Clement of Alexandria.</small>

[1] *Dial. c. Tryph.*, cc. 116, 117.

of the will of God, if they practise and teach the things of the Lord, being not indeed ordained by men, nor considered righteous because they are presbyters, but enrolled in the presbytery because they are righteous."[1]

Tertullian is the first to represent the Christian ministry distinctly as a priesthood. "The right of giving baptism," he says, "belongs to the chief priest, that is the bishop."[2] And yet Tertullian is still conscious of the larger and more spiritual view. "Are not we laymen also priests? It is written, 'He hath also made us a kingdom and priests to God and His Father.' It is the authority of the Church which makes a difference between the order (the clergy) and the people."[3]

Begins to appear in Tertullian.

Origen, as might have been anticipated, is still more spiritual, and free from narrowness. It is in Cyprian that we find the sacerdotal conception of the ministry full-blown, just as it is in Cyprian that episcopacy itself reaches its apotheosis. Nor is it without significance that, as Lightfoot shows, the growth of sacerdotalism was earliest matured in Latin Christendom, under the influence of heathen ideas of priestly intervention; and that we find episcopacy, apostolical succession, sacerdotalism, the idea of the Eucharist as a real sacrifice, all growing and ripening together as parts of one great whole, which by-and-by brings in its train withdrawal from social life, and celibacy.

But most developed in Cyprian.

[1] *Strom.* vi. 13.   [2] *De Baptismo,* 17.
[3] *De Exh. Cast.,* 7.

VI. Ministerial Support.

According to the *Didaché*, the unattached, itinerant ministry, who were constantly moving about from Church to Church, were to be lodged and entertained by each Church visited by them, but were neither to ask for money, nor to get more provision than would last them till they reached their next resting-place. *The Didaché on ministerial support.* Every true prophet also who settled in a particular Church, as he might do, was to be treated as worthy of his food. So far, however, as our manual enables us to judge, it was only those who had no worldly occupation, and no settled means of livelihood, who were supported in this manner. It is remarkable that no instructions are given in our Directory with regard to the support of the local office-bearers, the bishops and deacons, the reason being, doubtless, that they continued *No mention of support for bishops and deacons.* to pursue their ordinary avocations, and thereby supported themselves. "If ye have no prophet, give to the poor," it says. This state of things seems to have been general in the early Church, and to have continued for some centuries. The Church officers whose circumstances demanded it drew from the same fund as the orphans and the poor—from the voluntary offerings of the people; but it is beyond question that for a long period after apostolic times the bishops and deacons as a rule thought it more expedient to do as Paul did, that is, to earn their bread with the work of their own hands. *Bishops or presbyters of early Church engaged in secular callings.* The bishops and presbyters of the early centuries cultivated farms, kept shops or banks, practised the healing art, wrought as smiths and artificers of various kinds, pursued the shepherd's calling, attended the markets and bought and sold there. In the Cemetery of Callixtus in the Catacombs at Rome a record describes Dionysius as fulfilling at once the calling of a physician, and the office of a presbyter. We read of one bishop who was a weaver at Maiuma, of another who tended sheep on the mountains of Cyprus, of another who practised in the law-courts, of a presbyter who was a silversmith at Ancyra.[1] A certain Christian innkeeper of Ancyra, called Theodotus, who had shown great kindness to those who suffered from the Diocletian edict at the beginning of the fourth century, was himself threatened with persecution. He fled for safety to a village in the country, and took refuge with a priest there. "This priest ministered every day at stated hours in a village church, but at the same time worked a farm, and regularly visited the great market of Ancyra, driving his own cart, and selling his wares." Ultimately Theodotus was discovered, tortured, and put to death; while instructions were given by the prefect that his body should lie unburied, exposed to the birds and beasts of prey, and a strong guard was set to watch it, lest it should be carried away and buried by the Christians, who regarded such exposure of the dead with great abhorrence. The story is told by Dr. Stokes in his *Ireland and the Celtic Church.* "The evening," he says, "was cold and late, and the guard had lit a fire, and made a booth of branches, when

---

[1] For interesting facts and evidence on this subject, see Hatch's "Bampton Lecture," p. 147, *sq.*

the priest drove up with his cart laden with barrels of wine, the produce of his vineyard. They invited him to remain all night with them, as the gates were already shut. He learned whose body they were guarding, treated them plenteously to his best wine, made them all drunk, and triumphantly drove off with the body of his devout innkeeper." Professor Stokes adds: "As a sufficient evidence that the union of the clerical and secular office continued to much later than St. Patrick's time, I shall simply quote an inscription on the walls of Assos, in Asia Minor, telling us how the walls were restored about the time of Justinian, by Helladius, a presbyter and chief magistrate of the city, corresponding to the union among ourselves of such diverse offices as Dean of St. Patrick's and Lord Mayor of Dublin."[1]

We know that St. Patrick's father, Calpurnius, was a deacon, a farmer, and a decurion or town councillor; that his sister's son, Lugnædon, though a presbyter, was a pilot or navigator; and that, of the presbyters who attended on St. Patrick, one was a smith and another a maker of book-satchels.[2]

Long after the time to which our manual refers the occupations of the clergy were so extended that the exemption of the trade-tax granted them by Constantine was revoked by later emperors, so serious was the loss of revenue. It was considered in no way inconsistent with or dishonouring to the sacred office that those engaged in it should be thus employed. There is no trace of the idea that to be occupied in farming, or in some profession or trade, or in buying

---

[1] *Ireland and the Celtic Church*, p. 43.
[2] *Ibid.*, p. 85.

and selling, was incompatible with the office of a minister. On the contrary, "when the Montanists proposed to pay their clergy a fixed salary, the proposal was condemned as a heretical innovation, alien to Catholic practice."[1] The chief enactments of the early Church on this matter were to the effect that the bishops were not to take advantage of their position to buy cheaper and sell dearer than other people.

<small>Withdrawal from secular employment due to the growth of the sacerdotal spirit.</small> The withdrawal of the clergy from secular occupations was part of the same movement which proscribed such things as "worldly," and encouraged celibacy, asceticism, and withdrawal from the world as eminently "religious." The withdrawal of the clergy from secular pursuits was thus one of the higher tide marks in the progress of sacerdotalism.

VII. THE DIACONATE.

It remains to add a word respecting another class of officers mentioned in our manual, the deacons.

It is true that "the seven" of Acts vi., who were <small>Institution of the office.</small> appointed in charge of "the daily ministration," are nowhere expressly called deacons; but their office is described as a "serving of tables." Most expositors, therefore, regard this as the original institution of the office of the diaconate, and recognise the deacons of Phil. i. 1, and 1 Tim. iii. 8 as holding the same office as that here originated—a view confirmed by the requirement of the apostle that the deacons should not be "greedy of filthy lucre." It is indeed singular that the relief sent to the poor

---

[1] See Euseb., *H. E.*, v. 18, 2; v. 28, 19.

brethren in Judæa, subsequent to the appointment of "the seven," is given in charge of the elders (Acts xi. 29. But this only serves to illustrate the position held by the deacons all through the history. They appear as subordinate to and as assistants of the elders or bishops. They are associated with the presbyter-bishops as their assistants, not only in charge of the poor, but even in the public worship of the congregation. *Relation of deacons to presbyters or bishops.* *Their duties.* The bishops *and deacons* of the *Didaché* perform the ministry (τὴν λειτουργίαν) of the prophets and teachers; and Justin Martyr describes the deacons as distributing the bread and wine in the Eucharist. Afterwards, as I have shown, when all Church power became concentrated in the bishop, the deacons appear as his servants and attendants, as the eye and ear and right hand of the bishop.[1] They were employed both in the collection and distribution of funds; and, in connection with this latter office, it was their duty to visit the houses of the poor, enquire into their circumstances, and report to the bishop. They were to visit the inns, look after strangers, and find out every case of sickness and distress. It was at a later date, when the philanthropic spirit of Christianity began to wane, and to become subordinate to other offices which were thought more spiritual, that the deacons were withdrawn from such works of charity and mercy.

There is no express reference in our manual to deaconesses, but there is no doubt that from early times a female diaconate existed in the Church. *Deaconesses.* The word applied to Phœbe

[1] See *Apostol. Const.*, ii. 44; iii. 19.

(Rom. xvi. 1) might indeed refer to unofficial service rendered to the poor and sick; but Lightfoot, with most scholars, understands it in the official sense; and they are the more ready to attach this sense to it as they seem to see traces of a female diaconate in other parts of Scripture. Thus Lightfoot, Uhlhorn, and others take γυναῖκας (1 Tim. iii. 11), translated "wives" in our version, as meaning deaconesses; and for this interpretation the following reasons are adduced. (*a*) The term ἡ γυνή is employed in the early literature with this sense. See *Apostolical Constitutions*, iii. 19. (*b*) ὡσαύτως, according to the plan of the sentence, introduces a new category of Church officials. Cf. ver. 8. (*c*) At ver. 12 διάκονοι is repeated, for which there was no need if ver. 11 was still speaking of them. (*d*) The family relations of the deacons are first spoken of at ver. 12. (*e*) The wives of the bishops are not mentioned; why, then, the wives of the deacons? (*f*) There is no word answering to "*their*" in the original. If the wives of the deacons were meant, αὐτῶν would certainly be found, so as to render the designation intelligible. (*g*) If deacons' wives are intended, it is curious that *domestic* counsels should be given to the husbands and omitted in the case of the wives. Undoubtedly, owing to the greater seclusion in which, according to Oriental customs, women lived in the East, and the feeling which forbad their intercourse with men, one might naturally expect some such office as that of the deaconess.

Their service. Their service would be performed chiefly in the homes of the Christian people; and in this view the counsels given in 1 Tim. iii. 11 would be appropriate enough. They are warned not to be "slanderers," carrying gossip from house to house; and, as they would naturally have to do with the distribution of alms to the poor, they are required to be "faithful in all things." It is also certain that immediately after apostolic times we find traces of a female diaconate. Thus Pliny, in his famous letter to Trajan, speaks of having put to the torture two female slaves, who "were called deaconesses."[1]

It is remarkable, however, that for a long time after this, deaconesses so called disappear both in the East and in the West, and that we only hear of *widows*. "Widows" or "Presbyteresses." Many good expositors, who are at the same time familiar with the early history of the Church, suppose "the widows" of 1 Tim. v. 9, 10, also called " elder women " or "presbyteresses" (v. 2), were persons who, whether at this time formally set apart or not, were charged with certain ecclesiastical duties. They infer their ecclesiastical character from the fact: (*a*) that as it was held expedient that the bishop or presbyter should be but once married (1 Tim. iii. 2), so also it was required in the widows who were "received into the number" (1 Tim. v. 9), though Paul himself recommends the younger widows to marry again (v. 14); (*b*) that it was only widows above sixty who were admitted into this category—a restriction that would be harsh and arbitrary, if they were simply being admitted to the support of the Church; (*c*) that those admitted *must have brought up children*, whereas aged widows who were childless were even still more likely to need the Church's charity. At all events it is certain that very early we begin to hear of " widows "

---

[1] " *Quæ ministræ dicebantur*," Plin., *Ep.*, x. 97.

as an ecclesiastical order in the Church, who are charged with certain religious duties. They are mentioned by Ignatius,[1] by Polycarp,[2] by Hermas (probably), who relates how Grapte was commissioned with the instruction of the orphans,[3] by Clement of Alexandria,[4] by Origen,[5] by Tertullian,[6] and many others. We learn from Origen and Tertullian that one of their duties was to instruct the women and children. Lucian, in his satire *de Morte Peregrini*, c. 12, relates how when Peregrinus was thrown into prison, aged widows, attended by orphans, were seen waiting at the prison early in the morning. They are sometimes called presbyteresses or female elders.[7] Somewhat later, especially in the Eastern Church, we hear again of deaconesses, among whose duties was the assistance of female catechumens in the ceremony of baptism.[8] At this later period they were ordained by the laying on of hands.[9]

Often referred to in early Church history.

* * * * *

Conclusion.

If there is one word in which more than in another the essence of the Christian spirit is embodied, that word is "love"; and it is a most significant and beautiful symbol of the love that animated early Christianity that its first external institution was the diaconate, that the earliest permanent officials to which it gave birth were not bishops nor presbyters, not rulers nor even teachers, but

---

[1] *Ad Smyrn.* 6; *ad Polyc.* 4. [2] *Ad Phil.* c. 4.
[3] *Vis.* ii. 4. [4] *Pæd.* iii. 12. [5] *In Evang. Joann. Hom.* 17; *in Jes. Hom.* 6. [6] *Ad Uxor.* i. 7; *de Velandis Virginibus* c. 9. [7] *Const. Copt.*, ii. 37, and Origen as already cited.
[8] *Const. Ap.*, iii. 16; viii. 28; Jerome on Rom. xvi. 1.
[9] *Conc. Nicæn.*, c. 12.

deacons;—office-bearers charged with special care for the desolate and the poor, and with the administration of its philanthropies and charities. It is hardly less significant that as, in after times, the spiritual and the moral became subordinate to the ecclesiastical and external, love waned, and the diaconate either disappeared, or busied itself with other functions. No doubt the hospitals, asylums, workhouses, and other numberless philanthropic institutions which to-day stud Christendom, are the direct or indirect fruit of Christianity. We are, however, of those who think it a matter for regret that in this age the care of the poor and sick and maimed is left so much to organizations external to the Church, and that the diaconate is not still as primary and prominent as it was in primitive times. We do not know that we could close the thoughts and considerations which this ancient document has started, in a spirit more akin to its own, than by recalling and emphasizing the gentle, kindly, beneficent ministrations in which the religion of Jesus Christ set out on its career. In that spirit it went forth to grapple with and overthrow ancient heathenism, and to elevate and bless humanity. The work that yet remains for it to do is less in comparison than that which it has already done, the difficulties it has still to face are not at all so formidable in proportion as those which it has surmounted. And for the rest, this old book we have been studying unites with the voice of all history in teaching us:

> "It's wiser being good than bad;
> It's safer being meek than fierce;
> It's fitter being sane than mad.
> My own hope is, a Sun will pierce

The thickest cloud earth ever stretched ;
    That after Last, returns the First,
Though a wide compass round be fetched ;
    That what began best, can't end worst,
Nor what God blessed once, prove accurst."

www.ingramcontent.com/pod-product-compliance
Lightning Source LLC
Chambersburg PA
CBHW021953220426
43663CB00007B/801